BLACK TORRENT

BLACK TORRENT

LEOPOLD BUCZKOWSKI

Translated by
David Welsh

THE M.I.T. PRESS
Cambridge, Massachusetts,
and London, England

Originally published in Poland by Czytelnik
under the title "Czarny Potok"
English translation Copyright © 1969 by
The Massachusetts Institute of Technology

Set in Fototronic Baskerville (CRT)
Printed and bound in the United States of America by
The Colonial Press Inc., Clinton, Massachusetts

SBN 262 02064 5 (hardcover)

Library of Congress catalog card number: 78-107998

The journey and the night were interminable. Not until dawn did Heindl, dragging himself across the melting snow, reach Trojnog. After groping at the hut window, he knocked. His hot forehead touched the glass, and he said, "Open up, don't be afraid. Open up, you've no reason to hesitate. So you won't regret it later. You act as if you didn't realize what's happened."

From the dark hole of the door into the hallway could be heard the impatient whispering of someone exhausted from waiting.

"How do you feel, eh?" a man asked out of the darkness.

"Worse and worse. But now that it's happened to me, I don't regret a single moment."

"But why didn't you go out by this door? We went out to the stairs immediately after you, but you'd fallen flat on your face. There wasn't time to lift you. The Jews of Shaya's gang were looking for you, and so were we. In the mornings Cyrulinski and Ducat; in the afternoons Kunda and Flying-carpet relieved them. Kunda found Buchsbaum's grandson killed near Boldurki beyond the pond, and said that someone fired a dumdum at the statue of the Lord Jesus in the forest; and a little further along the path to Huciski a walking stick and tefillin were lying, and it was Kunda who brought it home. But you weren't anywhere about, the entire year. You'll have to justify yourself, for people say you brought much misery down on them."

"What if I did," said the newcomer. "It's the same as with that man who put a bridge over a swamp, supposedly as an act of repentance. One day this sinful man went under the bridge to listen to what people would say about what he'd done. And when people came, some cursed because the bridge was made of wood; others complained that it was too high and that a cold wind was blowing there, that there was a hole in it — as people do. You say the first man fired? I could also ask, 'Did you barricade the door as was agreed?' I had to get forage for the horses, cigarettes for Chaim, ointment from the pharmacy for boils. I had to try and get pictures of St. Anthony for Emilka, for she'd taken a fancy for some, and a whole lot of other things, which I won't go into. Each of us could have been first. I was sitting over a glass of warm milk. Kunda said, 'It's spitting weather so you should take a tarpaulin.' And I said, 'OK, I remember that Bernstein left a tarpaulin for a cart at Hanczarka's; let's go and get it from the old hag today, before we leave. She won't make a fuss.' Rozia put on a pair of trousers for the journey, because I advised her to. She stood behind a chair and pushed her dress into the trousers. And you, inside, were rolling a cigarette. You should have barricaded the door or fired at the door panel. Neither Szerucki nor Kunda had weapons with him that day, obviously. And when a shot was fired from that direction, you began shouting. Why in hell did you do that? And don't be surprised that even then I didn't trust you. It was like a smell that was bothering me. Nothing will save a guy when he starts to turn rotten, to stink like that. And you know that every moment of life matters, if only because someone always holds the winning hand of cards. There's no way to slither out of it. Sometimes informers succeed, but in the end their patron comes for them and they lie like cats, run over in the mud. You heard Ciszka beg: 'Oh, don't kill me! I'll serve you!' 'Son of a bitch,' Szerucki shouted, and gave the stool pigeon such a belt he almost shit. One could look at this little showdown with genuine sympathy, but that isn't the point. After all, it was only the beginning. Think what they did to Rozia. As they stretched her out for the rape, she said, 'I implore you, let me alone all of you.' It was then that you ran across my shoulders. Bear this in mind: Rozia was being suffocated by two fingers of a Mazeppa-ite gangster and couldn't breathe. It was essential to fire, every moment counted. Horse-face won't forgive you for that. You know, that man with the steely eyes and thin nose — he doesn't forgive anybody. You're weeping now for Rozia, but she should have been rescued. Nothing wiill help you, no matter how many confidants you have. Horse-face will come knocking on your door one day, no matter where you hide. He'll put an end to you."

"You're working yourself up," said the man from the darkness. "I've always told everyone you're a clever guy, but you've turned stupid tonight. Why the devil are you so down on me? Maybe it seemed to you that I had something going with Rozia. I tell you straight, I don't. But if you want, I'll tell you that . . . Szerucki — don't grit your teeth — Szerucki was hiding her mother at Huciski; he didn't let her out of his sight. But God knows it was they who went into the hallway. I was standing near enough to sniff you. And then the alarm clock went off on the commode; Szerucki jumped to stop it. 'All in order,' you said, and that fooled me. And I want to remind you of something else: you didn't have the energy. You were like crumbling bread. I can't afford to have it all pushed onto me. Admit your mistake. You jumped through the wrong door. And it was Kunda who shouted, not me. They were giving it to him in the belly; he threw his hands between his legs and groaned, drumming his feet as if putting out a fire. And the lamp went out from the racket. God knew who to join with — a shadow here, a shadow there. Rozia got entangled with me. But she was neither dearer to me nor cheaper than the cause. It seemed she was running step for step after me. It's all right, I thought for an instant. But meanwhile, you'd fallen on the threshold, and then Szerucki was running after me, not Rozia."

"No, not true. You should have gone back, lit a flashlight, and fired into the group. Fear drove you, and you thought, Oh, it's not worth it; as it is, things get worse and worse. Even as I was falling, I did not want to admit the thought that you were a man from whose eyes the sun had already disappeared."

"What do you know what I was thinking?" said the man from the darkness. "You talk like a priest filling a barrel with words very hastily. I understand your irritation, but why didn't you reflect? That might have illuminated more than one thing."

"Illuminated what?" asked the newcomer.

"Before evening, Rozia said to Szerucki: 'Talk to him about it. Horse-face wants to hide me at his place, but I'd rather not talk about it. I'd even prefer the other proposal, as I'd be nearer my father.' The thing is understandable — she wanted to be nearer the Sasow quarries. It didn't enter your head that the girl was suffering. She didn't want to get you involved."

"Let me tell you — when they came into the hallway, I was certain it was Horse-face. And though I'd never set eyes on him, I trusted him. But I couldn't afford to tell you that. I was at your place illegally. A guy who's been through a beating in jail is like a rat who's been through a great fire."

"Don't heap insults on him," said the other. "You want to mix something you don't understand at all with criminal matters. You talk like a man who's suddenly been punched in the head, before he manages to find out anything about life."

"There's no reason to get yourself worked up. What insult? The thing is only that I lacked faith, and it was that which led to such a situation. I can't help it. Before Tonka was killed, everything had a reason; no matter whether successful or not, everything seemed more bright; but now I brood and don't move a finger.

Once I broke down all doors to get her. Today I kiss the place where she fell. I don't expect anything, I don't look forward to anything."

"Did you ever see Buchsbaum?" asked the man from the darkness.

"The children of Hynda Glas found him a week after New Year's. He was lying frozen under a pine tree; the snow had melted a little under him, nothing more. A spongy face, and swollen. His gray beard on his naked chest."

"Who buried him?"

"Some two men or other who escaped from the Sasow quarries. The ironworkers believe that he still walks about there and collects half-frozen children from the fields. It comes from the fact that someone really does come out of the thickets to the little hill, and looks, with a hand on his forehead, at burned-down Szabasowa. By the shape, it's a man. It may be Gabe Gudel, the collector of dues."

"Someone from Szabasowa told me that Buchsbaum found little Kalma in a field near Pasieki. Where was she after that?"

"At Mrs. Arbuz's, who was a widow already."

"What happened? Arbuz was such a powerful guy."

"The Mazeppa gang came to take his cow away. It was night. Arbuz listened. There was a shriek nearby. A trail of light was coming from a fire. He ran out across the yard, cowering, clothes unfastened, an ax in his hand. Hearing rattling around the stable door, he rushed there, chopped at someone, struck once again . . . he struck frantically. He went back to the gate and hit the man at the gate again, with the blunt side. And then he fell. Mrs. Arbuz wept all through the night. In the morning, smoke weighed down with moisture spread over the earth and flowed through the forest, into the ravine and over the ravine. There was the stench of smoke and dead silence. The snow swept the remains away: rabbits left delicate traces; sometimes a magpie jumped after a mouse."

"And bear in mind who came to that fire. I was standing in the wild lilac; Mrs. Arbuz could be heard calling, 'Dear Jesus, but how did you get here? Eh?'

" 'One way or the other, you won't know,' said a second man to her. Mrs. Arbuz was standing with bowed head over her husband's corpse.

" 'Oh, Jesus! How quickly it happened.'

" 'Try not to get too upset. Creep into the heat and look for the tin can. It must be there near the stove. The head of the sewing machine should be there too.' And to think that Mrs. Arbuz lit the light that evening, got supper ready for the wanderers. And perhaps milked the cow. Jesus, just think of it! You crept into the heat and with a stick you pulled out a little wheel from the machine, a tin globe, and some wires from a bird trap.

" 'I thought you'd got it,' said the man at the side.

" 'Wait, you. After all, this ammunition might have exploded from the heat, and not a scrap of tin remained. Perhaps we could sprinkle some water here, because it's stifling me. Oh, how it's stifling me!'

"A sharp wind scattered the sparks. You, crouching, were pulling something heavy from under the firebrands.

" 'Well, is it there?' asked the other man.

" 'Too heavy,' you panted.

" 'You're a great guy, brother. Pull!'

" 'Oh, Jesus! Here, under the planks, someone is lying burned,' you shouted.

" 'Who is it? Eh?'

" 'Wrap something wet around your head and come here, help me. It's stifling.'

"And someone leapt into the heat. Who was it that leaped?"

"Chuny Shaya. We dragged out a roasted corpse. It was Rozia Arnstein. Worn out, we went to sit out the rest of the night in the gamekeeper's hut. Aron Tykies had made his nest there, and was building coffins for Poles shot in Cisna. He was baking potatoes in a brazier for himself and the children of the murdered Katz family, the Karawans, Propsts, and Hany Gutman, who had collected there. Some dog had attached itself to the children and went everywhere with them. They named it Bas. When winter came, Mrs. Arbuz took three of the children, and made beds for them in mangers. . . ."

This night we found a spy in the workshop of the gamekeeper's hut. He was sitting on wood chips by the stove and picking his teeth. Tykies was finishing off three little coffins. Kittens were sitting on his bench. As we came in, the man sitting on the wood chips said nothing, and watched Chuny Shaya's face, sunken, pale, with long marks under the eyes.

" 'Get up!' shouted Shaya. He searched him thoroughly. Tykies gestured at me significantly.

" 'Who are you?' I asked, feigning. 'Come closer to the light.'

"He came over, bristling. I struck his cap off. His forehead was damp. He had nothing to say. Chuny Shaya recognized him. But the job had to be postponed. We didn't want to dirty the keeper's hut. For the time being we sat and smoked. We pulled our boots off, put our foot-clouts on the tin stovepipe, and ordered the condemned man to put more wood chips in.

" 'A little at a time, you bungler; put them in and watch, for the tin is getting red hot.'

"Numbed, he put the chips in at regular intervals and watched over our foot-clouts. We rested, stretched out on the shavings. Accustomed to danger after the death of his children, Chuny Shaya went straight to meet the enemy and did not turn away from the most terrible things. Cold brutality and uneasiness had awakened in this calm and hardworking man. I saw him in the light — he was lying with both fists under his head. Watching Tykies at work, he smiled and gnawed his lips. With a rag paper wrapped around his index finger, Tykies was painting a cross on the coffin lid. Shaya immediately translated to me everything that Tykies said in Yiddish. He liked me, and was as completely devoted to me as a dog. I understood him and appreciated him at work, and for his commonsense, for sometimes his caution yielded us a great deal, especially when it was necessary to obtain something to eat at night. And he was a good psychologist too. It was he who revealed to us that Hanczarka, apart from her informing, was a chronic gossip.

"The night was tranquil; from time to time a shot resounded in the forest, and after it there was a rustling, as if peas were being sifted over a kneading trough. We just lay there, loosening our belts so our bellies also rested, and recalled this and that. We recalled how we once ran through a long ravine to the forest clearing. An autumn night was coming on, cold and damp.

" 'Death is boring now,' said the Czech.

" 'But a death sentence — well, isn't it? A death sentence on a horse, that's another matter. Read out and executed in public would be intolerable, in my opinion,' said the intellectual from Prague.

" 'But the behavior of the witnesses, defense, and prosecuting attorney would be interesting.'

"A conversation of this kind usually broke off, for we had to think of food, a warm corner, and sleep, or another flight and fighting.

"The man we'd condemned to death was rubbing Chuny Shaya's foot-clouts; he went over to the light and industriously scraped each lump of mud off with a fingernail.

" 'How terrible all this is,' said Chuny. We looked one another in the eye. And I thought to myself, Does some girl love this stool pigeon, this young bull; loudly I asked him, 'Do you have a woman?'

" 'Why not?' he replied.

"Chuny Shaya raised himself on an elbow.

" 'Just think,' I said to Chuny, 'a girl loves a man like this.'

" 'Maybe you'll take her place, eh?' asked Chuny.

"One thought flashed into heads simultaneously.

" 'She isn't in this area,' said the stool pigeon.

" 'No matter, we'll find our way to her somehow,' Chuny retorted gruffly.

" 'You know where she lives?' I asked, feigning surprise.

" 'Sure I know. I've written down every word in my memory.' Chuny glanced at his watch.

" 'Twenty before four. Take him outside and bump him off. But in such a way, you know, so he runs a little way, then get him in the back. But let him leave his boots behind. Take off your boots!' Chuny shouted, and he winked at me and whispered, 'We've got to do this orderly.'

"I rose and approached the stove, treading on the slats. The foot-clouts were beginning to turn crusty; I rubbed them in my hands. Suddenly plaster poured down from the ceiling, the light went out. In a flash I saw Chuny, with head lowered, leap for the threshold. A grenade exploded near the hut.

" 'Are you by the stove? Hand over the boots,' he whispered.

"I handed him the boots, and lying there, we pushed our feet into the bootlegs. Someone rattled along the walls with an automatic. And again a bang resounded through the forest. Various thoughts began sputtering in my head, like butter thrown into a hot frying pan, the first and most vital to get away, to creep into the hallway. Who was it thumping so frantically at the hut? We had to separate, for if they threw a grenade in — I was bothered also by the way the foot-clouts had got tangled, and I could not for the life of me push my feet any further than the instep.

" 'Chuny!' I shouted. 'See anything?'

" 'There!' and he pointed. They were visible through a crack in the worn threshold. A rocket winked with green light, and among the flickering trees some men were running into the brushwood ravine. These two men fired a few short bursts from the reserve in our direction. Unexpectedly the wood chips rustled, and something rattled off Tykies' bench. The whole room suddenly went up in flames, the dry pine chips flying to the ceiling. Tykies, dragging the glow with his feet, crawled over to us, still keeping his thumb on a black rag, and he coughed. We had to throw him into the back of the hallway with all our might, for he was pushing his way between us like a child.

"Yes, that was a bad night. The children were sleeping on straw in the attic. They didn't want to come down; scared, they burrowed into the depths of the attic, and we could hear the roof falling in at the back of the hut.

"At four, we were in the fields, the children jog-trotting after us, and a moment later, up rushed the dog. Tykies was worst off, as a snowstorm was pouring down in the fields and he only had a thin shirt on.

"We ran into the dark fields, and for the first time didn't know what to do with ourselves; while the children were walking beside us, they trusted us. The wind blew into our faces, stinging grit was flying about. We walked through the fields for an hour, then turned left through a forest clearing and plunged into the Podhorec woods. Chuny Shaya decided we would go to Pasieki.

" 'There we'll be able to burrow into some hay pile or other,' he said. We were mighty tired. There came into my mind, from goodness knows where, the legend of a forest goddess. The forest roars overhead, the neighborhood creaks, and underneath there's a green, moving silence. A bee is seeking buglosses. There are birds in nests. A birch is blossoming, with little golden wormlets on its branch tips, and is dark gray. On black forest water stand yellow flowers. When a man spends a night alone in the forest, an owl immediately appears to him in the shape of a beautiful maiden. She talks, jokes, but hides her lips cunningly with a flower or one hand so her beak can't be seen. How deceitful she is! She takes on the form of a maiden whom a man would want to love without limit. If you fall asleep in a forest, you immediately dream of her. Legends harass men on the move; so do apparitions and affectionate memories. When snow is falling, then a man in the forest's hearing torments him. A figure appears in every thicket, or the little house of a forest witch.

" 'Don't spread out, children,' Chuny whispered.

"We were still going through the forest. Snow was flaking

down. There was a footbridge over a ravine. No one was on the bridge. Cirla came across this way last winter — it had seemed to her that someone was standing there, like a transparent shadow.

" 'Who is standing on the footbridge in the black forest?' she cried.

"It was quiet and warm in the forest. Birches, covered with snow, crouched their branches to the ground. Glossy frost lay everywhere, and the forest became invisible in the sky-blue dust.

"Cirla had walked through the forest all night long, and cuddled her dead child. As she walked, she told it a fairy tale."

But what is a fairy tale?

I was living with Tonka in a brick kiln in Senka. We lived there quietly until fall. One night I went out, as usual, to get something to eat someplace. The night was black as a mare's udder. I could see only a tiny, flickering light near the forest, and I went to this light. As I got nearer, some people could be heard tittering inside, cursing, then something whined, and there was a shriek, as if they had mortally wounded someone who fell down. I peeped through a crack between the curtains. Sitwa was sitting at the mirror, combing her hair. A Jewish woman was standing on the threshold, cringing, covered in a black kerchief. Kurdiuk was standing in the middle. Sitwa could see him in the mirror. I too saw him in the mirror. He approached, raised one hand, and showed her a ring.

" 'Like it?' he asked.

"Silence. Then she said,

" 'What of it?'

" 'Here, I brought it for you.'

" 'What do I want with a ring?' said Sitwa, and she laughed dully, pulling hairs out of her comb. 'It's unpleasant even to mention,' she said.

" 'Unpleasant?'

" 'What do you want of me, why have you come?'

" 'I wanted to have a little talk with you today.'

" 'Very well. Sit down.' Sitwa, braiding her hair, turned away.

" 'I want to tell you everything in the proper way, from the start, so you don't think I killed Mrs. Ajzner only for the ring. I want to tell you so you know what it's all about. As I came in here, I kept wondering how to explain it. I decided to talk only about this matter, so that you would know . . . not about Mrs. Ajzner, Bernstein, Silberg, or anything else. That has passed, and now the question is, What will you and I have out of it? I want to talk about a certain man who is threatening to kill me.'

"Sitwa glanced at the window with her beautiful black eyes, and asked, 'What's happened to the dog, why isn't it barking?'

" 'Your dog is a stinking boot-licker.'

" 'Not at all.' Sitwa took offense, and kept looking at the window. It seemed that she could see my eyes at the crack. Kurdiuk stood motionless for an instant, then took a revolver out of his pocket, and cocked it. It was necessary to get away from the window. I decided to go further."

"Szerucki once told me merry things about Sitwa. He liked gossiping. Once a heavy snowstorm had caught him, and he barged in on Sitwa to wait for morning. He found three Hilfspolizei there. Sitwa was treating them to vodka, the gramophone was playing. The cops were lusting for her, and she in a dirty red robe, her legs crossed, was showing them French photographs. They howled with laughter, stamped their feet for joy, and she sang to them in a drunken alto voice: 'She was a tramp, she showed her piece of — !'

" 'Who's your mate?' they asked Sitwa when Szerucki began clapping her on the bare shoulder.

" 'He's all right,' said Sitwa. 'Drink up, lads,' she invited.

"The drunkest of all glanced rapidly at Szerucki and moved to the door. Fixing his belt, he grabbed his rifle. Szerucki hurled himself after him. The other man was well befuddled with drink. Szerucki kicked him in the head. The cop fell down and began yelling as if his spine had cracked. Szerucki jumped on his face, struck him with his heels, grabbed the rifle, and hit the door with his side. He fired at the man lying there from the hallway. Little boxes, papers, flasks poured off a shelf all over the door. In his agitation Szerucki fired three more times into the room until the lamp went out, then ran into the black, freezing fields. Yes, there was no fooling. I saw him later in the gamekeeper's hut. His shirt was hanging out; he was chopping wood with a blunt ax, sweat pouring off his nose with effort. It was necessary to light a fire in the frozen hut, for Chuny Shaya had brought Cirla, who was going to give birth.

"That was a wretched night. Kurdiuk ran out of the hut, and began firing at the thicket which I was standing behind. Then he fired a red rocket. I waited, crouching, then rushed into the fields and ran, ran, exhausted, hungry, without the hope of getting any food that night. Here and there stars appeared in the black sky, the frost was biting. I was passing a group of willows by a stream when suddenly someone came up to me out of the undergrowth, his voice, deep as though from the depths of a barrel, broke the silence:

" 'Who's there? Stop, or I'll kill you!'

"Momentarily, I couldn't find the right words for an answer; then something provided me with the phrase: 'It's all right, everything's in order.'

" 'Aren't you a local?'

" 'Almost not,' I replied.

" 'That means you were here once, and you certainly were born here.'

" 'Yes, something like that,' I said, and putting my face close to his, asked, 'Chaim?'

" 'Yes.' "

"I got to know Chaim in the fall of '42. I was sitting with him in Brandon's attic in Szabasowa, and shots were being fired around Kocjan Street, feet were clattering. We went to the ventilator and watched. The clouds were flying low, black with bright fringes. Fine rain was falling. Chaim shuddered with the cold as if it were cutting through his whole body. He watched and said,

" 'Like bees, only it's a rainy day, but like bees that have settled in a swarm on a branch.' The poor children, huddled together by the church, sat drenched in the street. They hunched up their wet shoulders. They had rounded up many of these children, and you couldn't see the ground for them. They jostled one another as if perched on a branch.

"Chaim watched, frowned, and rubbed the back of his neck hard. We couldn't see, but near the house someone whistled as though to a dog, and fired. These armed Ukrainians, the drenched children waiting for death, and the weather — all looked inhuman and terrible. Chaim shifted from one foot to the other, jogged his shoulders, moved away from the ventilator, then went back, watched, and again shuddered throughout his body.

" 'Something's suffocating me, but I don't know what,' he said, 'and there's a smell from it, as if they were rounding up sheep there.'

"The street was blocked with automobiles parked across it. The soaking-wet drivers, leaning on the mudguards, waited for something. Police wrapped in capes, stamping with their dirty boots on the children's backs, walked around, faded as autumn flies. Chaim fell down. I picked him up.

" 'I tell you,' said Chaim, 'these children were taught a song at school: "In Autumn, in Autumn, the orchards turn red . . ." Yes, it's started to turn red.'

"When he had made this statement, all the children in the street started whining, the automobiles roared in high gear, and shots were fired more rapidly.

"Chaim was deeply moved. Today he's different, he's acquired a gun. That spring, as I was running down burning Castle Street with him, he was already different. He had something with which to defend, and someone to defend. The cringing children cowered and ran after him; he called them together, for as soon as the fire broke out, they had scattered, rushed into a woodshed, burrowed into the darkest corners. The gasping of those not yet finished off did not interfere with his plan of action.

"Klara Wasicinska was of a different opinion about Chaim. She told me he used to lie for whole days at a time in the straw under the rectory shed, and only moved at night, straightening his back. He would walk about in the garden, and any horse's neigh would frighten him. She would have liked everyone to fight, chop, shoot at all hours of day or night. She was an impatient girl. Even a shadow under a plank gave her no peace. It must be remembered that after the first pogrom in Lwow Street, Chaim survived the death of his father-in-law and his mother; he sat through the whole night in a cellar with his dying wife, and it was not until morning, after making sure she was really dead, that he covered her with a straw mattress, took the surgeon's box and a bottle of disinfectant, jumped out of the cellar, and at once began running blindly around the ruins. After feeling his way to hard and level ground, he slowed down and took a penknife out of his pocket.

"That same night, Aron Tykies put out his cigarette in the hallway, wrapped a child in rags, and also feeling his way around the beams of the burned-out houses, went by the black meadow to the forest. After him, snorting, ran the dog of the late Arnstein.

"To the south stood a livid, dull barrier of forest. Tykies caught up with Chaim in the ironworkers' clearing. Their legs trembling, they crossed a line of aspens with dense undergrowth and crossed a second line, thinly planted with beech seedlings. It was already broad daylight when they entered the forest itself, old and lofty. The brushwood broke softly under their feet, like cotton. The soft, reddish earth was covered by a sharp frost which crackled like glass. The dog was running ahead. It looked back, then ran on at a steady trot, its muzzle to the ground. A leaf fell with a rustling noise.

"Tykies wanted to sit down and rest. 'I'm out of breath,' he said to Chaim. The latter patted the child, poked it lightly, evidently checking something — but a group of men appeared on the edge of a clearing. They waited for them to disappear, then they moved on, still faster, watching for an enemy to right and left. There, further on, a forest stream was flowing, and the path led to the right, near to the house of a lot-holder. They scrambled across the gooseberry bushes and the stream. Horse-face was sitting behind a thicket. He rose and approached them.

" 'Good day,' he said. 'Don't be afraid of me.'

"And the conversation ran like this:

" 'Who are you?' he pointed at Tykies.

" 'And who are you?' asked Chaim.

" 'You'll find out. I keep order in the forest. We shoot Jewish police, understand? I know you, but who's this?' and he again indicated Tykies, who was staring mistrustfully at the questioner.

" 'A carpenter, Tykies by name. What more can I tell you? Surely you can see that this man could never be a policeman.'

" 'And now tell me where you are all going. Now that I know you, and you know me, I want to know where you are all going. The carpenter can go where he likes. But you're a doctor, aren't you? Then come with me. I'll show you a sick girl, whose foot is swollen up like a jug. You can apply leeches or something, that's your business. The girl is dried up with fever like a wood chip, and has got so weak she can hardly talk.'

" 'Glad to help,' said Chaim. 'I'll do my duty.'

" 'Don't talk so wisely about "duty." Go to the hut and see the sick girl; later we'll be able to talk about "duty." ' "

"And Chaim went to the hut with him. An old woman looked at them out the hut window for a moment, and made a sign to Tykies. Horse-face went into action and shouted,

" 'Tonka!'

" 'Well?'

" 'I've brought a doctor, did I do right?'

" 'Ah, how disgustingly this illness has taken me. Do you think it is infectious?'

" 'It's dark in here,' said Chaim, 'hard for me to say. Did someone shoot you? How long ago? Come into the hut.'

"Horse-face seized Tonka by the hands and took her into the hut. Chaim followed, threw his cap down on the table, and asked for water. He drank, and looked at Tonka. He traced her black, sunken eyes, the pale, shrunken skin of her cheeks, and the red, tangled hair over her white forehead.

" 'One never feels the passing of time so much at heart as on a day in high summer,' said Tonka in her fever.

" 'It's already fall, miss. The bullet injured a bone,' stated Chaim. 'Under the circumstances I can't help you in any way. We'll check your heart, that's all.'

" 'What do you mean "check her heart," maybe we ought to buy an injection, surely you understand what is at stake.' Horse-face leaned against the wall and pointed to me: 'You, get a horse out. Write down what he's to buy. Tonka once left five silver dollars at Sitwa's, and you may be certain she won't tell a soul, there's nothing to fear.'

"Chaim wrote the prescription. I mounted the mare, Foundling, and set off.

"When I was leaving this hiding place in the brick kiln, Tonka had whispered in my ear: 'Look after yourself.' I wandered about gloomily that night, and the wind blew straight into my face; I thought to myself, There's something very wrong with this girl of mine.

"I crept into some hut or other. Everyone knows what it is like to creep in. It's dark, and you do everything by the touch or hearing, and still more by smell. I stopped in the hallway; snoring came from the other side of the door; I could smell pickled cabbage, harness, and mashed potatoes with buckwheat. I felt a loaf of bread under a sack of grain. I took the bread.

" 'Who's there?' I heard, and a ray of green light broke on me. But I was already in the garden. I jumped over the fence and ran downwards, all the time downwards.

"Meanwhile, Chaim had gone to Cirla's delivery. I found him still there in the morning, for I lost my way. Not until dawn did I return to the kiln. Tonka wasn't there. On the pallet I found her door key, the dearest souvenir.

"A year has passed since that time, but the memories of Tonka pursue me, I cannot rid myself of them. Since that time I have lived through many terrible things, and yet not an hour passes without her standing before my eyes; I see her everywhere. There's no way of proving that she is dead. But I know what it means to rot two years, loused up, in the fields, on the bare ground. A man can become obsessed."

When the German police drove into Szabasowa on their motorcycles, Gabe Gudel was walking along the street and tapping out the coming feast of Easter with a bone stick. They surrounded him, and the tallest of them hit the gabe on the forehead with a rubber truncheon. By the synagogue was a lime pit, and they put him into that pit, and after driving the boys out of the Mehuten school, they ordered that the unconscious Gudel be sprinkled with water. Driven by whips, the boys brought water and poured it on the head of the man stifling in quicklime.

On coming to his senses, Gudel stretched out his hands, seized the edge of the brittle earth with his fingers.

They ordered that Shames Buchsbaum be summoned in his liturgical robes. Two policemen brought him. The officer patted Buchsbaum and ordered him to read verses from Ethics over the pit. Shames Buchsbaum, scared to death, and ashamed of the crime, began uttering words permeated with sorrow and death with pale lips which clearly stood out against his red beard.

It was a hot summer day.

"Ha, ha, ha, ha!" the mob of police roared.

The boys brought water from a pump. The gabe seized the edge of the pit, and his skullcap fell off. And suddenly Buchsbaum, shoved by the scruff of his neck, fell into the pit.

The tall man, hands on hips, declaimed, Beloved sun, tearfully begged from the Lord God Almighty.

That was a bad sign.

From then on, Gabe Gudel walked about the world stupefied; he walked about the streets of Szabasowa and talked to himself, while his tangled corkscrew curls stuck out like those of a drowned man. All winter, the German gendarmes allowed him to walk about the town. They took pictures of him and showed him to foreign journalists passing through the Eastern front.

Most often, Gabe Gudel stood at the gate of the Jewish orphanage. Incessantly peeping under his armpit, where straw was stuck, he would thrust out his right hand in front of him with his skull-cap clenched in his fist, and say to the hungry children,

" . . . And the silence of the town? Which of you knows the silence of the town? A chimney is a silent town. Smoke may be the noise of a living town, but a silent town is smokeless, without the red glow of light, without the eternal flame of the Lord's Temples, without a word . . ."

The children, muffled up in rags, stood nearby and watched his lips during his monologue, and when Gabe Gudel peeped under his arm, it seemed to them that maybe he had something to eat there, and would begin to hand it around. Ah, frail and beloved miracles!

And a gang of spies walked the alleys day and night, led here and there by an invisible ringleader, pouring gold, pearls, pepper, and tallithin sewn with gold into a suitcase. German infantry on the way to Kiev marched along the broad asphalt near Szaba-sowa, tanks and artillery passed on broad treads, motorcyclists drove by, fast automobiles with radios, pontoons, ambulances, supply columns, field gendarmerie, espionage experts and agents, front-line and reserve girls. It went on interminably. Trains carried ammunition, heavy artillery, horses, sleighs painted white.

Lighting the candle one evening, Cirla said to Chuny Shaya, "Hide. They're coming here."

He barely had time to slam the door and run into the orchard.

The gendarmes came to Nudel's hut, and making a way for themselves with their knees through numerous children, dragged Nudel out to the gate and shot him. He could be seen through the window as he stood for a moment, pressed one hand to his ear, shrieked something, and fell down forever.

"We've lived to see accursed times," Mrs. Szerucki said.

Smoke was hanging all around, the town center was covered by fires.

Shames Buchsbaum fasted, was collapsing with suffering, and when Cirla gave him a potato pancake one evening, he held it in one hand, lacking the boldness to eat it, then gave it to his youngest grandchild. The men were being rounded up. They herded them, starving, dirty, barely able to drag themselves along, to the quarries, or to work on railroad constructions, or they shot them in the forest. And the human hearts in Szabasowa suddenly stopped beating, or else beat fast and pounded like crazy. Artillery rumbled in the East, the earth shuddered. They killed Mrs. Szerucki in the marketplace because she stood up for a Jewish child: "Everyone knows you did it out of kindness of heart, woman. Serves you right," said an Ukrainian policeman.

And the child remained, not finished off, on the sidewalk. Two little dead feet were lying on the asphalt, and its eyes were wide open to the warm summer night, cut through with the shrieks of raped girls.

"Oh, holy Jesus," groaned old Tombak, dragging himself along and collecting ends of German cigarettes. A horse neighed for hunger in a stable; there was no one to bring from the railroad station by droshky. And at dusk people walked with bowed heads, their eyes fixed on the ground.

At dusk firing began to resound in the workers' suburb; rockets flashed.

Tombak sighed deeply, lit a cigarette, wanted to show Josie the shortest way to Sawarynka, but heavy and boring rain was falling, and there was no way of telling when it would stop.

They went under the roof of a partly demolished building. The soaked horses, waving their tails, started into the empty street. It got dark. Immediately after the troops a train arrived, and after the gendarmes three civilians and a girl with a big dog stepped out. Then Tombak encountered them on Railroad Street, on Golden and Castle Streets.

"What are you standing here for?" they asked.

"Cab for hire."

"So what? Jew or Pole?"

"Pole."

They said he should drive them to the richest Jew in Szabasowa.

"And that colleague of yours, is he a Jew?" they asked. "Why is he tembling so?"

"He's old."

"And aren't you old? Confound you!"

Josie Propst pulled his head down into his collar. They lit a match, and the one in the tunic kicked Josie in the belly and ordered him to drive to the Jewish consistory. In a fatherly manner he added, "You should get a blanket for the horse, else it will lose it's marrow, and what sort of business is that, speaking frankly?"

Someone else from the group of people broke away, caught up with Josie, and got in. A flashlight from the sidewalk followed them quite far.

"Bultz will be here right away; then we'll go. Do you know Bernhaut?" they said to Tombak.

"Well?"

"Well, drive us to Bernhaut's," said Bultz, getting into the droshky.

"I know very well," said Bultz, "that it will be necessary to walk around all night, looking for them in the cellars. For an instant Jewish faces are to be seen; you switch off the flashlight, and the groping starts. I don't let any movement out of my sight. They have made pits under the cellars, and the thing is to grab them on the way to these pits. Then two matters are settled."

Suddenly they heard "Halt!"

"Criminal Investigation Office," they shouted back.

The gendarmes moved away, shouldering their rifles.

They knocked on the door.

"What's happened?" asked Bernhaut.

"You must open up!"

"Oh, Jesus," cried Turyca from the darkness; she was almost dead with emotion; she was stifling, but kept shouting,

"The children! Don't shoot the children! You're fathers yourselves!"

Bernhaut shouted loudly to someone. And a man with a pumpkin-like face came up to him and kicked him until the sound died away.

"What are you shrieking for, you fart?"

Bernhaut wanted to reply with his fists, but the pumpkin-faced man crossed the threshold and closed in on him with an automatic aimed at his chest. Nothing happened; in the darkness he missed. He went on smoking a cigarette cupped in one hand. Bernhaut's wife came into the hallway, wearing only a nightdress; she was stout and portly. She groped for her husband; he seemed warm, but he was breathing as heavily as though he had been dragging an anvil into the attic.

A plump hand with a bottle was suspended over the glasses.

"Remember, Tombak. Ask fewer questions and mind your own

business. Everything has been seriously investigated. Bernstein's diamond is in Szabasowa. No one has taken it away yet. Yes, we know there are various hiding places in the synagogue. But a diamond can be hidden in a loose tooth, in a nose, in the bowels. Well, can't it?"

But it was as though Tombak had not heard. He pursued the stupid narrative; he smacked his lips, sucked his mustaches, got red, and undid the padded waistcoat over his broad chest. The informer got another bottle of vodka out of the pocket of his patched raincoat, poured it, and munched a piece of withered yellow lard without bread.

"Well, can't it?"

"Can't what?"

"You know where Bernstein is hiding."

Tombak stifled his loathing of this horrible, brutal man with all his might.

"I don't want to," he retorted, when it was finally necessary to say something on the subject.

"Well?"

"Don't 'well' me, damn your eyes."

And, hunched up, he went out to see if the horse blanket had been stolen. He came back, sat down in his previous place, brought the *Krakauer Zeitung* out of his pocket, and shifted up to the candle. Set his eyes afire, son of a bitch, he thought.

A door in the hallway creaked; there was a cautious squeak in the kitchen. Black night was standing outside the window, sludgy and impenetrable as eternity. Tombak went out, and took the feedbag off the horse.

"It's a good thing you waited," said a girl, coming up to the droshky. She could be seen by a beam of light from a window, taking off her beret, removing a school badge. "They have killed my father."

"Oh, God!"

"Drive me to the bacon factory; I'm going to look for his body."

Bultz and Ciszka came out of the guardroom. They were walking together in silence.

"Here she is," Bultz whispered. "Come closer! What are you doing here, miss? A light, Ciszka!"

"What's your name?"

"Rozia."

"The rest?"

"Arnstein."

"Come with us, miss," said Bultz.

Tombak could hear the beating of this girl's heart; he crept cautiously toward her back and slipped an axle key into her hand. She made as if to strike, as though the entire burden of despair had come together in her hand, and struck. Bultz was hurled to the wall. Ciszka took over; her coat slipped off, but she wrenched herself away and ran. She could be heard jumping from the concrete into a field.

Afterwards, she used to come for the night to old Mrs. Szerucki's. The fear that Szerucki would perish in the war was born in her with savage force. She fell asleep with her curly head in the old lady's lap, and saliva flowed from her lips like a drop from a cut fruit.

"Get in!" shouted Ciszka, and waved his hand. "To Railroad Street."

Only a few people knew that Tombak could feign humility when he had to. He was cunning, secretive, slippery, crammed with thoughts of hate. He could drink without losing his senses, his eyes sharp, his ears vigilant — everything about everybody!

He clenched his dry fist and struck the horse. Ciszka, hunched, bald, little, as though he had no lungs in his shallow chest, inhaled cigarette smoke and leaned out with an agile movement to see if Tombak was going the right way.

"You're fettered by morals, Tombak."

"Why?"

"The *Landkommissar* must have this diamond. It would be worth your while to get involved. Drive to Jurydyka."

They went into Mrs. Arnstein's bedroom. Flowers were standing in the windows. Mrs. Arnstein opened a closet. There were ties hanging behind the door. Ciszka investigated everything closely. They lifted the piano lid; Arnstein's last letter was lying there. They took away a violoncello and radio.

Night was falling; only once a machine gun was fired in New Street. Not a single star shone, not even a spark was visible above the black town. The only light burning was in the Criminal Police guardroom.

It is not cheerful to stand still when there is an autumnal, dark night outside. A man's shriek was heard. They were kicking his shoulders.

Bultz sat at the back, revolver on his knees. The horse lifted its broken leg. A hoof clanged.

"You a Catholic? What sort of Catholic are you? You work for Jews on their Sabbath!"

"Jeeez!" cried the man they were beating.

"You spit out that Jesus!"

Not a single star. Horse-face's mother had come up and was listening. They were beating her son. She crouched and groped with one hand; the threshold was dirty, little pebbles mixed with mud. She knocked on the door.

"Take yourself off, woman, or we'll shoot. Don't interrupt our interrogation. The sooner it ends, the sooner you'll see your son. We won't punch his eyes out. Well, get away from the door."

"Open it, Ciszka. You're serving them. Are you afraid to open?"

"Don't hang about the door. You won't get anyplace."

"Why are you afraid to open? I want to see my son and tell the German something."

"This is no place for an old hag. It's a criminal matter. Understand?"

"Open the door," the woman shrieked, and banged her fist on it.

Tombak rubbed his nose and heard Bultz throw her down the stairs. She scuffled around the fence and fell down again.

Bultz came back to the droshky breathless. He asked,

"How do you feel, Tombak, eh?"

"Not bad. My shoulders ache a little."

"I too feel that my shoulders ache. Does he know anything about Bernstein's diamond? What do you think?"

"Oh, God. Who can tell?"

"What?"

"Who can tell?"

"Don't pretend, you dummy. We'll give you such a going-over today that you won't know what hit you."

Tombak said nothing, but clenched his fists until they sweated.

"Horse-face . . . who's he?"

"He's from a poor family. He's a porter."

"What do you know about him?"

"Well . . . a porter. His father was a porter, too. In his father's time, there was still work for a porter in Szabasowa, it was a transit station. But he was often out of work, and would dream away the summer in Rojowka. Sometimes on market days he'd jump onto a truck. In the fall they poured corn into the wagons. Planks, sometimes lime, God knows what, to make some money.

Everyone thought, Let him make something of himself. When he's dressed up, it seems he's a better guy."

"What does 'a better guy' mean?"

"A handsome bachelor."

"What happened between him and the Polish police?"

"How shall I say . . . he was a hard man, he bit the hand of anyone who wanted to have him jailed for picking pockets. For someone once set in circulation the nonsense that he was a pickpocket. What can a poor man do about that? People can call you what they like. You know how it is. When I think of it all, the only thing I can say is . . . Goddamn it. Surely it was God who sent down such punishment."

"And it was God sent you with your horse and droshky. We would not have been able to manage tonight! Eh?"

Tombak was silent. The shouting in the guardroom increased. Bultz walked around the droshky, and stopped in the darkness.

"There's only one thing I don't understand," he said, "why doesn't the animal confess?"

Tombak climbed up and straightened the blanket on his horse. Bultz went back, turning up his collar. In the glare his pumpkin-like face could be recognized. He rolled a cigarette.

"Mind, Tombak," he said, "mind you don't tell anyone what has happened here and is still going to happen."

They let Gabe Marasz and Spojdyk out after midnight; someone went out after them wearing a leather, gleaming leather, raincoat. And they called Tombak in at once. The whole corridor was swimming in water and vomit. A German in uniform was sitting in the bright room.

"Where do you want to get it?" asked some stranger. Ciszka was standing beside him, and nudged him.

"In the ear, apparently. Isn't that so, Tombak?" said Ciszka.

"And what did the gentlemen want?"

He told them he had driven up to the railroad station at dusk. It had not been possible earlier. Because they were unloading prisoners of war, the gendarmes allowed no one to stop in Railroad Street. He had not the faintest idea where Bernstein was, and his meeting with Miss Arnstein had been pure chance.

"You say you're telling the truth, do you?"

"Yes," said Tombak, "and I don't know why the devil I have to mess about here."

"Listen," said the stranger, brandishing his revolver under Tombak's very nose, "you, brother, old guts, you can mess about.

We'll smack you in the heart before you know what's happened."

"Don't scare the guy," Ciszka put in. "I'd advise you to go easy. He may come in useful in the business."

"Very likely, but he's a brute of his own kind."

"You can't talk that way."

Ciszka swung his hand and hit Tombak between the eyes. A second blow felled him. He sat down on the floor. Ciszka kicked him three times in the chest. Tombak grabbed a chair leg, tried to rise, but the soles of his shoes slithered to the wall.

"You, sir, investigating the Bernstein case, must know that he's primarily a moralist," the German said to Ciszka. "The environment of his influence must be decoded."

"Certainly."

"Very well. So that environment must be plunged into. Well, I think this will be the end for today. Do you perhaps want to appoint provocateurs? Also — "

Someone violently threw open the door to the corridor. A tall man in a lancer's jacket, pushed from behind, rushed into the room. His swollen eyes were bloodshot. He grabbed at his black, wet hair.

"Get up." Someone kicked Tombak.

Watching it all attentively, Tombak noticed that Bultz was not among those present. Behind the tall man was unshaven little Bilig, and he was holding a revolver in one fist. Everyone was silent a moment. Ciszka's lips curved in a smile.

"In order," said the German.

"Put that revolver away in your pocket, Bilig," Ciszka ordered, and he blew out the lamp on the desk. "You can all go."

The tall man in the lancer's jacket and Bilig went out in silence. After them went Tombak, cap in hand. His hair was matted with sweat and blood, and his right eyelid drooped down over his eye; he changed step like a drunk. On the driver's seat he cleared his throat. The blood was still pounding in his temples. The horse was pacing slowly, and someone passed the droshky. Tombak did not recognize who it was, but on the street corner a shadow came up and in a resounding young voice, seizing hold of the whip, said,

"Listen to me, Tombak, I know you. If it were necessary to hide someplace . . . can you be counted on? You know what I'm talking about. I could give you something. Agreed?"

"What can I say . . . but who are you?"

"Bilig."

"Oh, God!" Terrible myths in the dark night, everything stifled and hidden had assuredly emerged into the world this night. "What do you want? Get away. I've had as much as I want of this."

He thrust Bilig away with both powerful, hard hands. Someone wearing heavy boots ran up from behind. Suddenly a shot was fired. A man caught in the flash of a pocket lamp was writhing, and he ran across the street with his knees under his chin, and then, as it were, slowly straightened himself on the tips of his toes and fell with his head and chest against a tavern wall.

The night began to thin out a little. The man lying there in the darkness could be heard scraping his feet from time to time. The noise of heavy artillery, which was shaking the earth somewhere in the East, mingled with the whining of dogs and rattle of windowpanes in the pharmacy. The streets settled in a damp mist; everything was smoking with bluish dampness.

The trees along Cemetery Street were rustling, and the cannons thundered beyond the hills.

Shames Buchsbaum, liberated from the world and the Hasidim, was sleeping in a damp hallway. Toward dawn, Tombak knocked on the pinewood door. Holding his breath, he listened to the clattering on the plank bed. A clock in the room, choking and rattling its hands, struck four. Old Buchsbaum could be heard groping at the wall in the dark. The crooked shutter opened soundlessly.

"Cirla went into the country for bread today, and hasn't come back. She's staying the night there, for sure. I'm alone with my grandchildren."

"Things are very bad," said Tombak.

"What does that mean?"

"Someone may come here regarding the Bernstein case."

"Why Bernstein?"

"Did he have anything to do with you? Yesterday or the day before?"

"Yes."

"The German Criminal Police are after him. Watch out that you don't catch it."

"Do you think there's anything serious in it?" asked Buchsbaum.

"Well, yes. They may kill. Don't sit over the Talmud. As soon as it gets light, go into the cemetery and stay there all day. Jadwiga will take the children somewhere, perhaps she will take them into the bean plot."

Buchsbaum gave him a bony hand, and said in a low, clear bass voice,

"We can praise God that in the infinity of His Grace He ceded His majesty unto man. Even if I have to run away to the cemetery — I will let you know. I won't let anyone insult you. Thank you. Go back to your own people."

Without taking off his boots, Tombak lay down on straw in the stable, divided from the horse by poles.

"Here I am," he whispered to the dog; "don't be afraid."

The dog pushed its cold muzzle behind Tombak's ear and licked his neck.

"Let's forget once and for all. I kicked you, but now I'll scratch you a little behind the ears."

The dog coiled itself into a ball and whined. The horse snuffled through its feed in the manger, and a drain behind the stable rumbled. Then Tombak smelled smoke. He went out. Little houses immediately stood out in the glow. Bezkiszki's hut was on fire. The barn was empty. Along the way a murdered man was lying in a puddle; the chaff was full of the traces of people. On the dead man's forehead shivered the glow of the nearby fire. No one was calling for help.

The door was slightly ajar to the hallway; on the threshold of the room stood Ksawera.

"Where have you been all night?" she asked.

"What happened there?" he indicated the fire.

"Two men took Bezkiszki away and set fire to the hut."

He went into the room. A woman in a shift was sitting on the floor, her head against a little table; a child was standing beside her, frightened and spattered. Bezkiszki's wife was lying behind the stove, out of her mind, stretched at full length, her eyes closed. She rose when Tombak came in, leaped to the wall, and began shrieking as though to a stranger,

"What do all of you want? Haskel isn't here!"

Keeping by the wall, Tombak intended to go over and calm her, but he could not keep his feet. He said in a weak voice,

"Calm down. They'll question him, then let him go. Ksawera, take two buckets of water and put them in front of the threshold. Get dressed and watch for the fireguard."

But after a moment he rose, found a bucket, brought water, took an ax, and stopped on the threshold.

Some stranger or other, in a jacket and top boots, came into the yard from Mrs. Szerucki's little garden.

"Anyone come running this way?" he asked.

Tombak recalled having seen him someplace that night, and to get rid of him, said,

"Yes, someone ran by a moment ago. That way, to the cemetery."

"What can you tell me about Father Banczycki?"

"Father Banczycki is fat, with flat feet. He likes horses."

"And does he like Jews?"

"Who can tell?"

"Would you come with us to see him?"

"It's a long way. Something like twenty miles."

"That doesn't matter. Feed the horses, and we'll get there somehow. What do you think, can you trust him? To hide something at his place, for instance? After all, you once drove those refugees from Prague."

"I didn't drive them. Horse-face turned them out near the forest and drove them into the fields."

"Don't you remember where?"

"No, I don't. What happened was that Horse-face brought them one evening to me. They looked like brothers. I made up a bed for them in the alcove, but they didn't sleep until morning. Then Horse-face came, and said, 'Seems they've copped Paliczka. That really would be bad luck.' Then he came again, and gave a watch to the younger man, and told him, 'You must not leave later than four.' At that time we set out. I looked ahead. Nothing, only darkness on the road. Only crows walking about for winter corn. They thought someone might be standing hidden behind a barrier on the bridge to interrupt the journey. The young men were panting with exhaustion. 'It's a broken pine tree,' I said to them, to calm them. 'It happened just as I am telling you now. Father Banczycki had nothing to do with it. Surely there aren't any ambushes for people there. He's a sensible man.'"

The man in the jacket and top boots went away in the direction of the cemetery.

I was sitting huddled up, my head hidden in my hands. Everything was again becoming clear and evident. The clock had stopped at twelve. It was a full, bright afternoon. I found an old servant woman in Nadel's room, who told me in a tired whisper everything that had happened to her master a little while back. Opposite the window, Jewish laborers guarded by armed police were erecting a high fence. They were barricading the ghetto. Hoarse breathing came from the next room. Nadel was sitting on the bed, breathing on his spectacles, a tefillin on his head.

"Please take a look, I hate them!" he called loudly. His eyes were burning, and he raised his hands stiffly.

"Warm today," I said.

"Certainly is. The fall . . . a splendid time of year."

"There are mushrooms in the forest — "

"Don't speak of the forest. I shall never give way to the dominance of fear, and shall go out only in the event of fire. There are no plans either for the forest, or for men or space."

"Now there's still time in any case. Emilka feels good; she would like to see you."

"Emilka! There is no Emilka!" he shrieked, and started banging one hand on the wall. "You and I will be the cause of her death. Ciszka came and hit me in the chest with fists full of dollars. They wanted to take her, to hide her."

He gazed at me with penetrating, terrible eyes. It seemed to me I was standing in a persistent wind.

It was like this. Arm in arm with Emilka, in pouring rain, stumbling, we were running by terrible paths as fast as we could go into the fields. As far as possible from death. For a long time the cry "Emilka! Emilka!" reached us.

Nadel's flabby cheeks shook with laughter:

"No fear, sir, I'm unshakable."

After unwrapping a piece of paper and catching sight of a large gold coin, he contemptuously threw it out of the window. He was just about to open his mouth, to tell me what he wanted, and I had to leave, for at that very moment a secret agent was approaching. He took me to his place and began again:

"Look, we wanted to discuss a certain matter with you. Have you ever thought of earning good money? You could help us, and clean up. I have the idea it would suffice for a whole lifetime. You could stay in bed late, with a cup of genuine coffee, and no one would disturb you."

The noise of a typewriter came from the next room. The sound and clatter of carpentry work came from the square.

"One must keep one's mind off things a little," said the agent, stroking his whiskers, and he took his hat. "Will you have a beer?

I'll tell you what I intend to do. For the time being, I'll give you the right of reviling Krauts and a sack of oatmeal."

Tombak was sitting with his hands tightly clasped, rocking backwards and forwards, no one knew why. His eyes were closed. The agent was looking for something in a drawer; he opened the cupboard; finally he approached and put one hand on Tombak's arm. His legs in breeches jerked; then, having placed his left hand on the other man's shoulder, he raised his right hand and hit him in the face. Tombak's teeth chattered; there was a blueness in his eyes, and little ovules appeared. With each deep breath, something in him swelled; he began to feel enormous and fuzzy. But everything wavered; he thought something and began shouting insultingly. The agent threw some gasoline on his face and set fire to it. He had to put the fire out on himself with his own sleeves.

"I regard a confession as doubtful," said the agent to the sergeant major.

"Postpone the interrogation. What do you intend to do with this prick?"

Hands on hips, the sergeant began upbraiding the agent.

"Oh, this is awful," the agent defended himself.

"When one golden boy slanders another, then you — damn you!"

"I regard every detail as important."

"Intensity in work is important. Everything else is superficial and tiresome. Does he really know Banczycki?"

The gendarme took a newspaper from the pocket of his green topcoat and began reading out something from the advertising column.

They arrived after midnight and at once unharnessed the weary horses and put them in Tombak's spacious stable. Szerucki found a scythe by a rafter, went out into the garden, and in the darkness cut down two blankets of old straw.

The moon was rising, and there was a smell of apples piled in a heap under the workshop window. Szerucki went into the open stable and stretched out his hands before him. The manger was empty, a chain was hanging down, old dung crackled underfoot.

Two grenades exploded like two strokes of a cracked bell in the Foresta district, and shrieking arose there. Chuny Shaya could be heard drumming his fingernails lightly on the windowpane. His father-in-law, Buchsbaum, went out and was whispering there for a long time. And before a fragment of dark sky in the East grew lighter, Bezkiszki, Tombak, Bernaszewski, Mechuten, and Kweller knew that Kuba Szerucki and Chuny Shaya had escaped from the Bereza prison, and that they had brought the horses.

Tombak came first; he tugged his gray whiskers and shouted, louder than necessary,

"Well, thank God! You're back! But you've grown as thin as a dog."

Szerucki was sitting on a crate near the stove, soaking his feet in a wooden tub.

"How are you, Uncle?" he said, hoarsely.

"Good to see you back. Have a good sleep, and tomorrow we'll start doing an urgent job right away."

"What's so urgent?"

Pancakes were cooking on the stove. Szerucki looked away and turned them over: "Sit down, all of you."

"Some stranger or other is in Kant's restaurant, sitting and smoking a cigar," said Tombak. "He tells me to drive around Szabasowa, and asks questions about diamonds. And I was scared, I can tell you. To tell the truth, I'm scared of that man. He always has his hat pulled down over his eyes. He stares at you with big eyes, and it seems as though he doesn't see anything, but he does, the son of a bitch. He sees diamonds everywhere. And that stranger who took over Kalir's pharmacy, after cleaning the little plate of the weights with a cloth, sticks a match between his teeth and watches after us from the threshold. The man with a cigar waves a greeting to him, and we drive down Blacharska Street and Meisels, to New Street, and there he prowls around in the houses."

Szerucki rooted in his pocket and handed Tombak some tobacco.

"This, Uncle, is damned work."

"It is, is it?"

"Did a lot of police come with the Krauts?"

"Hard to say. Only Banczycki explained yesterday to Klara Wasicinska that these dark strangers with mustaches and bags under their eyes are the greatest plague. There are three of them, and one girl in fine stockings, with a dog under her arm. Well, and what will you be doing now?" asked Tombak, expelling blue smoke from his nose. "You'll have to drop the cartwrighting trade unless you take to making coffins, for there will be a demand for that merchandise. Yesterday they massacred seventeen men and women in the magistrate's yard. What do you think, everyone will want to bury their loved ones in baize coffins? What do you think?"

Szerucki squeezed a fragment of pancake between his fingers, placed his work-stained hands on his knees. "I'm not going to make coffins."

"Well, you're right. A young man ought not to do that. If I were thirty, like you — ha! — man! Everything ahead of me . . . But now one tiepin can set you on your feet."

"I don't understand a word you're saying."

"I think it might be possible to drive a pair of horses for a good distance. I see you brought a strong horse for the journey."

"It foundered on the way; it'll have to be left alone around two weeks."

"It's not foundering, Kuba. I looked. As I work it out, its hoof is swollen. Two or three days, and the pus will come out of the fistula, and it will be all right."

Old Mrs. Szerucki came into the room, swiftly blowing goat hair from the milk, which she placed on the red-hot ring.

"They killed Nadel yesterday; they took the horse, but the droshky is standing in Kowalska Street. You might give his widow some apples, and that will settle the matter. What do you think?"

"I thought of that. But do either of you know what has happened to Klara?"

"The Criminal Police took her. Yesterday they drove her children from Castle Street to the Small Market, and this informer tactfully said to them, 'Well, children, now you can hold hands, we'll go to the very end.' 'But sir, we don't want to go anyplace.' 'But I'm asking you to,' says that son of a bitch. 'I don't want to stand on ceremony with you.' Klara is not in Szabasowa. You ought not to worry about her. Her mother hurried over here to find out about her, and Samiczka told her that she would pay for having worked for Jews, and she said, 'Don't cry, old woman, because that won't help any. If she wanted, Klara could do well for herself.' "

"What does 'do well for herself' mean?" shouted Szerucki.

"Don't make a noise."

Szerucki rose, dried his feet on an army shirt, put his bare feet into slippers, and went to the window. Dew was glittering in the sunny yard. The withering mallows were covered with reddish dust.

"Drink the milk. Then go and bury the murdered Bernaszewski. Don't let him lie in a stranger's garden," said Mrs. Szerucki. She was, as it were, embarrassed; she glanced at her son and at Tombak, who was dipping a pancake into the milk.

"This day he was somehow odd, uneasy. He didn't want to do anything."

"Does Mrs. Bernaszewski know?"

"Yes, yes. She came and wrapped him in a blanket."

"If only he'd jump out of the window," said Tombak, and he frowned.

"Pah! Bultz jumped out right after him, and fired. He shot him directly in the mouth."

"Who took our cow?" asked Szerucki.

"Drink your milk," Mrs. Szerucki begged.

"That Bultz has a big belly on thin legs. Poland fed these bull-dogs," Tombak lowered his head, touched his boot-leg with his right hand, straightened up, and reached out a hand to Szerucki.

"Everything will be fine, you'll see. Once I talked to your late father about Bultz: 'Just look, Pietrek, at the way that shit is squashing bees.' He used to take them, you know — and he was still a little lad — he took bees and suffocated them in an empty matchbox. A bee was sitting on a plank, rubbing its little wings with its legs, as they do in summer. It was cleaning itself of every-thing that wasn't necessary for its flight; it rubbed its head and puffed out its sides, as a drone usually does. But he, damn it, took the box and bang! The bee started buzzing as though on a bass fiddle, and that was the end of it. He used to do that for a long time. Sometimes I showed your father. Then he started on dogs. To kill a dog with a stick is a big thing. First you need strength, and you have to be evil. He set about a dog in a corner and beat it to death. You don't have to say anything about that. I can see right away what you think of it. I tell you, anyone who kills bees can kill a man, and will kill Jews. Give me something to smoke. And you know what, Kuba — get that rifle down from the cor-nice, and bury it. Listen to me, I'm an old man. You think Chuny Shaya will survive what is happening now?" He stroked his whiskers; a lock of hair drooped from under his cap and hung over his right eye.

It is crowded and poverty-stricken on Cemetery Street. Crows sit on fences amidst ragged linen, cleaning their beaks and watch-ing children build sand castles in the alleys. Starlings flutter with a laugh around the tall plane trees behind the cemetery, and only yesterday Chuny Shaya's children stood by the fence and enjoyed the sun. In summer, the trees intertwine over the crowns of wild hops; dense blackberry bushes crackle underfoot. In the under-growth a surge of birds and the high blue grass veil the gray Jewish tombs. In fall it is quiet, mysterious, and rare flowers bloom in the half-light, and often huge dung-beetles and fat spiders creep into the hut. A spade clinks. In winter it is dense and deserted. Only reddish blue tombstones, topped with snow, loom, cosy for the night's lodging of rabbits.

"Now, go," said the agent to Tombak, sniffing his middle finger, greenish with nicotine.

Dogs are resting in the shadow of empty houses, curled into balls, lying motionless. Sunflowers in the weeds. But when a man passes the shacks of the ghetto, and sees himself alone on the deserted road to the railroad station, his previous noble certainty deserts him. He sat down on the scarp and stared ahead, though he did not see either the area of waving corn, or the villages surrounded by trees, or the clouds. But in this solitude no one saw him either, with his eyes raised to the sky. He decided to look for Bernstein's child.

"Yes, God's first gift — and his most beautiful deed — is life." He said it to himself, so as not to fall down halfway.

At every disaster mentioned in the most ancient of texts, a child dips its finger into a glass and lets drops of red, ceremonial wine, as the drink of joy, fall on the Bible. Across the sleepy cheek, half hidden in curls which emerge from under the little black Jewish skullcap, there runs an imperceptible smile.

What does a prudent child ask for?

What does a simpleton say?

Nudel had the biggest diamond in Szabasowa. It was as big as an ox's eye. Tombak used to drive Nudel to parties at the Star. The diamond sparkled to the street lamps in Jurydyka, and lit the way at crossings. Ah! With that diamond he could have bought up the most important German with all his politics! But Nudel is dead. One bullet brought him down on the threshold. Oh, God! And mice dragged the diamond away. It is quiet as the grave.

Tombak brought one hand out of the pocket of his padded burnous and plunged it into the air like a dagger, to kill some enemy or other.

Sparrows were pecking under the horses' feed bags. The train had still not arrived. A porter was standing on the threshold, picking an eyetooth, saliva trickling down to his wrist. Children were chasing a stray dog with a tin chamber pot tied to his tail, down Railroad Street.

"And I tell you, nothing makes a man angrier than a comrade

who's scared," Tombak said to Josie. "You explain this and that to him. Take when I was driving the financier and Father Banc-zycki from the railroad station. The priest said to the financier, 'Will the disappearance of the human race occur?' Then he lit a cigarette. The financier didn't reply. Finally he asked, 'What are you getting at, Father?' The priest asked, 'Aren't your children ashamed of you?' After the financier jumped out, on Carpenter Street, the priest said to me, 'That's a man with an oval face. So far no one in the world ever wrote a book about a man with an oval face. You know whom I'm speaking of, Tombak . . . there stands a tree stump with an ax driven into it, and a deaf angel is watching the huts. True?' "

Tombak quoted several pieces of advice:

"Josie, if they begin firing, don't be scared, brother. Don't jump off the box. And remember, a Catholic doesn't wave his hands when he's talking."

And old Tombak, the kindhearted droshky man, brought up in poverty, changed into a hard, unyielding man without a tear or mercy. Someone once said of Tombak that he had had some mother or other who fed him on berries in the forest, nursed him holding him in her woolen lap, and gave him a strange heart, like the wedge in a windmill. And everyone knows the wedge is the oldest and most important thing in a windmill. As the wedge is, so is the flour. But Tombak's life hadn't been wasted. And who knew the life of Josie Propst? Up to the age of forty, he carried water for the rich to bathe in, until a great sore opened on his shoulders from the yoke. Then he bought a horse and a droshky.

"Josie, no one here remembers you. Except Roth, but he's in Vienna."

Old Josie Propst, tall, with an eagle's nose and gray eyes, a tou-sled beard, looked like the picture of a saint. Once an old woman who met him behind the fence of Foresta's sawmill crossed herself and said some pleasant words.

"That was at one time in my life. Now I have a rupture, and I can't walk far. She saw me there during Easter."

"Ho!" bellowed Tombak. His terrible instincts cooled within him; they had survived his youth, his manhood, and into old age. Again he turned to Josie, tapping his boot top with his whip. I tell you . . . Blood, damn it . . . and I with a bayonet. Only remem-ber: a Catholic doesn't talk with his hands. This isn't a Jewish wedding."

"If you'd seen me, Tombak, when I was young and walking

with my wife." Josie, overcome with timidity, was telling him with some difficulty.

"I saw you, Josie. The Austrian secret agent saw you too, in 1905, ho, ho!"

Josie continued spinning his reminiscences; Szerucki and Chuny Shaya listened to him attentively. They had been searching the Zawodz meadow, through which two Germans were taking some woman to a shed in the town marketplace. A black horse was nibbling a mare's mane. Josie went back twice to the details of the killing of a Russian gendarme for raping his mother. Josie did not use empty words. After a short description of the killing of the gendarme Altanov, he sighed and declared, "The Creator appointed me an orphan in this world. But a man doesn't repent. It is only the past life of a poor man I am telling you of."

"Ah!" — Tombak brandished one hand — "the wind blows when a widow sows wheat. You don't know, Josie, that the life of a poor man lasts forever. Only like cattle, which live almost forever in poverty. Only creatures born from a double yoke are fortunate. The forest echo comes from a double yoke: the nightjar, the *anderduczka*, the *kurupietek*, and the *arpaniatko*. Josie, don't get agitated. The bullfinch, listen, the bullfinch flies high above the clouds to find out about the weather."

A civilian in a green trench coat, with a leather pilot's cap on his big head, came up to the porter's threshold from the stores. After him, step by step, was walking Bernstein's little son, barefoot and wearing only a shirt.

The train had not come. The noise of passing carts flew over from Szabasowa; a machine gun rattled far away in the forest.

The man in the leather pilot's cap was short, with smudges under his eyes, and had narrow hips; he cast stern looks around. He did not leave the range of his area: the railroad station, the square, the cabstand, and the guardroom with telephone. He said sweetly to the cabbies that his fervor in the service was nothing more than concern for order in the railroad station and that people ought to help him in his difficult work.

"I can sometimes be disagreeable to a person, but through that, some other person is saved. Isn't that so?" he spoke flatly and a lot like all men with an obscure past. Szerucki considered all Tombak's little talks with the spy as shameful. He intended to start the matter within a day, though only Chuny Shaya knew this. The case of Bernstein's diamond was a cunning stratagem of another kind, some acting in agreement with a cunning street urchin or other, and involving so much that it was hard to find out who had peached and who had committed murder in the cellar. All this comes from lying tongues. It stinks of death and is as tedious as dead and scattered flies on a threshold. Well, isn't it?

"No one is stopping us, damn it, no one," said Szerucki to Chuny.

Chuny's face was flushed; he shot furtive glances along Railroad Street. Whenever he shut his eyes, at once the phantoms of people running away in confusion through a storm of bullets appeared on a black sheet of glass, and his children, massacred on the corner of Korzeniowski Street. "I don't want you to show yourself with the children in daytime. Get some air in the cellar . . . a man must have the right to live."

"My hand is very heavy. Look, how the veins run," he lifted his fist under Szerucki's nose. The latter was looking at the ground, uncertain of the day's business, gloomy and withdrawn.

A shunter whistled in the station, a locomotive was pushing wagons with white-painted sleighs. From somewhere far away came the scent of autumnal space, sweet leaves and deal fumes from the sawmill. Horse-face, short, lean, with deep-set black eyes, was wearing a lancer's jacket. He was a man who, as had once been reported to the police, knew just how, where, when, and in what manner to escape from county jails. He had heavy jaws — he had bitten the fingers of a man arresting him.

He glanced into Chuny Shaya's eyes, scratched the back of his neck.

Tombak, pretending enormous satisfaction with the world, shouted, "My respects!"

"Oh, good morning," said the man on the threshold, touching his leather cap, holding the sleeve of Bernstein's child by his left hand.

"A cigarette?" called Tombak, and he snapped his fingers as one does to someone pleasant.

"For you, as a friend, eh?"

Tombak climbed off the box, straightened something in his right coattail, stopped close to the spy; they clapped one another on the shoulder. Tombak rolled a cigarette in his hand as though it were a dumpling.

Josie, accustomed to all sorts of tricks, patiently and calmly kept a tight grip on himself. He glanced at the sky.

"How late is the train?" asked Szerucki, and he also got off the box, pretending as he did so to be a resigned man with benumbed legs and an empty belly.

"Neither I nor you will be on top, boss." Tombak took the spy's right hand, struck the palm, and pressed it like pincers. With his left hand he bumped him on the head. The door frame responded. Puffy eyes drew to the crack. The spy looked around, seeking someone, but after Szerucki's blow, he was trembling with pain and sucked his saliva, as if trying to cry out. Blood emerged from his nose. Old Tombak fell down. Chuny dragged him from under the feet of the spy, who no longer had any idea what was going on.

Tombak jumped to the back seat with Bernstein's child and let the horse go.

Having raised the reins with leaden hand, Josie Propst set off last from the Szabasowa railroad station. Heavy bombers were flying somewhere over the blue, autumnal landscape. A porter, revolver ready to fire, ran down the little street as if afraid his indignation would end in some horrible mangling.

Josie Propst stopped his horse behind Foresta's sawmill. He tried to quench the flowing blood. His entire body was permeated with a pleasant warmth. He sat down, and with this softness bordering on unconsciousness, laid him down by some railings. The horse seized the droshky, and frightening those who were running away, drove with a rushing, clumsy gallop down the little streets of Folwarki.

His daughter wiped his tears. She too was vivacious, spry, and energetic. But she looked around the room incredulously. She said discontentedly to Josie, "He can't stay any longer. The child isn't dressed for his last journey from Szabasowa."

Everyone wants to help a hitherto detested child. A child is a star.

In tiny houses covered with tarred felt on the outskirts of Szabasowa lived the poorest ragpickers, street cleaners, and sawmill laborers. They went out into the countryside to earn bread by daywork. The poor wretches came back home in the evenings, preyed upon by shots in the little streets. All kinds of precautions were useless; someone always fell. A shot followed in the tracks of a man. Often, children on the threshold, recognizing their father by his step, lifted the bolt on the door into the hallway. Old women still wore rings on their fingers. When night fell, a mob of gendarmes and agents, shining flashlights, would go from house to house. Through the flashes and stifled blows, the squealing of children and breathless cries flew into the darkness. Night fell like a burden, the looting intensified into a frenzy. Longing for day as though it were bread or good health, the women awaited dawn, took their children and a few rags, and ran blindly into the fields. There they perished, dying of hunger and exhaustion. They spent nights on field edges, inside burned-out tanks or forest sheds.

After leading Cirla and the children by night along the path to Sewerynka, Chuny Shaya went back to the yard; he still wanted to get his sheepskin jacket and warm underwear for the children out of the chest. Someone fired at him twice from an alley, but missed. Chuny went back to the orchard, and stopped behind the stump of a hazel bush.

Before the great fire, the silence had hummed for a moment, an engine whistled somewhere far off. Then little fires broke out in three places. It seemed to him that rubbish was burning in a yard on St. John's Street; it was as though the fire were being stifled near the basement. But a moment later children ran out, chasing reddish shapes before them. They were crying out softly. And when the flames burst up, old people too ran into the orchard, waving clenched fists. Outlines of trees flowed out of the shadow.

The low clouds became reddish. A revolver cleaved a few rounds closer to the fire, and instantly someone there fell silent, his shriek cut off. The pond in Trznadel's garden was glistening, the white willows dancing against the dark-blue background of the potato patches. The old tinsmith Blum also rushed out, extinguishing with his bare hands a smoldering padded jacket. He glanced at Shaya, his eyes gleaming like glass. He asked,

"Did the children run away?"

He walked into the darkness as though led by tiny shapes creeping into a tunnel of black landscape.

As though in a state of unseeing fury, Shaya went back into the yard, looked, and bade farewell in his mind to the threshold of his house; he opened the stable, mounted a horse, and clinging to its mane, rushed out at a gallop into the orchard. Children were shrieking in the potato patches. Some woman or other, standing behind bean poles, was urging them in a whisper: "Be patient, children, be patient!" Further away, in the fields, more sensible people were burrowing into the heaps of dry manure. Szabasowa was burning, and everything surrounding it seemed plunged into a harsh autumnal dream. A locomotive whistled in the darkness, a sentry at the barrier was firing luminous rockets into the sky.

That was the beginning. Castle Street burned next night. Crossed hands leaned over the children in the glow. From the ancient wall, rifles sliced into the mud walls along Murarska and Rybia Streets. A droshky horse survived with its withers scorched.

It could still be seen in the morning, walking through the fields at Smolno, but dogs set upon it at a crossing. Children were running about the fields; Gabe Gudel met some of them and said, "Let us run about the dark sky to comfort the unhappy, lead the travelers, let us be a guide to wanderers, a ray of hope in prisons and in despairing souls. Go ye back to your homes, they will light candles on the table and serve fish, beans, and good cakes, which are eaten on the Eve of Forgiveness, and which are called 'cakes of mercy.'"

"What's the matter with you, Gudel?" shouted Kalma, "you're so pale and depressed."

"Run and find Chuny Shaya," someone said, "he has a rifle and will defend you."

And Gabe Gudel went by paths to the forest. There he found a tall tree, sat down, and lit a candle which trembled in his hands. He lifted his eyes to the sky, his lips whispering a prayer, but swaying, he tried in vain to link his thoughts with the uproar of despair, and instantly the cheerful candles on the table grew somber, and the cake of mercy seemed black and spattered with earth. Gliding in his mind through a crowd surrendered to groaning, he ran to get his parchment roll from a cupboard in the synagogue, and as the alms collector of each of the fleeing Jews, he asked for the sacrifice of a brief prayer: "That Chuny Shaya fight in good health. Let not the birch tree lose its leaves, nor the fir tree bow under the snow!

"May the bird swiftly slip away, may it be freed from the bird-catcher's net.

"Unknown pilgrims from towns and villages!"

"Cease from pursuing a transitory shadow, give yourself up to holy work; one phrase omitted or a badly written letter," said Gudel, "will make the work useless to others; through your error you will bring about the destruction of uncounted generations."

After August, the grass on the escarpments became reddish and withered. Pigs walked about the gossamer-strewn yard, looking for pickings. A crowd of sparrows burst from the brushwood into a bean patch and settled unexpectedly, like chaff thrown into the wind. The sky grew dull. In the mornings a slight, chill dew settled.

The summer was growing cold; only the forest still had active, silently prowling starlings in its dry lining. The rustling of these sparrows alarmed refugees from Szabasowa. The fast late afternoon fell flatly across stubble in a reddening beam, enclosing in a single color the trunks of young hornbeams scattered with groats of overripe sage.

In the late fall the Jewish cemeteries died. Green, mossy *maceils* carpeted the paths. Tanks cranked on the sacred paths. Men from the auxiliary police ransacked the stores, went into hiding places on the track of childish whinings, threw grenades at a shriek. Those spared ran into the Polish cemeteries, where they awaited night hidden among the graves. Dusk settled on the fields, little birds came down from the sky.

In Szabasowa, revolvers were firing into feather beds, into nooks and crannies in taverns, and at mites of living children. They beat gray-bearded melamdim stretched on the threshold of the temple. Young men, cowering, ran through the whistling and banging; they ran in groups across the plowed land or the ravines of field edges into the forest, and fell down in the dry undergrowth, breathless and agitated.

In the fall, the forest grass is white and smells of fish, is spider-webbed and springy. Cirla pulled up grass and thrust it under her child's back, then sat down and covered herself and the child with a black, woolen kerchief. She peeped through a crevice at the fire — heavy, tall. Distant fields with coniferous plantations twinkled with redness. Crows shrieked in the tension of blackness.

Then, amidst the uncertain days, snow fell. A white renewal for the hunt with dogs sniffing and for the spies tracking down Jewish hiding places in caves and holes in the ground. In dawns strewn with ice, there was a vague whitening in the window of the tile factory. The children of Hynda Glas came up, circuitously and cautiously. They looked into the smoke that was whiter than undergrowth. Arbuz at once came out to the children, and gave them a bottle of hot milk, baked potatoes, and the crust of a home-made barley loaf. In the forest depths a rifle rattled. A crow was sitting on the very top of an elm, it croaked: caw, caw . . .

Hynda's children did not know what this meant. Arbuz, parting the unshaven beard from his mouth, said, "Well, praise to the Highest, the bird is heralding spring."

The white frost resounded, the trees stood motionless, melting and blackening from within. Titmice and yellowhammers spent the night in the silence of snowbanks.

Policemen went into the shames' small room. A brass candle-stand hung from the ceiling, decorated with straw and bits of paper. Two warped beds stood against the wall, covered with brightly flowered bedspreads. The children with glittering eyes peeped out from behind the stove.

The bedclothes slipped off. Covered with a sheepskin, the shames crept out from under the bed.

"Why laugh, are your teeth chattering?"

Hynda had disheveled hair and was wide in the hips. Her hands together, she went up to the policemen:

"Hunechke!" she cried.

A shot upset all the pots on the stove. Hynda fell on Hunechke. She drew the ashes, with fire and baked potatoes, under herself.

The shames, covered with the sheepskin, stood in the smoke in the middle of the room, trembling.

"Why laugh?"

A candle stuck to the table crackled, and the flame began to go out.

"Go out into the hallway!"

"No, I will not," said the shames, dully.

"Well, then . . ."

"Don't say 'well' to me. I won't go out."

The man on the threshold knew that in that crowded little room, the thick-set shames would lay him out with one blow if it came to a real showdown. He shouted once more, in a broken voice,

"Stop!"

The door from the hallway creaked and Gail came in, smiling, looking for the eyes of the policemen and of the shames.

"I'm looking for you all. And you here, evidently, are terrifying a Jew."

Gail went out, his varnished top boots gleaming on the threshold.

After a second shot it was as though someone unknown had risen and was trying blindly to grope through an abyss. The shames rose again, thrust a hand out in front of him, fell down on the feather mattress. He suddenly sat up, overturned the table. He managed to escape to the other corner, a little to the left of the trail of smoke. He drew a pistol out of his boot top and fired into the black belt. He jumped through the window and smashed it out, along with the frame.

Trees in the cemetery were rustling. Rifles barked in the hallway. Swift footsteps could be heard in the dark alleys of the synagogue. They were breaking the windows in the tinsmith's little house. A black figure stood in the gateway. A flashlight searched through the snow. On the threshold lay a plank for ritual washing, pots, a torn mattress, boxes for carrying the dead, a yoke, a lamp, mourning boxes.

A foot kicks Moise Haskel recumbent on the threshold. Children rebound from the black dried leaves used to pack hut walls in winter, and run across the powdery snow toward the cemetery gate. They disappear amidst the tombs, crouching under branches weighed down with snow. Cirla is standing breathless in the rose bushes, listening intently, straining her eyes — maybe it's someone's whisper, maybe the spark from a cigarette.

"Stop, *tatele!*" someone shouts outside the gate.

After the rifle blow, Cirla fell face downwards in the snow. Boots ran over her. It seemed to her for an instant that she was a saint found in trash. By her eyes, clothing, and silence, they recognized her for a saint. Not a breath from her lips when they started hitting and kicking her like a wild animal. The sleeve of her blouse ripped off, but no longer did anything threaten her. Some men ran to Hesheles; laughing, they explained to the well-dressed man that it was nothing . . . a little trash had been gotten rid of.

A crowd of lively birds begins once again to cover the cemetery. Ladybugs and beetles hasten in lines across the sand toward the gate. From the hallway old Buchsbaum brings the children out to a green strip of grass with butterflies.

Warm, salty rain falls at night. Snails spawn.

The bells resounded somberly, as if someone wicked had covered their hearts with oakum.

Szabasowa was still smoldering. Stifling smoke hung over the ground. Children's voices resounded with despair around planks of the burned-down school. Coffins were standing in the narrow little street. Several men and women with shovels and a priest in a dirty surplice stood looking around. Cows with charred hair were lying in ditches, their eyes protruding, kicking up their hoofs. Yards were drenched in heat. In the mud lay bedclothes, glass from tiny windows, drain pipes, and tin kitchen utensils.

Smoke from the center of an anvil, embers kicked about. Sheep, with their wool smoldering, ran at a wild trot through the rough yards, near an open space; rebounded from a clay embankment at the crossing; and ran back between the legs of people who were busy digging.

Autumnal scarlet is reddening behind the huts and agricultural machinery, by the maidenly paths of phlox. In fine September, a bee flies up to the phlox. The undergrowth turns moldy; a cock chases ducks, tries to mount them with all the enthusiasm of a lover. The ducks squat. They like this wandering existence.

Cuddling the child, Cirla was running. She could see dahlias in the mud and rusty toads. A dog ran full-pelt after her, excited, his tongue hanging out, ears pricked. They ran past the haymaking into the forest. The child, like a rabbit suffocating in a sack, stretched and cried out. She ran with her heart compressed, sweating and feverish. Crows were circling over the violet forest, soaring, then descending vertically, then again rising with a cry above the sun widespread in the west.

Damp spider webs rustled in the forest clearings. In fall, the fields watch, the forest listens. A barren landscape is the enemy of a pursued man.

Cirla ran into the obscure hallway, jumped behind a coop, and sat down. Mrs. Arbuz barricaded the door. She carried the child into the room, laid it on a bench by the stove, and unwrapped it. It was wet and had marks of the hard swaddling clothes all over its body.

"When I look at the swaddling clothes of your child, my heart stirs within me," said Mrs. Arbuz. "It's as though I could see my own child, hear his voice, look into his eyes."

"Someone is knocking at the front door," whispered Cirla.

Mrs. Arbuz moved the curtains aside a crack. A tall woman was standing on the threshold. She drew her long hands out of her bosom.

"Give me water," she said.

"To drink?"

"Not to bathe a child, that's certain!"

Mrs. Arbuz sought long and clumsily for a quart jug, upsetting pots, making a noise, swearing to herself indecently. She peeped through the window to see if there was anyone besides the old hag. Her thoughts ran like a flood. Had she seen or not? She would set the hut on fire, inform, do harm, hateful old hag. Who was she? Had she once been a girl, and become so strange after

death? She has bleary eyes and a lot of fingers. She is hungry for
newly born children. She resembles a she-wolf, except that her
belly is bare. She has no fur. Someone said she is sometimes like a
ferret in winter. She comes reluctantly into a hut where a vicious,
swarthy man lives, slamming the door noisily, for he may suffo-
cate her and kill her the second time. She does not like a hut
where people make joyful noises and are hospitable to all.

Mrs. Arbuz took the ax, stood behind the door, and shouted:
"You — go away from the threshold, for I will wake my husband. And he doesn't like specters."

"You won't wake your husband," the hag replied.

"Why not?"

"Open the door, then I'll tell you."

"I'll open your head for you, you accursed specter. You think
people have already forgotten that in the depths of winter it was
you who went to Hutniski and caused so much misfortune there?"
Mrs. Arbuz held her breath until her chest puffed up.

"Well, go on prattling," said the hag on the threshold.

"You shaggy bitch, you. It was you, when old Skwarczynski
was dying beyond the forest and there was nobody else in the
room, who gave him a consecrated wax candle. His orphan
grandchild was lying in its cradle. The old man lit the candle,
which flew from his dead hands and set the bed on fire. The bed
set fire to the cradle. But instead of taking the child out of the fire,
you took a sheepskin."

"Because the sheepskin was mine, and I could not reach the
child."

"You could."

"No."

"Horse-face saw that you could."

"Then why didn't he grab the child out of the fire?"

"Because he is no man, but a spirit. A spirit can only see."

"Well, you and your spirit," the hag laughed, and she hit the
door with a stick. "Open up, and, spirit or not, I know you have
Cirla's child in there."

A patrol emerged palely from the bleariness of wind and mist.
They were going to the tile factory. Cirla lifted the rucksack with
the child and rushed through the back door into the bushes. Mrs.
Arbuz went out behind the stable and hung the swaddling clothes
on a box.

"Greetings, granny," said a policeman.

"Greetings," Mrs. Arbuz bowed.

A Mauser bumped on the policeman's rump. They searched

the bushes near the cow barn, kicked through the chips piled around the workbench. Two others ransacked the hut. Mrs. Arbuz's ears swelled, her hair bristled.

"Who did you have staying here?" one of them shouted from an open window.

"Come here, old woman. Who was staying with you?"

"Horse-face," said Mrs. Arbuz.

"Why did you have him staying here?"

"I was afraid. He came before dawn, ate a meal, cleaned his gun, slept a bit, then went away."

"What did he tell you?"

"He told me he is going to get you and will strangle you all, one at a time, each in an ambush. He said it will pay off, for each of you carries a pile of Jewish gold in your pockets."

"You, you old bitch, are fighting along with this Horse-face," said Kurdiuk, and he thrust the muzzle of his revolver under Mrs. Arbuz's nose. "Come, have a taste of that!"

They took away a watch, two carpets, skeins of wool, then fired several times into a dark recess and left.

When Mrs. Arbuz went back to the hallway, the alien hag was already standing on the threshold of the entry, and said directly, as if nothing important had happened a moment before:

"You ought to go to Szabasowa and clean up your man; don't let him kick around in the mud."

"Get out of my sight, I've no patience," Mrs. Arbuz shouted, seizing the ax. She ran up and struck the woman on the shoulder with the blunt edge. With a shriek the hag flew into the forest.

"Drop dead!" Mrs. Arbuz said as she pushed the door to and barricaded it.

Still clutching the ax, she jumped through the window into the yard. She threw the chain off the cow and drove it quickly into a clearing.

Wind bends the frail birches. It brings three clouds of smoke from over shot-up Szabasowa. Cattle bellow, and the calling of women drifts like an abyss: "Jeeeeesus!" as if someone sensible there was summoning the impatient.

Ashy mist flies like low-lying old slippers to an arched crack of reddish sky.

Mrs. Arbuz hears behind her someone burrowing in the bushes.

The cow rushes ahead, reaches a clearing, and shaking its flanks, throwing up its horns, hides in the undergrowth. Mrs. Arbuz goes down a gray track.

$\mathbf{F}$ather Banczycki sought neither power nor wealth. He wanted to break the power of destiny, to force that which had been alive to rise from the dead, to bring back to life that which no longer was. In the same way, Buchsbaum, after losing his grandson, repeated millions and millions of times in helpless despair, "I seek you from one synagogue to the next. I have traveled a long way," and then he would begin praying: "Shema Israel." And then: "Rid yourself of a weeping voice, for they are used silks, resembling standards which barbarians glory in. Solitude is slowly populating, and suffering will fly away on its black wings. The hubbub of evening is being born, shouts, quarrels, the crack of a whip, the banging of hammers, the rattle of carts, a great town rises out of the shadows, the smell of tobacco, the bitter pipes of wagoners, winds groaning under trees, myrtles, *lulebs*, the tick of an old clock, people checking harnesses by lamplight."

Toward the end of the year, Father Banczycki bought a pair of elk from Hungarian soldiers and took them to his farm. Paying no attention to the mockery of farmers from Huciski, he began feeding them intensively, cleaning them with brushes and bristles made for the purpose by Kweller.

The elks were sick, crippled, riven with fistulas, and scrofulous. Father Banczycki crept into their stable twice a night, strewed straw, laid dry straw, checked the hitches, and tended their drying scrofula. In the depths of the fall he covered the walls with leafy dry undergrowth, doubled their food, pampered the elk like a professional breeder. As soon as night fell, Kweller would creep out of a hole dug under the kennel, chop straw, draw water, carry buckets of hot water to the pigsty, get feed ready for the next day, or cut twigs for the stove in the shed by lamplight. He was dressed to look like an old hag, as it was known that Klara Wasicinska worked in the rectory. A tall, lanky girl, but strong and lusty, so she could take on seven peasants at a time.

When the first snow fell, the elk ran out of the stable into the blinding whiteness; they were clean and smooth, and they frisked around the orchard. And on the threshold Father Banczycki, "Whoa! Whoa!" He ran to the gate, closed it, and shouted: "Wasicinska! Brrr! Wasicinska!"

"What is it?"

"Look!"

Klara, hiding her hands, red from laundering, under her armpits, blinked with admiration. Her youthful eyebrows, black as coal, rose on her smooth, pink forehead. The priest surrounded the frisking elk with his fond gaze. Pleased with the young livestock, he set his legs apart and rolled a cigarette.

A week before Christmas, a little hunchback manikin came along the well-trodden path from dead Szabasowa to the rectory yard. Against the background of immense snowbanks and frost-covered trees, the figure of this little man seemed like a cloud of sparrows to the priest.

"Greetings," said the stranger, and he lifted his reddish cap.

"Gree . . ." the priest barely forced through his teeth, attentively investigating every little piece of the newcomer.

The stranger had a chapped face. There was long fuzzy hair on his chin, and a flat, ducklike nose hung down over his sunken lips that were stained with nicotine. Only the eyes of the hunchback were unusual, as though they were not his, but those of a man with bewitched beauty inside him. He had large eyes, rabbitty, bloodshot, vital, shaded by long and feminine lashes. His coat was crumpled, darned, patch over patch. Both coattails were covered with frozen snow, and instead of buttons, hazel pegs were stuck into the holes. He wore down-at-the-heel boots, rotten, with tops sunken over sewn clasps.

The manikin lifted his sheepskin cap again, and plunging his dirty fingernails into the fur, said softly,

"I would like to enter into your service, Father."

"Come, what use is your service to me, my man? I do my own work."

Tears rolled from the fine, womanly eyes of the hunchback. And these tears shook Father Banczycki's vigilance. He dropped his hands and went into the kitchen.

"Give him a crust of bread," he said to Wasicinska.

"Who?"

"Some poor man has come to the door. Curious," the priest added, "how beautiful his eyes are. Go and look."

And Wasicinska, drying her hands on her apron, cut a hunk of coarse bread, went after the priest into the hallway, and had a look. "Just like a little sparrow," she laughed.

"Isn't he!" The priest handed the bread to the frozen hunchback. The latter straightened a little bundle under his left arm, grabbed the slice with both fists, and began tearing and swallowing it as greedily as a dog. The priest, plunged into some joyful, fond plans or other, kept standing and watching the hungry, unassuming little hunchback, who was eating, breathing heavily, snuffling like a child. With mixed feelings of shame, sorrow, and grief forcing themselves irresistibly upon him, the priest asked,

"What would you want for your services? Eh?"

"Enough . . . to live on."

At this statement, the priest realized he was defeated, but he glanced once more into the newcomer's eyes, and thrusting out his lower lip with a cigarette stuck to it, said churlishly,

"Well, you can stay. We'll see what sort of a rascal you are. What's in that bundle?"

"What?"

"Are you deaf? What's in that bundle?"

"Two shirts, a blanket, and a horse comb."

"Evidently you're fond of horses, if you carry a horse comb."

"Sure."

"Have you any identity papers?"

"No."

"You can stay here for two days on trial. If I'm not pleased with you, I'll send you away. For no one can be useless in this world."

The frozen little hunchback took off his cap, turned red in the face, went up to the priest, and kissed his hand with a loud smack of the lips.

"You'll have to sleep on the straw, by the elk."

"Fine," said the hunchback, tripping after the priest.

The pigs were grunting impatiently behind the fence.

"That way" — Banczycki pointed to a ladder — "that way, up the ladder to the attic. The straw is there. Cut straw for the elk. That's the first thing for you to do."

The hunchback went into the stable; the livid and wrinkled back of his neck moved out onto his collar.

"Scared?"

"Who, me?"

"Then be off with you. Only watch the rungs."

But as the hunchback went around the fence, the pigs rushed at him and the bundle flew out from under his arm. Covered with shirts, the pigs recoiled, and a sawn-off shotgun rolled out of the rags and fell flat on the thin manure.

The priest pretended not to see; he broke a yellowish icicle off the thatch and smashed it on the threshold. Finally he seized a pitchfork and stuck the hunchback's dirty shirts on it.

"Here, take these shirts and go to the devil!"

"What?"

"Go to the devil!"

By some miracle, the reddish cap stayed on the head of the would-be servant, while his hump emerged from under his padded jacket and fell, in the shape of rolled foot-clouts, into the snow. Banczycki hit him on the back of the neck. He jumped closer. His cap slipped down over his forehead, and he threw it off with a hot hand and again was banged between the eyes with a pole. But the stranger treated the priest to a knife; there was a crunching noise, and they crashed down onto the packed ice. Banczycki brought his legs out of a confused tangle, gathered himself up, scuffled out from under the stranger, and stood up. After jumping up from a squatting position he wiped his eyes and kicked the other's knee, rammed one fist at the peak of his nose, and crashed down on his rubber soles. Now the stranger began kicking Banczycki on the back of his neck. Both smelled death. Disheveled, they throbbed; pressing against each other with the last of their strength, they bit and stabbed. Bang, bang, bang. Sudden blood flowed. Banczycki fell down. He got up on his elbows, a hand went under his armpit and froze, his forehead settled on the snow.

Wasicinska managed to hit the little sparrow with a yoke. He fluttered his hands, fell on his back, rapidly jumped up and ran out of the gate, dragging his coattails, and disappeared into the wintry weather.

Klara and Chaim carried the priest into the room, brought him around, and looked after two cuts on the back of his neck.

"The devil take such blows;" said Chaim, "you forget you're over fifty."

"But I have a good nose, don't I? I sniffed that he was a spy right away."

"Did he have whiskers?"

"Whiskers? Hm. All spies don't have to have whiskers."

"Let me tell you something. Do you know who he was?"

"Well?"

"The sign . . ."

"Devil take the sign. A spy like any other."

"How come?"

"He came to look for a pearl in the barley," the priest replied.

"That's a peculiar philosophy. But let me take a look at your pulse."

Chaim put his thumb to the priest's pulse.

Father Banczycki's rectory stood under linden trees, on broad stone foundations. Frozen leaves slipped down the shingles and blocked the gutters. Brushwood was heaped with bean stalks and leaves in the yard. A cart with the reins thrown over it stood in the carriage house, wheels soiled with mud. A shed on four poles extended from the stable, and near it beehives were placed like a building, opening inwards. There were traces of pigs in the gateway.

When Kweller entered the premises, breathless and wet, Father Banczycki waved one hand toward the porch. He went into the stable.

"I seen Buchsbaum today," said the farm laborer to the priest.

"Is he still alive? Well, what then?"

"He said, 'Greetings.'"

"And what did you say to that?"

"Me? Nothing."

"Why not?"

"It isn't right."

"Why isn't it?" the priest lifted his stick as though to strike, and shouted: "Are you going to give the pigeons their feed or not?"

"There's no jug. Nothing to put it in."

"Oh, you wretched spirit. I'd have fed them out of my cap by this time."

"Damn the pigeons," the laborer hissed, and he wandered away behind a straw-cutter.

From the stable threshold the priest looked toward the gate. He struck the planks with his stick. Snow slithered down.

"You don't look after the little pigeons, which means you're a heartless person."

"Well, the devil knows best. It's impossible to please you anymore."

"That's not the point, you soulless individual, whether to please me or not. I declare despairingly that you are wicked."

"Why wicked?"

"You have no pity for the birds, which means you also lack pity for your mother, as the heartless usually do." Banczycki shouted, and he shook his fist.

The pigeons slithered underfoot like corn sheaves; they cooed, seeking chaff. The priest went to a corner of the threshing floor, gathered millet into his coattails, went out into the yard, and scattered it thickly by the threshold, flicking the lap of his soutane with his stick. He came back and said calmly,

"From today on, don't go into the kitchen for food. I will bring it to your hiding place. I will carry out the hot feed for the cattle. Don't come into the kitchen for anything. And if you don't like it, then plan your life differently. The pigeons were just a test. You can expect worse things in your life. I do too."

Banczycki's nose turned purple, his cheeks came hatefully together like the skin of a trodden-on puffball. Without waiting for a reply, he walked calmly toward the gate. The piglets ran after him.

Kweller, small, in a black burnous, was standing there at the gate. A sheepskin cap was pulled down over his chops, and a tail of gray beard was visible against his collar; he had sharp black eyes.

"It's good that you're so small, Kweller. You can hide successfully under a kneading trough."

Father Banczycki looked around. The laborer, carrying a bundle of trefoil, went up to the stable door, threw the hook off with the tip of one boot, and jumped over the threshold.

"A child is even smaller," Kweller whistled hoarsely.

"Yes, a child is even smaller. And when did your daughter-in-law give birth?"

"Before the sowing. She gave birth one day, and the next day they killed her."

Kweller pulled off a twig with a black fingernail, broke it in two, and showed the priest.

"If only he'd turned the muzzle to the left, she would have lived."

"Oh, *Materdea!*" Banczycki groaned.

"And how is it?" asked Kweller, throwing the twig away.

"All right, supposedly. It wants . . ."

"Milk?"

"No, not milk. Measles is a terrible thing."

"And a bullet is not terrible?"

"You talk nonsense, Kweller. A bullet in the leg is more terrible."

Banczycki put his stick on his shoulder, scratched his forehead with his thumb. They stood silently for a moment. Then both went into the summer veranda, scattered with logs, bundles of brushwood, packages, and trash. There was a rabbit hole in the foundations near the kitchen. Banczycki had enlarged this black hole with its friable walls in the heat of the summer. He had carried away the earth in a basket to the garden, and scattered it there.

"There's straw on the bottom, you can sleep. Does Gail still have a dog?"

"Gail? Surely. Kurdiuk has a dog too."

Kweller slithered backwards into the hole. Banczycki put a bundle over the exit, estimated the verisimilitude of the muddle on the floor. He went out.

An old hag was rushing vigorously from the pasture straight to the rectory, dragging her long skirt.

"Greetings," the old hag hissed. She rubbed her oval cheeks with the back of her hand.

"Greetings," the priest withdrew his hand. "Don't kiss my hand, what use did it ever do anyone? What have you to say, woman?"

"Wolves have suffocated a Jew in a field edge around Przepastna."

"How do you know it was wolves?"

"Kurdiuk said so."

"Who to? You?"

"He told me. He says they will multiply through the winter and go around eating people."

"And who might you be?"

"I am Varvara, and I go begging."

"I see," the priest grumbled, and began talking disjointedly; he leaned toward the old woman: "The wolves are not increasing, but they come from man. There are damned souls who turn entire villages, many people, into wolves. These wolves run away into the forest, they attack Jews. At dawn they go home with the belongings of those they have killed. Who is lying dead on the field edge around Przepastna?"

"The old tinsmith Kweller."

"Did the wolves maul him badly?"

"He's still alive, but they will carry him off tonight," said the old hag somberly. She asked for water. She drank it without removing the half-liter gourd from her lips. Once again she surveyed Father Banczycki from his boots to his bald head, and went away across the pasture at the vigorous pace of a farmhand.

"The black depths of all possibility," Banczycki whispered, and he began mashing potatoes in a wooden tub. Piglets flew into the hallway grunting, jostling each other with their snouts.

Heindl is turning the pages of a notebook. He extracts the details of someone's beautiful face from his memory. And he orders: "Now forget me; I am a faithful dog, wandering with children in a certain far corner of the earth. And because the Lord of the world sends misfortunes only as a punishment for sins, and wishes to preserve the innocent from death in terrible sufferings, so children have not suffered without cause. During the feast of Estear, alm-seekers dress up as dancers and perform various arts for merriment, as once they did before King Asseverus. Gabe Gudel, surrounded by a little group of children, will disappear under the tall black pine trees where everything which ever existed is preserved, as in a tomb: a square covered with snow is to be seen, a house, tombs, illuminated halls, heads bowed over books, huge stables, the sound of psalms, a porch of moss-covered brick, pieces of broken porcelain, in the corner a traveler's stick and small bag. Here someone who was alive a moment ago had written, 'What does a wise child ask for? What does a simpleton say? What's this? And what's this?' "

From the dark hallway they went into a room smelling musty with vinegar. There was a heap of dirty linen lying by the wall, straw mattresses, and a commode with overflowing drawers; a cupboard was hanging across the door and in it a skirt, children's knickers, and rusty books. Little flasks stood on the rusty stove, dirty jars, a linden flower in newspaper, wire for beating cream, and a candlestick. Instead of crusts of bread, as Mis Kunda had predicted they found a corpse in a closet. A fat bloated woman. She lay with her hair disheveled, right hand on her calf, the left pressing a red skirt to her belly, flies, wasps, and moths were creeping over the little windowpane. And there, further on, someone was moving in straw scattered from a mattress. Mis went up to this straw and poked it with his foot. A little girl in a dirty shirt got up from the floor, sighed, and sat down. This little girl was somewhat like Kalma.

"Come with us," said Mis.

She went after the boys, cowering, hands crossed on her chest.

They went up the lime-sprinkled stairs to the upper story. There, in a huge hall, right in the middle, stood a chair with a worn-out seat. The walls were smoke-stained, with a great many nail and bullet holes. Over the entry to the next hall was a black plush tapestry, with gold embroidery. Cups stood on the chimney-piece, and near the stove were half-burned stockings, balls of wool, packets of needles, buttons, and a child's small chair. And they went on further and further without finding anything for food. Dudi staggered. They saw the same everywhere. Broken mirrors, papers, chairs, plaster, pillows ripped open, heaps of smashed rubbish, and corpses shrinking in rags, sitting on window sills. A draft carried bits of paper and moist wind from the fields. Butterflies flying around the empty rooms, their wings sparkling, alighted wearily on the bronze candlesticks.

Over the burned roofs stood the lilac-colored distance, mingled with white clouds, and the sound of summer was wafted from one horizon to the other.

There, in a green meadow, amidst sheep, children were quarreling over a ball made of a pig's bladder. The boys were wallowing, pawing each other mischievously, and set off in a chase across the open space splashed with geese droppings. The dogs were tearing up holes, earth scattering behind their tails. A little stream was rippling, horses snorted, and there was no end to time. Telegraph poles stretched into the distance, smaller and smaller as they went, and swallows sitting in the wires looked ever smaller.

When Dudi tried to catch up with Mis Kunda without falling down from exhaustion, the shadows on the floor doubled and his step faltered. And in the cellars there was not a crust of bread either. Only a sheet appeared from a barrel, and from under it a black head on a thin neck. Two black eyes looked at Kunda. A woman scrambled out of the barrel and ran into the empty cellar, dragging behind her something resembling a squashed centipede.

A draft blew, and a door creaked behind them. Someone's footsteps made a crackling sound. Dudi looked around. A young woman covered with a green shawl stood in the light from a little window. Before he caught sight of her face, the memory of his mother came back to him. Or was it perhaps this woman who had given him a handful of berries through the fence? Or was she the girl who loved Horse-face?

Black, gleaming brows and eyes, her lips smiling. His mother had smiled thus, with full lips and dimples in her cheeks.

It was difficult to make out the color and shape of the man

standing by the synagogue. He was moving, and held something in one hand.

"Is it a gendarme?" whispered Kunda.

"Yes." He approached, grew in size, staring into the hallway, loading his gun.

"There are more of them," said Dudi.

The gendarmes were standing along the fence as if waiting.

The lads fled through the cellars to a stokehole of the brewery. They peeped through a little window. To the right were dark lindens, shading the roof. In shadows under the trees lay murdered people. Close to the little window someone was walking over glass; the door creaked. An old man came out on the sidewalk in front of the brewery, vomited, pulled his black frock coat on as if he were cold. When a gendarme went up to him, this man raised one hand, slowly looked around all four corners of the world. He could be heard saying, "I am a knife grinder."

The gendarme put his left hand on his hip, went up and hit the grinder on the head with his revolver. A thin snake of a smile played on the gendarme's lips; he looked from the right corner of his eye to the brewery roof, spent some considerable time examining the walls. The grinder sat for a moment and then, throwing himself on his back, turned on one side, and it could be seen that his eyes were sunken, his bald head drenched in blood.

At night Mis Kunda and Dudi crept through the wires, ran a long time over the fields, found some straw, and after burying themselves in it, slept until morning. Who knows how long they would have slept had it not been for a farmer's dog which frightened them away from their lair? Driving it away with a stick, they went by the meadows to the Styr.

They could see their reflections as, without moving their feet, they leaned their heads over the water. Cheeks puffed, hands wide apart. They chased a gudgeon from under a stone. And to scare the gudgeon out of the slime Mis Kunda splashed with his hand — water splattered off his back. They rose and brushed themselves off. Disappointed, raising their knees high, they gazed; where would the gudgeon appear next?

"There it is, there it is," Mis whispered.

The sun was burning, the flies biting. An old woman came up from the direction of Pasieki with a bucket full of rags. Pulling her dress up, she squatted on the bank.

"There it is!"

Mis seized the gudgeon in one hand, rose and walked along the bank, balancing. The fish, gleaming in the sun, fell onto a dirty shirt. Dudi grubbed in the loam, put somewhing on his left hand, and sniffed.

"Whose boys are you?" the old woman called, beating a sheet.

"Daddy's and Mummy's," said Mis; he picked a leaf of grass and pushed it into his mouth.

"Tssk! That's not nice," the old woman hissed.

Two airplanes were cruising over Szabasowa.

"That's not nice. I had a son like you. He wouldn't have answered in that manner," the old woman shrieked, and her voice clattered over the water. "Terrible thing. Death came in at the door. Instead of coming for me, it came for him."

She straightened herself; as she was drying her hands she looked at the boys' naked shoulders, spattered with flies, at their white buttocks. She wanted to tell them what had happened to her son.

The boys, setting their elbows on their knees, gazed at a small bank of stones — a gudgeon had leaped there. Could it have hidden itself in a snail shell, gleaming white on the bottom?

"Come, touch that snail. Don't be afraid, I'll hold you."

Dudi plunged his hand in, lowered his head, till his left ear was covered with water.

"It's deep."

"Touch it. With one finger, gently, gently . . . don't stir up the water."

"What?"

"Don't stir it up, you're stirring it up with your feet."

"Am I?"

"Stop up the hole."

"It's slippery, it will fall over."

"I can't see anything. Don't stir up the water."

"What?"

"Take my foot, gently, for you will shield it. Well, grab it with your whole hand."

"It's deep, it seems close, then it reflects so that it is close."

"Don't stir up the water, just be quick, else it will get away. If we could catch five of them, there would be enough to make soup."

"I can't, it's too deep," said Dudi. He opened his mouth as if to smile, his lips trembling.

"Catch hold of me and grab, just be quick, quick. Don't stir up the water with your feet, Dudi, damn it!"

Dudi seized Mis's hand, plunged in his side, neck, and half his head; bubbles emerged from his nose.

"Got it!" he shouted, and spat out water.

"Keep your finger on the hole."

Mis Kunda also thrust a hand into the depths, leaned over like a reed, groping for Dudi's calf.

"Hold it, hold it. Is this your leg?"

"Don't push me."

"Squeeze. Are you holding on?"

"Ooooh," Dudi groaned.

"Dear God. I can't see anything."

"Let's rest awhile," said Dudi.

"Sit quiet, it will swim out again."

"What are you doing there?" asked the old woman, blinking.

"We are catching a golden snake."

"Well now, fancy that!"

Dudi went out on the bank, ashen-faced, with his sunken belly — he stood there for a moment, placing his arms apart, as if they were strewn with boils.

"Fancy that, fancy that," Kunda mocked her.

"Do you lounge about like this all day? Who is pasturing the cows? Tch!" the old woman hissed and stamped her foot. After a moment she went on more quietly, as if to herself: "Who gives them food, that would be interesting to know. And it is not allowed to catch a snake. What did it do to you? Why kill it? A snake is a peaceful dumb creature. And it likes to be useful to man in time of need."

The boys put their pants on and sat on the grass, huddling their bony shoulder blades. A sparrow crept in to the gudgeon in the shell.

"And it was so," the old woman went on, "the Virgin Mary had to pass the night in a deserted mill. They kept her there; as usual St. Joseph spent the night in the yard with the donkey. And the night was dark, and there were no stars, no matter how hard you looked for them. But here, look — a light was flickering in the millrace. What was its cause? Why a light there? St. Joseph drew near the light — ach, here, here — he looked, and at the bottom through a wide window he saw a tavern room. A candle was standing on the counter. Inside was a great company of people with knives and pikes. Ha, thought St. Joseph unhappily, what's to be done? Then a snake swam out from under a bridge and said, 'Why are you so gloomy?' 'Robbers have a lair under the mill.' 'Wait,' said the snake, and it changed into a miller's boy, and said, 'Don't be afraid, pray to the Lord God.' He let the water flow from all the millraces, and the water flooded the robbers, and just the candle floated. And as it floated down the river, it was no longer a candle, but became the blessed snake. And just today you have to catch a snake, dear boys."

Dudi's small, melancholy eyes gazed at the old woman; the flies fidgeted on his little cheek that was covered with pimples.

"I wonder whose boys you are, eh?" the old woman droned on, hawking.

"We have no daddy or mummy," said Mis, and he pondered and added, "because we lost each other in the crowd when the Germans dropped bombs."

"Ah, Jesus beloved. I knew at once that this was it. Would you pasture a cow, then? I would give you plenty to eat, and right now there is beetroot soup on the stove. Well? I'd get my money's worth, eh? Come along, boys." She rose, seizing her bucket.

The boys, hungry and weary with the heat of the sun, followed her. They walked to the hamlet of Pasieki. The noon time was hot, and there was no one in the fields. Only larks sang, high up, and poppies were red along the field edges.

"Oh, God," the old woman groaned; she stopped, put the bucket down, and clapped her hands.

"Go on, boys, straight ahead, and as you pass the hayricks, on your right will be a thicket. Sit down in that thicket, and wait."

Mis Kunda and Dudi found the hay, turned right, and sat down in the thicket of young willows.

Then a young, fat girl came and led them along the field edges, amidst rye, close to the forest. In the depths, surrounded by a stumpy cherry orchard, stood a peasant hut covered with a red and white roof, with a wide and low shed, a black hayrick, and beehives further on. In the middle of the yard stood the old woman feeding hens, with a dog sitting by her, a big black mongrel. It sat and looked calmly at a crumbled egg, and saliva dripped from its muzzle like a blue thread.

"Give them dinner," said the old woman, and pushing them gently by the shoulders, she took the boys into the hut. She asked them quietly:

"What's your name?"

"Mis Kunda."

"And yours?"

"Dudi."

"Well, now, what's to be done? How about lice, do you have lice on you? Eh?" said the old woman. She knelt down looking for something under the bed; she moved vases aside and looked behind pictures.

"Pour them soup, Klara. I'm looking for that comb, the lice-killer."

Klara served them white beetroot soup in a large clay bowl, with two aluminum spoons, and she cut four slices of bread, right across the loaf.

"You ought to make the sign of the cross," said the old woman.

And Dudi, looking at Mis through the tears that veiled his eyes, closed his fingers, raised one hand to his forehead, and shivered. The dog, moving its wet nose over his calf, sniffed his trousers industriously. They slurped the soup, threw lumps of the bread into their mouths. Then sleep took over, and the spoons drooped more and more from their hands, and the flies settled more and more tranquilly on the edge of the bowl.

Everything they had experienced hitherto vanished like smoke, and Dudi felt he would do anything for this woman. "We'd even fight," he wanted to tell Mis Kunda, but the latter, his head bowed, had fallen asleep where he sat.

And Mis dreamed that Kalma came, and said, "Your father is lying dead in Meiseles, go to him." And he could see his father pouting his lips, beckoning, and puffing; a fly crept into his mouth, buzzing, and would not let him sleep. People run away to the gate, and gendarmes run there, and the fly disappears into the darkness. "Daddy?" There is no reply. Szerucki sticks his head in from the hallway, signaling: "Run away! Run away!"

They shake a net, and a little bird suspended on horsehair rocks toward the sun; "Hold on!" a cry is heard. "He may be pretending he's dead!" And a hand seizes the small body, warm and vibrating, throws it into a sack. Oh, you song of the field, how sweet you are, song of the field. Someone speaks in a bass voice. The bird, still moist with dew, falls into the bag. Faces lean over it. They are listening:

Easter time has come.
In the forest the cooing of doves resounds.
The fig has already sent forth buds,
The stem of the vine is blossoming,
Arise, my beloved!

And then he dreams he is going as early as possible to school, like always, and like always he finds the old melamed saying prayers by the window. Doesn't he ever sleep? He sees his sunken cheeks, the thin hair of his beard which he plucks and twists. When one hair remains in his hand, he places it between pages of the Book. Father among six kings, who are Buchsbaum, Laiba Shorr, Haskiel Karawav, Kanchuker, Spojdyk, and the ritual slaughterer Kojfie. They sit down amidst red feathers — there are plates adorned with flowers, in front of each a dish full of water, three "azim" loaves, a jug full of sweet liquor, ground almonds, ginger, chives, raisins, and eggs baked in ashes. Mother places a savory-smelling carp on the table, the flame of the seven candles flickers. Mother lifts him in her arms. Does she know that the prophet Elias himself has left the burned-out town forever? And Kunda sees the prophet Elias, weary from the heat of the day, as he walks along the field edge through corn ricks to the enormous forest of a ravine, a high cloudless sky, creaking carts and stacks of nicely cut grain, women carrying loaves of bread. People are hurrying to the little towns, for soon a sparkling star will appear.

The yards of Szabasowa were already overgrown with thick undergrowth, wet burdocks could be smelled on the burned ruins, scarlet reddened under overturned fences, and peonies damaged by fire had faded. The crooked alleys were empty, but amidst troughs from burned cellars black stoves stood, with silent wag-tails sitting by them. Oats sprouted on the paths. Charred cherry trees were spun with cobweb.

In the morning, the joy of birds resounded in the gleam of dew. From the pink East, a warm river flowed into the high sky. Jasmine was scattered on the lake by the cemetery, bronze dust strewed the mirror, and the depths were not to be seen, nor the reflection of clouds, nor the fresh greenery stretching like frogs' plankton. Blackthorn shivered at the gate of the crossing of Szerucki's place, pushed by the merriment of sparrows, and beetles dried out on the thorns.

Horse-face crept into the orchard and looked at the burned cherry tree for the last time. Once, leaning against it, he had kissed Emilka's warm lips. He turned to the yard and knelt on the threshold, on which his mother had stood in March to scatter grain for the hens. Then he pulled a burned ax out of the ashes, and looking around at Tombak's dark and silent hut, he strode into the cemetery.

Shames Buchsbaum saw him from his hiding place, and wanted to call out.

But a dog on three legs jumped out of Hanczarka's hut, and ran up, whining. After it, a gendarme, jamming his cap on, pulled a revolver out of its holster. He fired until it howled, and went back to Hanczarka. The dog lay shuddering all over. Mis Kunda went up to the dog, smacked his lips, and patted its knee with one hand.

On Cemetery Street, carpentry work started in the fullness of dawn: a chopper rang behind the apple trees, a cross-saw cut notches. In the shade, a wooden hammer banged on builders' blocks. Behind Buchsbaum's hut Jewish laborers were building a high fence, driven on by rifle butts. They were barricading the ghetto. A plane tree bloomed above the laborers; it threw down bugloss on the little trees, on the guelder roses in flower, and the summer weather inhaled all this.

And as soon as it was morning, hungry people walked the alleys here and there, in ragged coats. Their staffs thrown away, they shaded their eyes, collapsed on the sidewalks. Children and young girls ran away through the huge gardens, but the muzzle of a rifle sought out their backs. One shot after another rang out.

The wind roared. At noon the sky grew puffed up with clouds. It was quiet and warm, and a sad, ashy rainbow began to glow for a while over the black forest. Rain was coming.

In the old cemetery, birds flew away into the fields, and only the burned grass made a noise, crackling underfoot. Children lurked in the dense undergrowth, hiding behind tombs, throwing stones into the wrinkled pond, at the dogs running in line. Under the wall, in the black water, stood trees; the wind gathered up leaves, and carried their scent and the smoke of the burning frames of Foresta into space. Little girls were talking in the undergrowth:

"Do you know that each flower doesn't smell of itself, but of honey?"

"No, autumn flowers don't smell of honey. The dahlia, for instance."

"Did you smell it? In the autumn?"

"And do you think that little birds don't have a scent?"

"We talked about the birdies already."

"In the forest everything smells."

"Even a mushroom?"

"There's a mushroom. Oh, let's smell it."

"If you got up on tiptoe, then you'd see very big fields on the other side of the wall, telegraph posts and a road that goes someplace very far away. On a fine day you can see a little white town on the hilltop. My daddy was born there."

After gazing attentively at a dead man by the wall, the children stroked a sorbus tree and went near the morgue on the grass.

"I know. That's his father who is killed."

"No. That isn't his daddy. His daddy was tall."

"Just so. He was tall, but he fell down."

"Really?"

"No, that isn't my daddy. Daddy is coming back home tonight."

"Little golden bird in the black forest . . ." a little girl cried.

"I'm the little golden bird . . ."

"An old witch with a beard and protruding eyes!"

"I'm the old witch with a beard."

"Kill the witch with a beard."

"But I know," said Kalma. "I know who's the old witch with a beard."

"Who?" ask the boys.

"It's the woman who came to a hut and handed out onion peelings to all the children, while she ate bread and butter, as if she had horse's teeth. But the thread broke, and the old witch fell off the stove onto her head."

"Kill the old witch with a brick!"

"We'll take the bread from the witch," the children shouted.

The children pretended to take the bread from the witch, they picked grass, cut hunks of bread with their fingers, and began eating, swallowing saliva.

"Run, the dog wants our bread."

"Stop, all of you. I'm wounded."

A man was sitting under a tombstone, head bowed. In place of one eye he had a bloody stain. Flies had settled on his mouth like a wreath.

"Let's go away from here."

"That's a thief, children."

"But, but . . ."

"Why are you running?"

"What do you see?"

"Some man is coming."

"Where do you see him?" The children stretched their necks, looking at the gate.

"There he is. I can just barely see him."

"Point to him."

There was nobody in the place the children were looking.

"Is he coming along the alley?" asked Kalma.

"No, among the graves. He's coming here," said Bernaszewski.

The children quieted down; someone fired behind the grave-digger's little house.

"Maybe it's Horse-face?"

All the children bent down, looking into the alley, and Kalma said,

"No, it isn't Horse-face, for he walks by night."

And again someone's steps could be heard, the grass rustled, twigs crackled underfoot. There was a rumbling, and someone coughed. Mis Kunda came out into the alley, rumpled and ragged and said to Dudi Tykies,

"Want some bread? If you do, come with me."

Mis Kunda had red curly hair, like wool on a sheep. He was a strong boy, supple as a thong, and he moved his shoulders as he walked. He talked louder than was necessary, and laughed until your ears rang. The first in fights and in showing off before little girls.

He liked Dudi, for he often saw Dudi's father and his own sitting behind the cemetery wall smoking cigarettes in their cupped fists, taking council together. Then, when they shot Mis Kunda's father, it was Aron Tykies who made the coffin and helped with everything at home. Then his mother died, and on the day after her death, Aron disappeared. He disappeared and did not come back from Meiseles.

Maybe he joined Horse-face's gang? Anyway, who was this "Horse-face," the boys wondered, this uncatchable, mysterious man whom people nicknamed 'the jay' because he had a long nose and pointed chin? Who is he, and where can he be met? In spring they used to sit under a sunny wall and think about this man for a long time. They never saw him. They often heard about him, and built up his image in their imaginations. They knew that Horse-face had thousands of ways of killing Germans, that he had many revolvers, a great deal of money and bread. They knew his life story from Mrs. Szerucki's and Tombak's tales.

"Come on, Dudi," said Mis, and smiled. It was hard not to trust him.

Dudi Tykies rose and went lazily after Kunda.

"Where are you going?" asked the children.

"I'll bring you bread," said Mis, and he pointed at Kalma.

"What about me? And me? And me?" the children asked.

"No, Kalma loves Horse-face; only she will get bread."

The children walked down a wide path, stopped between some trees, formed a circle. Kalma touched the chest of the first with a finger, and counted out:

One, two, three,
Mother caught a flea,
Put it in the teapot
And made a cup of tea.
The flea jumped out,
Mother gave a shout,
In came Father
With his shirt hanging out.

"Nasiek, run to the chestnut trees. Over there! Turn around!"
All the children sang:

One, two, three,
Mother caught a flea . . .

"Anielka chooses!"

An old woman sits on the roof,
Rolling herself tobacco,
Up rode Cossacks,
Give us, old woman, some tobacco.

"Jozia, run to the chestnut trees. Don't look!"
All the children sang:

One, two, three,
Mother caught a flea . . .

"Choose, Knopf!"
"Tonia, run to the chestnuts! Don't look!"
All the children sang:

Mother caught a flea,
Put it in the teapot . . .

"Bernaszewski, choose!"
All the children sang:

Mis-ter capt-ain!
Playing on the organ,
Eeny-meeny miny-mo!

"Elza is running away! There she goes!"
All the children sang:

The flea jumped out.
Mother gave a shout.

"Run away! Gendarmes are coming," Kalma whispered, and the children, like startled hens, fled crouching into the distant suicides' corner.

It was growing dark already; rain began to sprinkle. Klara went into the cemetery and let the children know they could come back. She hid her face, and wept.

"What's the matter with you?"

Klara felt that all the children were looking at her.

"Control yourselves. Now, be quiet all the way to the cellar."

The children, hungry and exhausted, cuddled up to each other and fell asleep at once. And Klara, Cirla, and Hynda Gidel sat down on the threshold, awaiting a new day. In front of them loomed in the darkness the little bed of Mrs. Arnstein's child, who died that morning.

Josie Propst was snoring on a droshky in the shed; the hungry horse grumbled. Josie Propst had driven to his own place in the yard, pretended to be calm, muttered something, standing on the driver's box, looking ahead somewhere. He held the reins in his sweaty fists. In falling, the horse broke a shaft. Josie also staggered, and it was only with a great effort that he managed to take the halter off. Then he fell into the back seat and shut his eyes, not wanting to see the ground. He began realizing what had already happened, and what still awaited the remaining children. When he came back, his grandchild was not there. The women sitting on the threshold listened. They were breaking windows at the gravedigger's house.

Once, at night, someone knocked on the windowpane, someone's footsteps rustled at the door.

"Who's that?" I pulled on a sheepskin jacket, stopped in the hallway ready for anything.

"It's Tombak."

"Is it really you?"

"Yes, certainly. I'm on my way. My boot hurt my foot, it ought to be bandaged . . . and if you allow me, I would like to rest a little, and in the morning I'll be on my way. Oh, God!"

The heavy man rolled into the room and at once sat down on the ground. He took off his wet, battered boots. He hung his foot-clouts on the little door of the stove.

"Oh, this journey! Thank God there's a hut in the forest on the way."

"Did you recognize me?"

"No, I didn't recognize your voice. One doesn't know many people. Do you know me?"

"I do," I replied.

"And who are you?" asked Tombak.

"I'm the man who bought a rifle at Mrs. Szerucki's for a kilo of tobacco and five kilos of flour," I explained.

"Yes, he used to have a rifle. He has been a restless man ever since he was little, he had that kind of nature. Everything in Szabasowa is different now. There's no trace left of my hut, no trace of Szerucki's property. The grave of Szabasowa is slowly being overgrown with brushwood. From the ruined railroad station you can only see the broken-down church tower and a factory chimney with holes in it. There's mud in Railroad Street."

"And the house of Josie Propst?"

"Nothing. I go there to mourn over it all. Yesterday I was in Cemetery Street. Nothing. A weasel has made itself a track into the basement, and there's continuous firing in the cemetery. They killed such beautiful girls . . . They lay in a line on the snow. Ah! They cut down the trees — just to think that those trees remembered our fathers and ancestors. Once, in spring, they used to whisper to their girls under those trees."

"You must admit that Szerucki is a brave fellow. A man that's grown one with truth, isn't he?"

"Hard to tell. People say he prints false money and harms our people by that."

"But is it true?"

"Gail was telling old women in the market: 'You ought to kill that bandit with pitchforks. He forges birth certificates for Jewesses.' I was tempted to find out more about him, but you know the way it is in the market. They round up peasants for labor; wandering little Jew kids lurk there, and they chase after them like rats, under carts, around stores behind the counters. So I think to myself, What's it to me, I'm hungry myself, I lost my horses. I've no refuge or warm corner in my old age. Oh, God! Keep a wise and pure forehead in these dark times. It can't be helped. Yesterday, I saw some man watching me. Well, my man, what do you want, I think to myself. He watches, he comes in my direction. I must admit he had cheerful eyes. He came up, and he asked,

" 'Do you want to earn some money?'

" 'Well, now,' say I, 'why not?'

" 'There is a woman in a certain place who must be driven to a safe spot. Maybe there's someone who would play the part of a relative, and take on the responsibility for her?'

" 'Well now,' say I, 'I'm a poor man. How do you think I could help?'

" 'Someone important in Szabasowa told me you could settle it. You're in contact with certain people. There's a little money for this purpose.'

" 'Yes, yes, yes, this isn't to be for nothing.' And here I think to myself, what sort of man is this? He looked around thirty, with a cheerful and honest eye.

" 'It would be undignified to show dislike to me in such a position. I feel that you'll fix it for me,' says he.

" 'Very well, but where shall we begin, sir, where?'

He indicated with his eyes a young woman who was standing alongside, looking at me very attentively. What's going on, I thought; to what cunning have people been reduced? This stranger pushed money into my hand and went into the railroad station. I counted the money: there was fifteen thousand. The girl was standing beside me.

" 'Let's go,' I say to her.

"And she says,

" 'I am glad to be going to live.'

" 'Oh, God! It's a long way, can you manage?'

" 'Yes. I've been in one place six months.'

" 'How come that gentleman trusted me? Who can have given such a good report of me?'

"She gazed at me as though wanting to find out if I were joking, and said,

" 'I don't know, sir, that is their business.'

"By five o'clock we had arrived. The girl was pleased, happy to be far from Szabasowa. She was young, and she believed that happiness doesn't leak away between one's fingers."

"Where did you leave this girl?" I asked.

"That's hard to say. Only one person knows."

"Klara Wasicinska."

"You know her?"

"I've known her for a long time, ten years. Do you want something to eat? There's potato cake."

"No. My stomach's a bit out of order. How hard it is to get away from spying eyes."

"What do you mean?"

"I met Ciszka on the way. He pretended not to see me, but I immediately understood everything. Death is walking behind us. Ciszka walked around us once more, then came back again. Take a look, I think to myself; who likes what, everyone likes something. Once, in the spring, I was driving just such a young man from Prague. What was important to him? Well, he looked at the green fields, at a brook; he threw up his head to the sky. He would have gone through the green world like this, endlessly watching and listening. He told me about his country. He stopped on a path, pointed: a little mouse was running along, out of breath, peeping at us with its tiny eyes. Well, everyone sees something different. Ciszka also sees his own things. I took care of the girl and came back. There he stands, shamelessly gazing into my eyes, and he says two words; it's as though someone had spit and blown into my ear."

"What words?"

"Two words: 'Hands up!' And he pushed his hands into my pockets. He took the money. Another secret agent appeared. They took me under the arms, and brought me to the chief of the gendarmerie.

" 'Alexander Tombak?' the gendarme begins. 'Come closer to the table. You must answer my questions. They stopped you doing a certain job. What happened?'

" 'What?'

" 'Was the woman you took to Huciski a Jewess?'

" 'Hard to say, surely she wasn't a Jewess,' I reply.

" 'We know about that. Very well. But why did you do it? You drove her out of Szabasowa. Jews spread typhus; you will be sentenced for sabotage.'

" 'What?'

" 'Quit saying "what?" We know all about it. Why did you drive a Jewish woman with typhus into the countryside?'

" 'With typhus?'

" 'Don't play the fool,' says the gendarme. 'We'll smack you in the mug, you'll tell us everything.'

"They hit me, the worse was Ciszka. He has already learned various tricks — he's learned how to beat people. They locked me up, and I had to chop wood for a month for the whole guard post, bring water for baths, take the dirt away from the privy, and sweep up the snow. That's what I got. And so much fuss was made of this that every secret agent recognizes me from a distance. I can't move at any price until dusk falls."

"And this little Bernstein you all rescued by the railroad station?" I asked.

"Everything healed up. Szerucki drove Bernstein to Huciski. I went back home. The night passed quietly. In the morning I wandered into town, to hear what people would say about it. No one knew anything, no one was interested. People had too many troubles of their own. I gave Klara Wasicinska an accurate account of everything, but she says that the man who was keeping little Bernstein is dead now, and that the gendarmes are no longer interested in the matter."

"What's happening in Szabasowa? When were you there last?"

"I was there yesterday. They are carting out the rest of the Jews to sandy ground and shooting them. After cramming a truck full, the police and gendarmes sit on the people's heads, and drive out to the sand. And the Jews tear up dollar bills into little pieces and scatter them along the street. Are such scraps of dollars worth anything? Maybe I could collect them and stick them together?"

"I don't know. But what happened to little Bernstein? Was he spared from the Huciski pogrom?" I asked.

"No, he wasn't. He was burned to death with the children of Manka Skwarczynska; there they killed Mrs. Malecki, Mrs. Zelaznya, Suchcicki and his children, Katz, Mrs. Orstein, and someone else who was unrecognizable."

"Chaim at Banczycki's place?"

"He had to run away from the rectory," Tombak replied, "because a large patrol went there and surrounded the yard. Klara told me they attacked after midnight. A man with grenades in his belt shouted, 'You, priest's crap, tell the truth! Any weapons in the rectory? Any Jews? No? Then we'll take a look! And this man' (he pointed to the man in the door), 'if he hits you in the face, don't tell your mother, and don't try to lie down and sleep with him, or you'll get poxed up. And we'll take a look for weapons; maybe there's also Jewish gold; your little priest has certainly accumulated a lot of Jewish sheepskins in his trunk. He sits here, and the peasants support him. What you don't say, he'll spit out, knight of the Heavenly Maiden that he is!'

"He walked around the dining room, opened drawers, shook out rags. A third strolled in, taking huge steps, stopped in front of a picture, crossed himself and then spat at the glass. He had fat and gleaming cheeks, as if bees had been stinging them. He went up to Klara, and said,

" 'God forgive me, a sinner, God protect what you have between your legs.' He pretended to be crying. 'Fasting, fasting, and I have a craving for warm little feet.' The man at the door laughed.

" 'Will you give me it?' the puffy man said to Klara. Klara sighed. 'Well, my pretty, answer — yes or no?'

" 'No!' shouted Klara.

" 'I'll take it myself, then. Will you?'

" 'No!' Klara shouted again.

" 'Then stand against the wall, damn your ass!'

"Then someone fired behind the pigsty, and a green rocket lit up the yard. The Hilfspolizei had piled looted things on a sledge. A carter was standing by the horses' muzzles. Two shots replied beyond the garden.

" 'Well, let's go,' said the puffy man, pulling on the priest's sheepskin.

" 'Where's the door? Where's the door?' asked the second, and he walked from wall to wall without finding the exit.

" 'What will happen if it's them?' the puffy man was impatient.

" 'Get a grenade ready, and hang on to it.'

"And it started. All the windowpanes overlooking the yard flew out at once. Bullets spat all over the walls. Klara, on her knees, found the lid to the cellar and fell into it. In the cellar was a hole dug under the stable, the hole that had saved Chaim from death several times. Klara found him lying in the depths.

" 'Is that you, Klara?' he asked.

" 'Yes,' she replied.

" 'What's happening up there?'

" 'Please be quiet, no one knows what will come of it.'

"But Kweller was sleeping in the stable, and the shots woke him; throwing on a topcoat, he ran out and crept through broken undergrowth to the hole under the dog kennel. He told me he could clearly hear what was happening in the rectory yard. The cops fled into the gardens, leaving their horses, sledges, and loot. A moment later, some men rushed from two directions. He recognized Horse-face's voice, saying loudly to someone, 'You, go with these horses to Helenka, take the short cut.' And the other man said, 'Give me a couple of cigarettes for the journey.'

" 'I don't have any,' said Horse-face. 'When you bring the horses, Mrs. Orlovska won't begrudge you some tobacco.'

"The man with the horses left. Kweller crept out of the hole and recognized Chuny Shaya in the group. They talked a moment, but the shooting began again. Kweller dropped and began creeping on his belly to his hiding place. Chuny Shaya and Szerucki caught a cop in the garden; they took him to the brushwood by the gate, and a shot was fired.

" 'Well?' Horse-face cried in the darkness.

" 'Everything's fine,' Szerucki replied, and cleared his throat.

"When Kweller crept out, he saw the man they had shot in the undergrowth stand up and start to run away. He was falling and running, but Szerucki shone a flashlight on his crouching shoulders, and another shot went off.

" 'What are you playing at?' shouted Horse-face from the rectory threshold.

"A few footsteps thundered in the hallway and 'Chaim, everything in order?' was heard. Szerucki said to someone, 'Go and search him, maybe he has some cigarettes in his pocket. Take his identity papers. If he has a pocketknife, take that too.' "

"Where was Father Banczycki that night?"

"He'd driven with those young elk to Szabasowa for the first time. He expected to buy a few drugs there. He settled what had to be done, and drove away from Szabasowa rather late. In Lipki, three men sprang out at him, as though from underground. Two held the elk, and one put a muzzle to the priest's forehead.

" 'Out of the sleigh!' he shouted.

"Banczycki rose in silence. He still didn't know who the men were. He stuck his hands in his pockets, and asked,

" 'What's the matter?'

" 'Take your hands out of your pockets and don't ask questions. Put your hands behind your back, and double back to Szabasowa. And don't look around.'

"These same robbers went to Huciski in the priest's sleigh, and looted the rectory," said Tombak. "They expected to discover Chaim there, as someone had already reported to Gail that he was hiding in the rectory. Next morning Banczycki walked to his house and yard. Heavy silence. In the snow, trampled by many footsteps, lay an eiderdown quilt, by the threshold was a pair of winter boots near the well a pillowcase, a sheepskin jacket, and a bundle of linen. The floor in the hallway was scattered with plaster, chairs in the kitchen overturned, flour was sprinkled about. The lid to the cellar was not properly shut. He lifted it and called, 'Klara!' Nothing. He walked through all the rooms. There wasn't a living soul anywhere."

"You said that Klara and Chaim were sitting in the hole under the stable?"

"They were," Tombak replied, "but Horse-face found them, and asked,

" 'Are you there, Chaim?'

" 'So what? Here I am.'

" 'You can come out now, everything is OK. You must take your tools, Chaim.'

" 'What for?'

" 'You're coming with us. A man came from Szabasowa who is seriously wounded. And you can take the opportunity of learning a lot of things from him. He's called Knopf. He says that the Liberman family is hidden in the Balaban vault in the old cemetery.'

" 'Where is this Knopf?' asked Chaim.

" 'In Helenka, at Mrs. Orlovska's place. We have to get there by dawn, so no one will see us.'

"Klara Wasicinska went with them, because she was afraid to stay at the rectory alone."

"But the hens? The pigs? Who was to look after them?"

"Faithful old Kweller stayed," Tombak explained to me, and he went on: "Chuny Shaya, Horse-face, Szerucki, Klara and Chaim, and some three armed men went through the fields to Helenka. They reached Pasieki. And suddenly they saw a broad belt of fire in front of them. The red glow was winking and rocking under a low sky. The Orlovska homestead was burning. It was clearly visible as Orlovska's from the distance. Someone fired a little to one side, in a dark pit. Someone else barked back with shots, and a grenade exploded. From that direction a pair of startled horses rushed, their whiffletrees ringing over the frozen mud."

" 'See that?' said Szerucki. 'Father Banczycki's elk!'

" 'Look, lads,' Chuny whispered.

"He was the first to notice a group of approaching people who emerged from the furrows of a field path."

" 'Stop!' shouted Horse-face, and the group halted.

" 'Who's that?' — but nobody answered. A whispering was heard, as if they were talking together. Several fell to the ground.

" 'Flying-carpet?' asked a man's voice.

" 'Speak out. Czaczkies?'

" 'Yes, that's me.'

" 'What happened there?' Horse-face and Szerucki went in the direction of Czaczkies.

" 'They burned down Orlovska's place.'

" 'Did Knopf stay there?'

" 'He was hiding in the stable. He's surely been burned to death.'

" 'Can we get close to the fire?'

" 'We couldn't. They are firing from two machine guns.'

" 'Who's that with you?'

" 'There are seven of us. There is Swistun, Ozieg, Kin, Bacewicz. There's also Kalma and Elza.'

"That same night they fought their way through the forest, and on finding a convenient cellar on a burned-out site in Huciski, sat there until morning. Chuny Shaya and Szerucki went back to the rectory. On the way they decided it would be necessary to slaughter the piglets for food. But they were surprised to see the priest at work. He was drawing water, while Kweller was sawing planks in the shed for boarding up the windows. Two large pots of potatoes for the piglets were cooking in the kitchen, with millet groats in a smaller pot. The priest, in his sheepskin jacket and cap pulled well down over his ears, turned to Chuny Shaya; he was a little tipsy, and he laughed and said,

" 'How did you lads come to let them wreck my place? I feel like singing to you: play on, music, better play to me, or I'll knock you on the head. What's become of Chaim? And where is Klara?'

" 'They are with our men at Huciski. You didn't come back from Szabasowa for a long time; one might think something bad happened on the way.'

" 'They took my elk from me. I barely got back, a rotten journey.'

"Banczycki told them everything in detail; they stood in the kitchen over the iron pot, pulled out the cooked potatoes, and ate them with enormous relish. Blowing on a steaming potato, Szerucki said,

" 'Knopf was burned to death in Orlovska's.'

" 'Where was he burned to death? The cook from Arnold's pharmacy told me yesterday he was not seriously wounded; he left Szabasowa in the evening.'

" 'He got to Orlovska's for the night, and there death met him. We were on the way to him. Chaim was going to inspect his wound.'

" 'He knew a lot, did Knopf. I tell you, he had a radio on him. A radio would have been very useful. The Germans have got a thrashing near Stalingrad, and now, I tell you, everything will be different. Tell Chaim this, he will be glad. If you know in the evening that the road will be safe, then come, for I feel very dull on my own.'

"Father Banczycki drank a little potato water, then rolled a cigarette, and said to Chuny,

" 'There are some of the late Buchsbaum's things here, your father-in-law. You didn't like him, I don't know why, it isn't my business, but there are a few of his things left. He asked me, if you were spared, and if you brought up a son, that the things he left after his death be transferred to his new grandson in God's world.'

"Chuny Shaya wanted to tell Banczycki something more, but somewhere, as though around Huciski, a rifle rattled. It fired a long time, as if pushing back running fire. Szerucki managed to fill the pockets of his top coat with potatoes; he ran into the orchard, looked a while, and at once turned back with the shout:

" 'Horsemen are on the way here! Kweller, back to your hole, quick!'

"The priest jumped into the cellar.

" 'How many are there?' Chuny asked.

"They hid behind the well boarding. Three horsemen were already in the yard. One gendarme, two police. Old Kweller, unluckily for him, came out of the shed, crouched down so as to get to his hole through the undergrowth. A gendarme rode up, and shot the tinsmith three times. He was certainly hit in the back, for at first he flapped his feet, then ever more slowly; it had assuredly seemed to poor Kweller that he had reached a safe corner. Chuny Shaya raised himself a little from behind the boarding and shot the nearest man, whose horse, evidently not accustomed to noises, jumped on its hind legs to the gate, knocking him off into the snow. The policeman tried for a moment to raise himself on one elbow."

"You say that there was firing around Huciski? What was going on there?" I asked.

"It was terrible," Tombak replied. "Szerucki will tell you all about it. He was saved, Chaim and Horseface and Kalma; the others perished."

"Then it all agrees, Buchsbaum did leave some things at Father Banczycki's place," I said.

"Yes," said Tombak, "but no one knows what or how much. Chuny Shaya has said no more to Banczycki on the matter. It was getting more and more crowded in the fields and woods. German 'pacification' units and Ukrainian Hilfspolizei were tracking down people in the Torjnoga district. Maleckie, Podlaski, and Hallerczyn were burned down as Jewish communes. One blaze after another flickered in the sky. Kalma fell sick with typhus, and Chaim's boots wore out. Banczycki's winter boots were too small for him. Chaim had to sit for a week, inactive, in a hole behind Przepastna, until one day Horse-face brought him a pair of good boots from a dead gendarme."

For the winter, Horse-face placed Mis Kunda and Dudi in Podlaskie, at Mazurek's. The boys had no boots. Mis wrapped his feet in rags to go out into the frosty yard and help Mazurek on the farm. He cut wood, chopped straw. One winter night after midnight, just before Christmas, the Germans set fire to Podlaskie. Mazurek's hut also took fire. The entire village was encircled by red flickering light. Black shadows ran across the snow, and the bitter smell was suffocating. It was terrible. Fire was crackling everywhere. People ran breathlessly, not saying a word, running no one knew where, for on the field edges and paths machine guns sliced at the legs of people running. Only women, not understanding many things, carried out holy pictures and blessed the fire with them. Somewhere, someone was trying to let cattle, horses, or pigs out of stys, or untie a dog. Pigeons flew over Mazurek's hut in the red smoke. The dog crouched, whined, and squirmed. Mazurek, Mis Kunda, and Dudi ran into the fields and sat down behind a manure heap. Alongside lay a dead woman, some little old man ran past with a child in his arms, and from under the shrine at the crossroad a machine gun sliced people, and a raised voice calling "Halt, halt, halt!" could faintly be heard. The boys already had more than one thing behind them; they knew a lot and had experienced a lot. Breathless women ran beside them, with sheep after them. Ceilings could be heard falling in with a dull rumble, rafters sizzled, and it seemed that the whole world, all around, was covered in sparks, smoking with pink mist.

Mazurek could not endure it; he jumped out, crouching, and ran after the sheep, but he at once fell down and did not rise again. Mis Kunda and Dudi burrowed deeply into the manure, and stayed there until dawn. The Germans went away, laughing and whistling. A few scared survivors gathered; they stared at the burned-out site and collected the dead. Mrs. Mazurek stood over her husband like one accursed, shook her head and squeezed her skirt in both hands.

In the afternoon Horse-face came, collected the orphan children, dressed them in unburned garments, and took them to the rectory, for it, like an island, stood still untouched by the conflagrations.

Chuny Shaya and Szerucki killed the piglets and Wasicinska cut them up. They cooked food for the children in a large laundry basin, and put them to sleep on the dining room floor strewn with straw. Two men stood on watch day and night in the undergrowth on the road to Szabasowa. For almost two days and nights it was quiet, but at dawn on the third day Szerucki ran in and awoke Horse-face:

"Get up!"

"What happened?"

"Someone is coming in great strength."

"That's nothing new. The children must be taken to Trojnoga. Wake up the children. And tell Banczycki what's happening."

Klara took the children away. Only Mis Kunda stayed with Horse-face. Klara said that when she was passing the forester's hut, it seemed to her she could hear Tykies planing and hammering — but all that was left of the forester's hut was its stone foundation. Inside, a hillock of drifted snow lay, with burned nails sticking out of the damp walls; a steel angle gauge, already rusty, was hanging up. By evening they had come to the cliff near Trojnoga.

"Let's sit down here a little," said Klara, swallowing tears. She herself was in despair, completely exhausted; she had begun to hate the world and people; it seemed to her that no one wanted or knew how to cope with what was going on around.

Thick snow fell all day, until late at night. In the evening, as they had arranged, Szerucki was to come to Trojnoga with news of whether they could go back for the night.

Nine children were sitting in a crevice in the cliff, Klara with them. They were waiting. Night came, the first night without fires or shooting. Toward morning Klara fell into a cramped sleep. The children dozed, covered in Banczycki's quilt; only Dudi did not close an eye. Every rustle in the forest brought him to his feet; he listened and stared with his black eyes.

Aron Tykies did not find his Dudi again. As late as summer, someone informed him that his son was spending the night at Mrs. Arbuz's. He went there immediately, but had to return. The road was picketed, because that very day, a lot of children had run away from the ghetto in Szabasowa. Somehow it worked out luckily that a terrible storm, with thunderbolts, came up. The sentries by the fence on Cemetery Street hid from the thunderbolts in the gravedigger's deserted hut. Young men took advantage of this moment to escape. Three fell.

No one knows how Tykies died. He vanished without trace. Weiss, who escaped from the Sasow quarries, said he saw someone dead in a ditch by the road to Huciski. Szerucki saw this corpse, insists it was not Tykies, but certainly Brodzki. He recognized him by a scar.

In the beginning, Klara and three children survived. Three of them, the strongest and quickest, escaped through the deep snow into a pass behind Podlaski. They were Kalma, Dudi, and the Janicka girl. Some days later, Horse-face met Kalma in the forest. She was already alone in the world. Louse-infested and combed to the last. From her narrative, it emerged that Klara had died a most terrible death.

They found Klara's body. Kalma led them to the place. Horse-face and Szerucki buried her on the edge of a field.

Chuny Shaya was not with them; he was in bed seriously sick with typhus. Horse-face no longer believed Chuny would recover. His sickness began in this way: after a long night's march they had crept into a hut behind Podlaskie. It was morning. Chuny stood by the stove, and stayed there in silence for an hour. He was racked with fever, and had to hold on to the stove. He did not touch any food. Later he said he had been bothered by a stupid and persistent thought: he counted the days. He thought there would be a first day, then a second, and that on the third day he would die. He would fall somewhere in a field; Horse-face, Szerucki, Chaim would come up, measure him with a rifle to see how long his grave would have to be —

He stood an hour by the stove, with his breath coming as fast as if he had been running, his legs becoming weaker. He drank a lot of water.

"What's the matter, Chuny?" asked Szerucki.

"I'm going to lie down here on the ground; now, don't get mad. I haven't the strength to go any further."

"Well, now," said Szerucki, "you must be sick."

"That's it. Something has happened to me, I don't know what."

"We'll call Chaim, he'll take your pulse."

And they went off. But they did not find Chaim at the agreed-on place, only a lot of tracks in the snow, nothing more. One track of boots with nails in the sole led to the river, to the other bank and the Huciski ruins. They searched all the cellars and potato holes there, but there was no trace of Chaim. This was their most terrible day. And meanwhile Chuny became completely sick. He took off his boots, filled with water, the foot-clouts black. He crossed his hands over his belly and closed his eyes, for he was acheing. An hour later he opened his eyes, and shouted, 'Let me get up!'

There was no one in the room. The housewife and children had gone into the forest for the night. Already people were afraid of staying home during the night; they preferred to be in the forest; they had learned from the pogroms at Huciski and Podlaskie. Chuny was lying alone in the darkness. He used to say he could smell horses all night, it reminded him of a stable in Szabasowa, where he and Szerucki had once beaten up Bultz. Afterwards they had dragged him into a latrine ditch. Then someone had brought him three bays. He gazed a long time at their manes, and finally he mounted his Arabian mare, took off the shackles and bridle, and wrapped buckles around it and around his own hand. And he thought that in case anything happened, he could strike the horse's flanks with the bridle, and flee still further, and get beyond the burned-out ruins, provided the fields were dry.

Horse-face came in the night. He gave him something to drink and covered him with two dirty blankets, for there was nothing better in this wretched hut.

A little village, lost among ravines and hills. In spring, birds repose on the greenish trees. An eagle skims over the neighborhood, seeking pheasants and rabbits. Woods, ponds, sparse brushwood. The faces of all the children sitting around the campfire can be seen, but no one will find the dear, lost child again.

"Go with this man, you," said Horse-face, pushing old Raphael in the chest. "Through the short cut at Gontowa. Stop at Skwarczynski's place in Helenka."

"Can you give me a couple of cigars for the trip?" Znajda asked.

Then this stranger went up to him, and thrust a pack of cigarettes into his fist.

Then the shooting started. Raphael began twisting and dragging himself on his stomach; then they took the stranger, took him into the undergrowth, and fired a shot. Raphael went up, lit a match, and saw he had a stain on his forehead. The stranger jerked up and began running away. He fell as he was running. An electric torch flashed in front of him, as though someone were waiting there, for he ran into a pig knife.

They ran in the direction of the forest. Some woman covered her face with both hands and stumbled in the furrows. Someone fired again from the brushwood. They were running across swampy, soaking fallow earth. Sparks flashed under their eyelids, their hearts suffocated. They slowed down in the brushwood. Faltering, losing her way, the woman fell.

"Run, run," she whispered to her son.

Unconscious, with delusions of Kurdiuk, she lay in the cold gulf of brushwood. Somewhere further ahead someone shouted, "Stop, stop, stop!" And a shot exploded, it echoed in the forest. Life was going on uninterruptedly; after tearing herself out of the hatches of oblivion, the woman supported herself and got up. All night she carried a burst-open bundle on her back. Old and thick grass crackled underfoot. Snow started to fall. The field was like clay, a fine mist was hanging around the forest, and snow drifted in the furrows and around the field edges. The wind hit the face, cold and biting.

When the night came down, the soft ashes of Boldurko crept out behind the wide fields to the north, the grave pile of the village.

Chuny Shaya wanted to dart across the highway, but a group of peasants in sheepskin jackets appeared under a lamp on the side of the railroad track. He squatted down behind brushwood. The group disappeared into the darkness. He crept over the pasture fence, hastening his step outside the circle of the railway barrier lamplight. Fine rain and snow were falling; his feet sank into squelchy clay, his boots weighing like logs. Dogs in the north part of Old Szabasowa sniffed someone, and ferocious barking resounded. Beyond the bridge Chuny encountered someone who leaped back. A gun barrel could be seen against the background of sky, and a safety catch clicked.

"Good evening," Chuny whispered.

"Who's that?" The silence rang. The stranger retreated backwards.

"It's me," Chuny extricated his revolver from a pocket. He who's first is master.

"Who's 'me'?"

"If your voice has changed, then damn you," Chuny went up; they embraced and kissed.

"Jeez," Horse-face whispered, 'I might have killed you. Why didn't you shout out at once? Eh?"

"You were to wait at the tollgate."

"Someone is lurking at the tollgate. Difficult to make out who."

They moved along the field edges to the south, reached the forest, and leaving the tollgate on their right, sat down on a tree stump in a clearing.

"Got any money?" asked Horse-face, scraping lumps of mud off his boots.

"Cirla left five dollars at Sitwa's. She was supposed to sell them. We'll have to take them back on the road if she sold them. I wonder if the lover of that ragbag will be at her place? What do you think?"

"Well, I think so. At such dark and wet times a man is drawn to a woman. How soaked my boots are! Hold the rifle. Damn, I have to fix my pants."

Two railroad trains flew to Semperka, rattling heavily in an abutment.

Around the tollgate someone fired, once and then again. Something rattled in the undergrowth. Several figures were running, flashlights at their feet. A thin girl could be seen running in the flashes, men with rifles after her. They could have reached the girl with their barrels. The man running closest shouted,

"Stop! Or we'll fire."

They ran across, and ever finer little spots of light twinkled on the dark earth.

"Rozia," said Shaya.

They ran out after the band of ruffians, tripping on tree stumps at every step. The shrill cry of the girl mingled with rifle shots. Horse-face breathed heavily, cursed, and fired. The light jumped to one side, and someone in the group fell down. Shaya extricated himself from the circle of light.

"Halt! Halt! Halt!" someone shouted in a bass voice.

Chuny fired three times from his pistol. The beam of a searchlight found him, quivered, and went out. After a moment, little lights began glittering in the fields, but they were already further off, running along the railroad track. Horse-face ran along the edge of the forest, something rustled alongside.

"Rozia!" he called. He heard footsteps behind him, squatted down in the brushwood, and again whispered, "Rozia!" But it was Chuny who approached, crouching all the time, searching the ground thoroughly. Then he lay down beside Horse-face, breathing heavily.

Now they could see, in the distance, beyond the railroad track, sparks scattering from the north, and a green streak of bullets from machine guns was going from the beech forest to the Boldurki tollgate. Black piles of manure leaped into relief in the light of a rocket. And now, until morning, it was quiet in the forest. Black clouds did not descend from the sky. A giant was flying over the railroad track.

They found Rozia next day in a clearing, her left hand shot through. They pulled the coat and boots off the dead bandit.

A month later Rozia recovered. Again a fresh plumpness filled her body. She helped Arbuz in the farm work. She peeled beans, ground corn, cleaned wool, or plaited straw for baskets.

Sometimes Szerucki came, and they would sit on a bench under the window. Arbuz told tales and tried to whittle shingle, but any sound brought him from the table to the threshold, to sniff about.

That night Mrs. Szerucki was not sleeping either. Leaning one elbow on the cold pillow, she listened to what the man who had been shot was telling her son. Kuba had brought him in in the evening, and that wound of his, on his left side, stank unbearably in the warm hut.

Kuba Szerucki was sitting on the mattress. He smoked one cigarette after another, until he felt faint.

"My brother was looking impatiently for his ticket," the stranger's tale went on. "He reached into the pocket of his pants and froze for a moment. Yet the ticket must be someplace. He searched his vest . . . Finally he pushed it out from under the belt of his little pocket. He showed it to the gendarme, and this changed the picture. But not for the better . . . as might be judged."

" 'Why did you throw away your weapon at the last moment?'

" 'I didn't throw it away,' says my brother, 'because I didn't have it on me. I'm a free man.' He concentrated, and beyond the flood of words on the subject of what he had been doing, as he was struggling with emotion, he dictated to himself that he must not be devoured. He began again, exactly as before: 'I set off from Belziec. My mother lives in Semperka.'

" 'You animal,' the gendarme interrupted him. 'If you don't stop lying, I'll shove your face in the mud.' Clasping his hands behind him, he went up to my brother, gathered saliva in his mouth, and spat in his face. He said,

" 'Show me your whistle pipe, dear.' He brought out a weapon, came still closer, and shoved the barrel at my brother's nose.

" 'Let me alone,' my brother said.

" 'You love your mother?'

" 'Yes.'

" 'Pipe on the table!'

"With a swinging blow he hit him on the ear. My brother whispered something and fell unconscious, with his head on the threshold.

" 'And the bitch of your god?' he asked me. I said nothing; you will admit it is hard to reply to anything like that. He hit me, but I held out. I can say that after the blow, I felt, or perhaps it seemed, as if a sound had settled obediently in all the crannies of my head at once, and the squeak of an uttered word was a whirlpool which carried off everything into the distance, like an autumn wind on a path.

"He gave you a good going-over," Szerucki put in.

The sick man turned to the wall. Szerucki opened the window, listened. The rain and wind were blowing in the forest, and a dark autumnal expanse charged itself with its own song, as an old woman used to say.

"But I held out. I sought my brother with my eyes; I could hear only heavy stumbling in the passage, near the duty officer.

" 'What's there?' a gendarme shouted.

" 'He fell down,' was the reply.

" 'Can't you lift him up?' he said as he went out to them. 'Who was it?' he asked on coming back.

"I said it was my brother. What do you think, was that a good answer, Szerucki?"

"God knows what you mean by that. I don't know."

"Then I'll tell you, Szerucki. A man must wait a moment for a good answer. Even when he's answering himself he must wait. The thought of my loved ones running away someplace, creeping quietly through deserted alleys, took my breath away. The same would have happened to you if you were married and had children. Your child walks alone through the fields, and everyone there attacks him, they kick and flay him. What do you think of that?"

"I think you are overdoing it. Nobody will touch your child, he's in a good spot. It will cost you money. What else could be done?" Kuba replied gruffly.

"Szerucki, you'll hide me in case something happens, eh?"

"OK, OK. Sleep a while."

"I shan't be able to. Tell me, Szerucki, who fired at me? I would like to know that before I die."

"I wasn't there. They thought you had Bernstein's diamond on you. Well, didn't you?"

"May I die like a dog, I didn't, Szerucki, surely you believe me. I had nothing to do with them. I only lived there. And I am very glad they were mistaken. That's their false point of view. When Mrs. Bernstein left the house, it was well into dusk. I swear I wasn't able to see where she went. One of two places: the Jewish Council, or Samiczka. Then she came back, and Bernstein asked, 'What happened?' He lit a match and gazed at his wife. 'I've decided,' she said, and nodded to me, 'we've thought it all out beautifully.' But this had nothing to do with the diamond. It was about a place for their elder child. It was a subterfuge in front of the servant girl. Then Bernstein could be heard floundering about in the garden, the gate opened, and Bultz and Ciszka came in, those men from Criminal Investigation. Bernstein sat down on the threshold and leaned back against the door. They didn't move him. They took the servant girl. All I said to Wasicinska was, 'Behave yourself, little Klara.' Well, and afterwards nobody was there; evidently they believed the diamond had disappeared along with Bernstein. If I'd been well, I'd have extricated myself from the mess. Sooner or later."

"There is nothing to consider. The question is for them not to find you here. I haven't any ammunition for the Mauser, my entire supply is one magazine."

"Yes, you were very sorry," said the sick man, and he sighed deeply.

"But how do you feel? Drink a little of this herb tea, it's cold, but even so . . ."

"Do you think there may be infection?"

"I don't know," Szerucki replied. "Take the jug in both hands. Yes, some horse doctor ought to see you."

"I'd like you to understand, Szerucki, what it was all about. The suspicion still exists that I have this diamond. But I've had enough of it. Everyone, even Father Banczycki, thinks the same. I can feel it. Nobody wants to know me. That can be proved."

"Come," said Szerucki, "you're rambling and vexing yourself. Take such a matter for instance: I had no ammunition when I took you on my back — to some end or other. They like going on the track of that diamond, as you know."

"Yes, I know. You can speak freely of certain things."

"Rozia gave up her place in my hut to you, you're lying in the warmth. She is in the stable loft. There is no question of bullying; I'm just telling you how it is. Rozia has no shoes, no warm clothes."

"I can't recall who Rozia is."

"Daughter of Spojdyk, the water-carrier."

"You're right," the stranger recalled. "There was also a Rozia Arnstein."

"Yes."

"Excuse me, that's it. This is a serious matter."

Szerucki groped in the darkness for the door.

"I am considering something inside," said the stranger.

"Are you?"

"It might have been this way. Are you leaving, Szerucki?"

"Don't think up tricks. Spit it out."

"Where are you going?"

"All this won't let me breathe," said Szerucki, anxiously. "I'm afraid they may track you down. That would be a strange tune. Lie down and don't get up."

The sound of someone prowling in the mud under the windows had been audible for several minutes. Old Mrs. Szerucki was snoring by the stove, mumbling as she did so, as though suffering from fever.

"Take this, Szerucki," said the stranger.

It was terrible outside, wet and dark, and their boots sank as if they were walking in tar. Szerucki went into the stable to scatter feed for the horse. He stood for a moment on the threshold, listening.

Every night there was a fire. As soon as dusk and the black sky closed tightly over the earth, red glows bloomed over Szabasowa and Talesni. Often reddish clouds with smoke under them hung low until broad day. Often a distant conflagration seemed to be the moon rising, or dawn. Often fire broke out so close that the walls of huts in Zalesie, standing among the autumnal leaves, looked as though they were spattered with blood. Pieces of burning paper, straw, and such flew high from the fires; human groans, the squealing of animals, the wail of children could be heard amidst the crackling.

Somewhere far in the east a searchlight was probing the sky. Automobiles whined on the highway near Szabasowa. The wind brought the smell of the swamp.

Szerucki stopped up the pantry window with a sack and lit a candle. In a pocketbook permeated with the perfumes of a barbershop, there was, in addition to an identity card in the name of Julian Brodzki and seven thousand zloty banknotes, a letter, closely written on four sides: "My dear and only one," wrote the woman, "someone tapped lightly yesterday at the cellar cover. Someone's footsteps came up and withdrew; I could have pushed out the straw over me with my hands. And I did. Your messenger came out of a dark place, and gave me a letter. Your letter, my dear. If only you could know what is happening to me. . . . Little Jurek is asleep at my feet. He is clutching the bottle of milk Mrs. Arbuz sent us. I gave her that which we agreed upon at home. I don't walk about this cellar, so as not to rattle anything, but if anyone were listening, he could hear me and Jurek whisper. People often come to the stable overhead. In the night the mare bangs its hoofs; obviously she has already conceived, and the female elk too. Is the village in which you stopped deserted? How far from us are you? What a terrible night, full of pain and hopeless care. There are a lot of broken bottles on the ground. It is even a good thing that there is so much glass here. I stop the rat holes with it, but that does not help. What should I do? I am afraid they will bite Jurek. He is asleep and doesn't wake. I wanted him to kiss this letter to you."

Szerucki barred the door and supported it with a block. He decided to take off his boots and doze a little before the journey. He went back to the room and threw Brodzki's wallet on the table.

Any poor person could easily wheedle anything he wanted out of Szerucki. Awareness of someone else's need touched his tranquillity to the core.

"You'll get over your feelings about me," Brodzki began.

"Listen, let's talk seriously. Try and sleep a little. I'll leave before dawn, I'll stop at Father Banczycki's to ask for a doctor. Banczycki will see to it. My mother will manage what is required. But try to get some sleep, you'll suffer less. They chose a fine name for you — Brodzki."

"You think it's a bad name? I paid twenty dollars for that name!"

"It's all criminal, damn it," said Szerucki, and he curled up on the mattress beside his mother. The swift hands of the little old woman plunged into his hair.

In the night, snow fell, and the dawn smelled like a frozen blanket. Time mingled snow and sunlight. Warm rivers flowed across the sky, and shadow chased shadow across the earth.

Szerucki jumped off the low cemetery wall and trudged wearily and dully into Shaya's yard. The wind was banging blind window frames. Fresh footsteps led to the stable. The droshky lay on one side without its front left wheel. A hen was standing on one leg. Hewn logs were lying in a corner, along with a discarded horse blanket.

A funeral was moving along an alley from Zawodz. Swaying, the people walked after the coffins and drew out a sad song of discordant wailing. There was nobody in the crooked alley to the railroad station.

Szerucki went into the hallway. Shaya's children were sitting there, eating underdone potatoes. A dog was sitting beside the children, waiting for peelings, and by it lay a hammer and pea stems. The room was dark and quiet as a grave. Someone was standing in a dark corner, cupping a cigarette in his fist. Old Kweller approached and said,

"They're in the stable. They want to take the mare."

"What mare?" Szerucki put one hand into the pocket of his jacket that was stuffed with something similar to a horsehoe. "Where's Chuny?" he asked.

"He's somewhere around. Take it easy. It's always necessary to take it easy."

"Damn, 'easy,' " said Szerucki, and went out into the yard. He caught sight of the legs of Chuny Shaya fidgeting behind overturned planks in a corner of the stable.

He crouched and crept behind the planks, leaning with one

hand on a rafter. Chuny pressed Szerucki's hand. From the black interior came a rustling, as though someone were tying haystacks. Szerucki, who always fired too soon, did not even put a hand in his pocket.

"A mare's moment of birth is often difficult to guess," someone said in a bass voice inside.

"Rub her udder. Are there beestings on her udder?"

"Right away . . . trrr. May the devil . . . trrr. May the devil take it. There are no beestings."

"And her hindquarters? Rub her hindquarters."

"She will kick."

"She won't. A high-ribbed mare never kicks, you prick."

"Trrr, damn you." He scraped a match.

In the light, Szerucki saw Bultz.

"The sinking in of the hindquarters is a sign that she will foal any time."

"Hindquarters normal."

"What do you mean 'normal'? The prepuce is removed, you prick. And there are certainly beestings. Light up! Trrr . . . light up. What's that, if not beestings? An Arab mare is delicate."

"You certainly milked her," the man in the Olympic jacket laughed, and went up to the door.

Szerucki was first to fire into the darkness, more or less in the direction of the man in the Olympic jacket. A silence resounded, and at once three shots replied. Szerucki felt a burning sensation in his calf, and fell over a tightly packed hayrick.

Feet clattered on the floor. With held breath, Bultz shouted, "Damn you. Who's that?"

"Give it to him," said the man in the jacket. Knocking the door down, he ran out, pulling the reins with him.

"What are you doing here?" asked Szerucki.

"Well, what?" Bultz was standing with his revolver half out. "Be off, or you will get yourself stamped on."

"Say that again."

"Leave the mare and be off," said Szerucki, and he stretched his left arm into the darkness.

"And I you! You!"

Shaya came out on the planks. A shot resounded in the yard, and someone shouted loudly. Footsteps ran behind the stable and died away. Water dripped by the threshold. Chuny flew into the stable and struck at once with the blunt side of an ax. Bultz rubbed his brow with one hand, his cap flew off, and his hand slowly moved across the back of his neck and over his close-cropped hair. His legs gave way, and he fell into some straw with one outstretched hand, as if he wanted to greet someone and tell them lots of things.

Chuny Shaya muttered, throwing the ax aside. His cheeks were red, and he was biting his lips. Bultz was gasping for air, as though he wanted to sigh deeply once more. Szerucki came in and kicked him. He was standing on a package near the dead body, and was feeling his calf, shot through from the side. His leg had reddened with blood.

Shaya put one hand on the mare's mane.

"Sweating," he said, and spat. "A man has a strange taste in his mouth. You know, blast his eyes."

"Cheer up, Shaya, for perhaps it really will foal. Eh?"

He wiped his mouth with the back of his blood-stained hand. A cloud flew briskly like a shadow across the yard, and snowy grits sprinkled down.

"What are you groaning for? Cover him with straw. Who did you shoot behind the stable?"

"It was he who fired, Ciszka."

"Whom?"

"Spojdyk, I guess."

"You, what's going to happen to my leg? Eh? Damn it. Cover him up, Chuny."

"Cirla came around, Kuba; she told me last night that she came." Shaya pushed a little manure onto Bultz's face with the tip of his boot, and staggered. "If only it would lighten up somewhere in this world." He repeated: "Lighten up," and he went out.

"What are you groaning for, Chuny? It'll all work out." Szerucki tied a piece of string around his knee and rose.

"It will."

Two magpies flew into the yard, and with bristling tails peeped into the stable. Shaya puffed his lips, sniffed, spat, and began dragging Bultz over the threshold. The mare turned around in fright.

Szerucki helped him, then went out and took some loose snow in his hands, pressed it into a ball, and wiped his fingers with it.

"The mare must be taken out and allowed to disappear," he said.

"Give me the toolbox."

His joints crackled as Szerucki pressed several pitchforks of manure down on Bultz's chest with the whole weight of his body. Gulping air, they carried the corpse behind a latrine in the marketplace. Bultz's dead fingers stuck into the earth, but the earth was rotten and slipped down from his hand.

Alongside the traces of the magpies, staggering tracks went behind the stable. The poor water-carrier Spojdyk was lying there. He lay face down, as if he wanted to swim in the snow-flavored clay. And one more solitary track went beyond the broken-down fence and into Railroad Street. Two women with headbands were standing there.

Szerucki went into the room.

"Take it easy, old man."

He drank some water and spat out sand.

"God, how my leg hurts. Do you hear, Kweller? I shall have to lie on my backside for a long time. Do you hear, Kweller? Be easy, it was worth doing that way. Do you hear, Kweller?"

"Where are the children?" asked Shaya.

Snow was scattering, it grew dark in the room, as though a cart of hay had driven into the yard, shadowing the window.

"If they kill us now, well, it's all the same. I feel like lying down a little more. Since I got back from Podlaskie last night, I haven't taken my boots off. Do you hear, old man? And Mama comes up to me, for she peeped into the oven, and she says, 'Don't get undressed, you have to go to Szabasowa.' Oh, God, it's as though they flayed me!"

"Nahum!" Shaya called in the hallway.

"The children are waiting in the cemetery," said Manka Kurpinska, coming out of an alcove, loaded with a feather mattress and basket. A bright ray from the door settled in her dark eyes. Her thick lips had turned purple from the wind.

"My dear girl, the mare is going to foal. When it happens, we will look for you." Szerucki's strong fingers seized Manka's warm palm, and he pressed his knees to her thigh. Such heat flowed through her as though she were standing naked by a stove.

Shaya was standing as if turned to stone, his hand hanging down, black with earth and manure. The sirens of the Foresta sawmill howled at noon. Jewish laborers were walking along the road from the railroad station, surrounded by six mounted police. There the wind erased their footmarks, and a mist of snow scattered over the signpost. At the corner something happened: one laborer fell down, several ran off; then a shot was heard, faintly, as though someone crouching and unconscious had banged his head on an empty beehive. A train with cisterns rolled by to the east.

Manka went behind the cemetery with the featherbed. Szerucki, his calf beginning to swell, sat down in the hallway on an upturned bucket, groping at the crust forming on his leg, and lit up. His knees began trembling, and he shoved his hands into his pockets. He heard Shaya whistle through clenched teeth, and had to run for it, without arguing. It was as though a spider web, biting death, had emerged from both sides of the hut. He tried to dodge out on his injured leg, rebounded to his left leg, and jumped over the low wall.

The man who first came into the yard was Samiczka. Stout, with a feminine face, he blinked as though he wanted to draw attention away from his harelip.

Beyond the cemetery Szerucki and Shaya wiped their feet and set off calmly along the highway to Stock. At the barred door of a tavern stood a short, bandy-legged peasant with a whip in one hand, who smiled at Shaya.

"What jokes are they playing on you? Who's there?"

"Take a look, you'll get a hint."

Szerucki wiped his frosty cheeks on his ragged sleeve, went in, closed the door behind him, and felt that he was sick. A sharp uneasiness enveloped his head; his eyes met two rifles leaning in the corner, and the street was suddenly filled with running. Someone breathless shouted: "Ruuh!"

He should have lain down, fallen under the feet of the man running up. There was no time to retreat to the door. From a squatting position he hit the first with his head in the pit of the stomach, and jumped into the passage. A large privy stood in the yard, a folded ladder and fire hook hung on the fence. Snow was whirling in the empty space, and smoke threw about sheets stinking like burning rags.

"This is your little business, you son of a bitch," he heard behind him, and his legs at once changed into ice. But he turned and began to make a way for himself by firing. Some *baudienst* or other had hidden behind the planks. In the black hallway Szerucki could still see the flashes from his own Mauser.

Sometimes it is strange in summer. Even at dawn a cloud flies with thunderbolts to meet the sun, a warm wind chases straw around the fields, raising a bluish dust on little paths. It was not yet day, but already thunderbolts were banging over Szabasowa.

Gabe Gudel, Mis Kunda, and Dudi were sleeping in the fields on stacks of trefoil. When the wind began blowing the withered leaves off his shoulders, Dudi woke up and he nudged Mis with his foot.

"Get up, it's raining!"

A roaring approached. The first great drops fell on Dudi's forehead and bare knees. He gathered up trefoil and put it on his back. He wanted to cover his knees, but somewhere close by a thunderbolt struck. Thick, oblique rain began and Mis Kunda, awakened by the cold moisture pouring down his back, rose on his knees, crouched as though to pray, not making out yet what was happening. He covered his head and shoulders with the trefoil. His hands were soaked. Water flowed over his shoulders, down his chest and belly. It bit at his shoulder blades. They decided not to move for they had learned that when a person doesn't move, the water does not chill so; it flows away down the spine to the backside. It is a little warmer.

Gabe Gudel was lying alongside, but he did not even shiver. Rain drenched his face, and his eyesockets filled with water.

"Maybe Gudel has been killed or wounded?" said Dudi.

"We'd have heard if he'd been killed."

And again there was thunder and lightning overhead, until it seemed that the sky had been ripped into fragments. The boys crouched down to the earth and held their breath, waiting for some terrible mountain to crash upon their backs. Dudi said something, but Mis did not hear what.

The steady, heavy rain poured down on them. It flowed around their eyes and into their mouths. Finally Mis Kunda jumped up and began running blindly, and searing fire flashed over the ground, and another thunderbolt broke, covering the entire sky with its noise. Bang, bang, bang — the earth groaned, and far from the rear the echo and roar resounded, as though the forest were breaking.

Dudi ran after Kunda. They ran to Smolno. There it was possible to hide in some pigsty not yet burned down. Dudi closed his eyes, but the flashes of the lightning claps penetrated through his closed eyelids, the cold rain permeated his entire body. Mis Kunda covered his eyes with his left hand, and ran; Dudi could barely distinguish him from the stream of gray water. Wind struck Dudi's chest; he spat rainwater out of his mouth and rubbed his eyes with his fists, and his pants stuck to his body. Mis was already on the other side of the highway. Then Dudi caught sight of another danger: a cart packed with some men or other was standing on the highway, and around the cart were several policemen with long rifles. The water roared thicker and more gloomily, and it veiled the cart and the long rifles. Dudi ran across the highway and jumped onto an escarpment. He looked around. These men from the cart could be seen running in all directions; someone there called out loudly, and a shot was fired.

Dudi caught up with Kunda, and shouted to him, "Where are we running to like this?" But the latter, as though he had gone deaf, heard nothing and ran on further, lifting his knees high. Dudi staggered, breathless, and when Mis Kunda disappeared for a moment, he was seized by despair: it seemed to him a thunderbolt had killed Kunda — he would open his eyes and be alone in the world. Somewhere further on a thunderclap resounded briefly and flatly.

"Dudi!" he heard behind him.

Mis Kunda was sitting under the little wooden bridge at the crossing to Sewarynka. The still unburied Mrs. Ceigier was lying there, a child close by her.

In the afternoon the rain stopped, the wind carried the clouds away to the north. A white, thin little cloud arose from the fields and meadows, then faded away after crossing the height of the forest. It dissolved against the background of the sky. The field footpaths steamed under the sun, the grass rose, and drops trickled down stalks of corn. On the telegraph wires to Szabasowa, raindrops hung, then flowed down into the loops, and fell off.

A little girl was walking through the mud, drenched, pale, gazing with distended eyes at her feet, her lips trembling. Whistling and shots could be heard. The little girl frowned, raised her hands and ran, slipping on her bare feet on the tiring road. From behind the corn three policemen could be seen coming down off the roadside escarpment, looking into the fields. Their eyes were seeking someone, and they talked loudly. Mis Kunda watched their every movement, listened to what they were saying.

Together, Mis and Dudi darted from under the little bridge and ran without looking back, across interminable fields to the forest. The policemen, breathless, thundering heavily on the field edges, ran after them.

"Horse-face and Chuny Shaya will kill them at Przepastna," said Mis. "They will ambush them and kill them off."

This rifle, with which Chaim went to a confinement today, was carried by Kurdiuk yesterday. Horse-face met the boys on the edge of the forest. They were sitting there naked, drying out their rags. Chuny Shaya thrust one hand into his pocket, and produced a lump of wet bread. The bread was dissolving into grits. He divided these grits into two handfuls, and gave them to the boys.

"How would you both like to join the gang?" asked Chuny Shaya.

"We would," said Mis. "Horse-face's gang."

"Good. Take your drawers and we'll go. It will be necessary to get them some clothes," said Chuny to Horse-face.

They took the boys to the gamekeeper's hut and fed them, and in the evening Horse-face brought the coat of the dead Kurdiuk to the rectory, and asked Klara to cut out two little pairs of pants.

Rozia was not at the gamekeeper's hut. She had made up her mind. What she wanted to do, she did. Her father was toiling hard in the quarries, and she wanted to be with him. She went there one night and disappeared. Someone talked of a girl's dead body near the barbed wire of the Sasow labor camp. Horse-face went to see; he came back toward dawn and said nothing. Some days later he told Chuny Shaya:

"Suddenly, with my sharpened hearing, I caught some rustle or other in a nearby pile of gravel. It's all the same to me, I thought, so I jumped over and shone a light under the wires. The light was in my left hand, and my right hand was outstretched to the right, and I had a finger on the trigger. A slow little stream was flowing by the wires; its course had been blocked by stones and a small overturned boxcar. The water rippled in breaches of the track. Rozia's legs were soaked in water up to her calves. She lay stretched out on her back. I had to leap over and crouch behind the pile of gravel, for a sentry was shooting at my place until the water splashed. I made up my mind to sit it out and look at Rozia once again. I wanted to kneel down and see everything accurately, so as to remember for a long time. Do you think that if I had managed to get through the wires a second time, do you think I would not have kissed her on the brow? I thought just as I am telling you. Meanwhile, there was shouting around the sentry post: 'Halt! Halt!' Someone also jumped out of a neighboring heap; I fired in that direction and heard, 'A friend!' We ran together, side by side. Someone shouted: 'Horse-face?' And I: 'Szerucki?'

" 'We can slow down,' said Szerucki, 'they are not coming after us.' "

After Arbuz's murder, Cirla hid at the house of Klara Wasicinska's mother. Old Mrs. Wasicinska made a hiding place in a bay of the barn. Cirla sat there all day, and at night she came into the room. By the light from the stove, the women plucked feathers, peeled beetroots, or wove chains of onions.

Chuny Shaya came later. After scraping his boots on the threshold, he looked at the women crouching in the corner.

"Dark in here."

He came into the center of the room and took a breath.

"Everything all right here?" he asked.

Cirla put one hand on his arm.

"Where's Nahum?" she asked.

Chuny seized her trembling hand and led her to the bench.

"Why should I hide it, sooner or later it will have to be said: Cirla, Cirla, you mustn't . . . He's gone, he's not with us any longer, they killed him."

Chuny's voice became gruff, as though something were lodged in his throat.

"Chuny," whispered Cirla, and she fell down by the bench.

Chuny Shaya said nothing, he did not try to console Cirla. Silent, he sat in the corner by the stove and gazed at Mrs. Wasicinska's shadow dancing high up on a wall.

Cirla was weeping. Mrs. Wasicinska sat quietly, staring into the fire. A fly calmly crept over her forehead.

Szerucki tapped at the windowpane. Chuny hurried out; on the threshold he cocked his rifle.

"It's very bad," said Szerucki.

"What do you mean 'bad'?"

Szerucki pressed his fist. From the village could be heard the clattering of carts.

"Horse-face was here just now; he says we must beat it; he went with the boys beyond the rectory. He says German police are gathering in the hamlets; they are setting up machine guns on the crossings."

At dawn Buchsbaum dozed; his grandson, cuddling to his grandfather's belly, was fast asleep, covered by the tails of his halat. Buchsbaum was tired of the night-long flight and was agitated by the firing. Gendarmes had been looting, out beyond the Huciski hayfields and around the hamlet of Helenka since early morning, trapping peasants for labor. Someone armed was there, and he had fired at a gendarme with an automatic pistol. There was an uproar, a wild shriek, and three grenades exploded. In a moment people could be seen fleeing in the direction of Buchsbaum. And soon afterwards, several men on horseback rode into the meadows, crossed the river at the ford, and galloped into the brushwood.

"Run for it!" someone shouted.

Buchsbaum shuddered and lifted his grandson. Two boys, then a girl, were running alongside. He had time to whisper to his grandson,

"We're running away."

He seized the child by the hands and immediately started running. The forest clearing was very thin, the undergrowth low. Crouching, Buchsbaum ran heavily, forcing himself on with the remains of his strength. There were a few seconds of quiet, and suddenly a shot was fired. There was a whistling noise, and they heard a shout:

"Halt!"

Buchsbaum was already near a thicket. The last of his strength was going, and his heart stifled him. He let his grandson down to the ground.

"Follow me," he whispered.

A gendarme rode up, aimed a short volley in their direction, drew his bridle, and jumped after a girl.

"Halt! Halt! Halt!" he shouted after her in a clear tenor voice, as though he wanted to say something nice to her.

Buchsbaum fell down immediately, but his grandson ran a few more yards, then seemed to trip. His head fell on his breast. Buchsbaum rose, and seized the dying child. Blood was flowing from his grandson's mouth, running over his cheeks, into his hair. The child was still stammering something. Stiffening with despair, Buchsbaum realized that this was the end, that all was now over. Everything that was the most terrible was behind. Unafraid, holding his grandson, he gazed back: there, they were bringing Mrs. Ciper and her children out of the undergrowth. Buchsbaum carried his grandson's body down a crooked path into the black forest, and he laid him very quietly and carefully on some moss. An hour later Chuny Shaya came after him. They buried Nahum under a maple tree.

Buchsbaum was no longer impatient. He sat in the undergrowth and guarded the grave, lest foxes tear it up. Sometimes

Chuny Shaya sent him a slice of bread and a bottle of milk. The shames did not leave his grandson's grave; death found him there.

" 'Mrs. Arbuz . . .' I had to blink, I went closer, I had to go closer. Something was lying by a scorched wall.

" 'Mrs. Arbuz,' said Szerucki, pointing.

"The heart and liver of Mrs. Arbuz were lying there. I looked at them for a long time. Then Szerucki said:

" 'First time you saw that? It's simple, man.' Then, as though recollecting something important, he went to the burned-out stable. On the floor of the burned-out granary lay heaps of smoldering grain. We raked them aside, wishing to get at what was underneath. There was a faint hope that maybe something had been spared which we might grind in a handmill for pancakes. Roast piglets lay among the black firebrands. In the yard, scattered elk, hens, and ducks had been completely burned; only ash was left. Orlovska lay shot by the well. Her daughter's hands had been axed; she had no fingers. Of the entire farm, only a cat had survived. It was sitting motionless by the dead woman, its nose in the snow. Nothing we were doing in the yard interested it.

"Suddenly Szerucki ran up to me, and said,

" 'Five men are coming in our direction.'

"I looked and saw armed men with dogs coming toward us. Dragging our feet, we ran out of Orlovska's yard.

"Mrs. Arbuz's heart and liver remained unburied; foxes dragged them away in a few nights. We were there a week later. Fresh snow had covered the burned-out site of the hut, only titmice were sitting in the cherry trees and a milking stool lay upturned to the cloudy sky."

"Sitwa was concealing that tearful poet who was with us in Szabasowa, but one night three guys with lordly manners, as she said, came to her, and said,

" 'We think madam will allow us to see him.'

" 'Him? What's going on here? You gentlemen haven't told me what it's all about,' says she.

" 'Now we can get several good witnesses. These two gentlemen, if you please, madam, will bear witness that Tolek isn't a Jew.'

" 'He is now being interrogated at the police station, things are working out very well. Maybe you gentlemen will take the trouble to go to Szabasowa now, to the Criminal Police, and make statements. This is working out beautifully!'

"And the swarthy man with the gloomy expression — as Sitwa

said — took a step forward and hit her in the face. The other, pretending to defend her, groped at her. They searched the attic and cellar, and beat her silly.

"They found Tolek. The eau de cologne gave him away. Sitwa had looked after Tolek, and she fed him. He rested, slept well, and sprinkled his hair with eau de cologne. This betrayed him. It was simple: in the attic there was a covering of planks by the rafters. And Tolek lay there. The spies were already creeping out without finding his hiding place, but one caught the smell, and said,

" 'I smell scent. Hey, there!'

"They followed the scent to the hiding place and pulled Tolek out. Sitwa says they carried him into the room, as he was rigid with fright. He said nothing. He fell down on the floor."

Once Buchsbaum stank of wind, another time of snow. Daily he gave death the slip. Lice and the itch, hunger and cold devoured him. The wind tousled his gray beard, rain beat down on him, thunderclaps harassed him, a spy was on his track. He met him in the summer. Birds were whistling in an interminable landscape and the heat of the sun. Buchsbaum was walking after Flying-carpet.

He was already without his grandson. They were walking along a high field edge; harvested ricks of corn flapped. Across the path were many trampled footprints, some photographs lying about trampled by a boot. Further on, trampled corn and someone lying there killed. He lay with his face to the sky. There was a red stain on the shirt of this corpse, and greenery thrust into his mouth.

Flying-carpet searched the dead man. In his shirt pocket were some cigarette ends drenched in blood; under his shirt on his chest was a scapular with mercury, such as men from the Sasow quarries wore.

Going down into the valley, they could still see smoke from Szabasowa; the trefoil was blackening in piles near Lipki. The sky was violet in stretches to the right and left of Szabasowa, and a reconaissance party could clearly be seen on the horizon around Stock. Szerucki's hut was glowing with fire on a violet curtain. The last hut was burning up on Cemetery Street; the smoke drifted straight and very high.

They went down by a field edge into the valley, to Mogila. This was a Sunday in early fall. In Mogila, carts with new ladders were standing in the yards, harnesses were hanging under sheds, sowing groats and bags also. Cows masticated, horses were combing down their manes, elk gamboled with tails up around the yard. But there, beyond the beech thicket, Huciski was perishing. Groaning people were digging graves for their families. The village was burned out. Only here and there, beehives amidst sooty orchards were spared. Czaczkies' old horse came to the burned-out homestead of his owner, leaning its nostrils on the boarding, his gray tail hanging down. There I saw Father Banczycki.

"A horse is a clean creature," said an old woman, holding yarn, to the priest. Her skirt had holes from fire, and her eyes were stupefied.

"They must kill that horse now," the priest pointed his stick at the horse's burned flanks; "matter has collected; its perineum will take fire at any moment. Czaczkies would not be angry. As for you, woman, why are you holding that yarn?"

The woman did not reply; she nudged with her spiky foot unburned rafters, metal lids, melted glass, and little dishes for feeding bees. The frame of Czaczkies' hut was still smoldering, it stood out toward the sky with no door frame and a ripped hinge. Scraps of burned paper, leaves, and the like were blackening in the little garden; a dog was lying by the stable ruin with swollen skin like head cheese.

Banczycki recognized Buchsbaum.

Neither said a word to the other, but they shook hands, and Banczycki took him into the fields.

They walked through meadows someplace, to Przepastna. And Czaczkies' son in top boots came to the site of the fire, and crept into the hot cinders and raked them with a stick. He aged that night. It seems he was looking for his mother's body. She was to have picked bread out of the oven, put it in a bag, and brought it to the forest before dawn. Kurdiuk had taken away the cow in the evening as he knew very well what was going to happen that night in Huciski.

Szerucki came later. It was already late in the day. He came with some man or other. They gave their horses a drink, hobbled them, and set off for new cattle. Immediately a crowd of mosquitoes began buzzing, crowding around the horses' tails. Spreading out sacks, they sat down on a field edge. In front of them was buckwheat — still young as yet, but behind stood stacked corn like a gray whetstone. Who will regret losing this corn?

Evening was coming. At this time of day cattle always came back from the pasture. And when it grew quiet in Huciski, the rest of the survivors went to find places for themselves, and suddenly an enormous mountain of smoke, swollen, disturbed by sparks, stood over the fields. Smolno was burning. From there came the cries of women, children lamenting, buckets clanging. The glow lay along the west; to the north beyond the forest the sky turned dark-blue, strewn with flashes, as though mute cannon were firing beyond. A sorrowful evening star also appeared in the sky.

"What star is that?" Szerucki asked his companion.

"That one?" he pointed at the sky. "What can be said about a star? It's the evening star — there's an evening song and an evening bell."

"It must have been there forever, since the beginning of the world, eh?"

"Yes," he replied, and he began telling Szerucki about an experience with his father and brother. "It was in the spring. My dream opened up and something was left of it, like the echo of a wedding song. Still across the knocking, a rapid little stream seemed to be running, women were beating clothes with washing sticks, a deep pre-spring sky stood outside the window. The dawn was coming fast. But the orchard was still dark. Someone was standing on the threshold of our house, and was knocking. My brother came back at dawn. He went into the cart house and dug out this stranger. They came into the hut and sat down. The stranger looked at my father with his eyes screwed up.

" 'Must eat something,' said my brother.

" 'Yes, we must,' said my father, but he did not stir. After a moment of silence, rolling a cigarette, my brother mentioned meeting Horse-face, that the job was in the final stage, only ammunition for the machine gun was lacking. But some acquaintance who had escaped a few days ago from Belziec promised to try and get some.

" 'What acquaintance?' asked my father.

" 'Do you want me to push a shovel into your head?'

" 'You, you loafer. Don't mess up my life with any Horse-face and shooting, so there!'

" 'Don't prattle, for Christ's sake,' said my brother in a cold fury, and he stood up from the little table.

" 'What do you mean "for Christ's sake"?'

" 'Well . . .' he went up to the old man; there was a creaking in his broad chest; he spat underfoot and went outdoors. He stood a moment on the threshold, his heart swollen, he said, with youthful, restive grief. He went back into the hut and got tobacco out of a box. My father, in silence, took his sheepskin jacket and went out. My brother went out after him.

" 'Where are you going?'

" 'That's my affair," said the old man 'but come with me to the cart house.' He winked significantly and shufflled ahead, bad-tempered and constricted.

" 'This is a hunted man,' said my brother.

" 'And you, aren't you hunted?' My father thrust a fist into one pocket and whispered something, as though stupefied.

"I went back into the room. The stranger was still sitting there motionless, looking incessantly at the window, and nothing else concerned him.

" 'There's a little of yesterday's milk left over; maybe you're hungry,' I said.

" 'Does your father know anything about me?'

" 'No, surely nothing.'

" 'I am Brodzki. I escaped from Belziec; my wife is hidden here in the neighborhood. Your brother knows all about it. All that counts now is for your father to change his feelings toward me.'

"But meanwhile, a gendarme on horseback rode into the yard and shouted something. Two horsemen from the auxiliary police were standing outside the gate. Brodzki looked out the window, his wide-open eyes resting for a moment on the shouting gendarme; then he ran out into the hallway and up a ladder into the attic.

"Gendarmes and police prowled around our village all that day, looking for hidden Jews.

"And I know where the wife of this Brodzki was hidden — in a dog kennel. She sat tightly curled up, holding her child between her knees. She sat through the whole day in this manner. At night, when we lifted the kennel, she was almost dead. For a long time the child would not open its eyes. Stupefied, she did not realize who we were. She took us for agents, and had to run out into the dark fields again, for a patrol appeared and fired three rockets. We too had to take off from the village.

"This forced march exhausted me. I had passed several sleep-less nights; the ground was soft as it is in spring, and I had the itch all over. Somebody was moving in the thickets; it was hard to see who was running away, who was chasing. That night I met Cirla for the first time. She was sitting in a field edge, her hands thrust into the sleeves of a frayed coat. I took her to Mrs. Arbuz; she laid down straw for herself in a corner of the room. Toward morning Mrs. Arbuz came back from Huciski and asked:

" 'Cirla, do you still have milk in your breasts? For, if you have, you should go and feed Kweller's grandson. He is in the rectory at Father Bancyzcki's place.'

" 'You should — ' said Cirla, and she pressed her hands to breasts flat as boards."

Next day Szerucki found Chaim in the gamekeeper's hut near the Trojnoga forest. Tur-koc's widow was giving birth, and Chaim sat by the stove waiting for the newly born child. Szerucki stayed the night with Chaim. He sat on a tailor's stool, drawing on a cigarette, rubbing the bolt of his rifle without thinking. The woman was shrieking with pain. Chaim went up to the patient, placed his hand on her forehead, and said kindly,

"Come now, come, it will soon pass."

"Dear God," the woman in childbirth grittted her teeth.

Two tiny children were sitting under the bed, and no pleas could get them out.

"I'll show you something nice," said Szerucki. "Why do you sit there and get in Mama's way? She is sick, poor woman, and she will be angry with you."

But the children squeezed still more deeply into the dark hole.

"See him?" Chaim turned to Szerucki and pointed.

A big black cat was sitting on the stove, gazing at the woman as she writhed in pain.

"You must do something about that cat, Szerucki, else it will pounce on the placenta. I feel it will."

"You think a cat could?"

"I don't know for sure, but I am afraid it could. I don't like this cat."

"It certainly feels the housewife is suffering."

"Never mind what it feels. I bet you, Szerucki, that it will pounce on the placenta."

"Then bang it on the head if it does."

"I prefer you to listen to me. Take that damn thing out."

"What if it bites?"

"It won't. Stroke it, then grab it by the scruff of the neck, but leave your rifle."

"You're talking nonsense, Chaim. Let the cat sit there on the stove."

"What do you mean 'talking nonsense'?"

"Let it sit there, I say. You're too jumpy. There's no harm in it sitting there. I never heard in all my life that a cat likes human guts."

"You're a coward, Szerucki, you're afraid of that cat."

"Come now! Me afraid of a cat!"

"And how."

"I swear to you that I'm not."

Chaim went up to the patient in silence, and Szerucki went out of the hut and stood on the threshold. He stood thus about a half hour, and listened. The sky was starry, frost crackled, dogs were barking far off. When he went back into the room, Chaim crouching astride was working hard on the patient, and he said through his teeth,

"Get that cat out of here for Christ's sake, and light the stove."

"Why blame the cat? It's sitting there quietly — let it."

"Szerucki!" Chaim shouted, and he turned and threatened him with a blood-stained fist.

"Where is it now?" he glanced at the stove; the cat was no longer there.

"Don't make a fool of yourself, and light the stove."

Szerucki chopped up some pine wood, then crouched by the stove and struck his cigarette lighter. The woman was howling so that his ears rang. The children under the bed were crying. Szerucki blew into the fire. The candle was dying out; its tall flame flickered a few times, then the light shrank to a handful.

"Did you light it?" asked Chaim in a different voice, as though something hairy was caught in his gullet.

Szerucki puffed. A wide glow flickered over his thick lips, nose, and wrinkled forehead, and when he took a deep breath, supporting himself on his shoulders, his face looked swarthy and green.

He puffed faster and faster until everything brightened, and a merry flame crackled. The great shadow of Szerucki's head began to dance on a wall.

"Put some water in a pan; it must be heated," said Chaim from a dark corner.

Szerucki went out into the hallway, looked for water, rattled about and swore, then came back, and said,

"No water."

"Isn't there a well in the yard?"

"I'll take a look."

He went out, taking a bucket and his rifle. His footsteps could be heard under the window. After a moment someone came into the hallway, someone's hand sought the handle. Chaim called,

"Kuba!"

Nothing. Chaim opened the door, shone his flashlight around, there was nobody. In the yard, dawn was coming. Szerucki did not come back again.

Not until spring did Flying-carpet meet Szerucki. Szerucki was lying on the forest edge, resting after a deadly forced march, with sunken eyes, almost stupefied with exhaustion.

"Where in the world have you been?" asked Flying-carpet.

"Awol," replied Szerucki, "I stepped out of the hut for water for the woman in childbirth; the spring was about thirty yards below. I'm coming back with a full bucket. I was in the gate already, when someone runs out of the hallway. You know how it is. I reached for my rifle, then I say to myself, it's some girl. She ran out of the hallway and into the pigsty. I followed her. To this day I'd swear by my life it was Tonka. She ran into the forest, and I too ran after her, and shouted."

"Are you certain it was Tonka?"

"Yes."

"You were seeing things. People often see things. Gabe Gudel also used to see things. Whenever he walked past me in the forest he was rambling frantically; most of all he used to see Szabasowa. He wasn't a stupid man, but he saw things. He grabbed me by the hand and pointed to some town or other in shadows under the trees."

" 'Listen to me, man,' the Gabe whispered; 'that's a town. In it there prevails the purest Czarist officer's rigidity, the genius of street-sellers connected with the genius of creators embroiled in profanity. The last fifteen minutes of reading out the legal code, the intellectual authorities of the population, with smiles on their lips, hats revolving on display, new patrons, shopwindows stuck over with strips of paper and black rain for identifying those who, warned in advance by the police, do not go into town, and those who went out into the black rain, apart from a lesson for the town, will always be held in the same contempt. The town! The lesson of these sprinkled by the black rain gave the police a paper, in which at every moment they hang up a picture of the death sentence for the townspeople. I know the police," cried the Gabe. "They keep everything to themselves. Especially the chief of the section of the Great Secret always marks off at night typical sections regarding our town, its streets, women, children, and provisions."

" 'Calm yourself, man,' I said.

" 'You're just the same,' the Gabe threatened.

" 'No, I'm not, calm down,' I asked.

" 'Do you love your town?'

" 'I do.'

" 'The roofs, chimneys, and high places of our town are bristling with harpoons thrown at birds, since the police are afraid that eggs brought into the area of the town will upset the equilibrium, and begin to resuscitate everything once again. Even our sacred books, which they consider unnecessary now. But who has not defiled the books thrown under the foot of those who are leaving?'

"All that Gabe Gudel said was not entirely meaningless. Chaim, for instance, listened to him very willingly. As a man listened willingly to a fairy tale told by old Politynski. About the forest echo, for example. The old man put his feet up on the stove and told the tale. It was dark in the hut, the child of his daughter-in-law sucked her breast until it almost hiccuped, and the old man talked of the forest echo:

" 'A man was walking along, and when he stopped on a bridge he saw many ducks floating in the water, and golden fish, and these ducks and fish began to flee, for people usually fired at their heads, or threw stones. So the man begins throwing breadcrumbs, which he had obtained from a bear, and he went further, for he mended people's boots on the way, and so he lived. Then he stopped in a wood so thick that not even a scrap of sky could be seen. He stopped to take a dram. And a white figure in a blue robe appeared to him there, twelve feet tall, and said these words to him: 'Dedicate apples and two candles placed cross-wise to Saint Blaze, and you will sell them to people for sore throats.'

"We're getting off the subject. Do you think it could really have been Tonka?"

"It could have been. But what happened to her? The woman in childbirth might have known, for it is not out of the question that Tonka visited there. How did Chaim know, for instance, that she was going to give birth? He never saw her before in his life; she no longer had a husband, the children were too small to deliver messages. No one of the family around."

Father Banczycki was left entirely alone in the rectory. Some kind of sickness bothered him; he lay in bed or wandered aimlessly around the chilly rooms covered by two blankets. Snow lay in the yard untouched by human traces. One day, a half-stupefied woman came to the rectory, lit the stove, cooked some potato cakes, and went back to the forest at night.

On the day before Twelfth Night, late in the evening, Chaim and Flying-carpet went to the rectory. A feeble light was flickering in the kitchen window. When Flying-carpet approached and peeped through an unfrozen crack, he saw part of Father Banczycki's face. The priest was in a sheepskin cap, coughing like a hoarse dog, his face swollen with effort. There was also someone else present: the end of a long laugh was heard. Chaim claims it was Gail, a secret agent from the Criminal Police. The conversation must have been going for a considerable time, for Gail was giggling. He could be heard tapping a finger on the tabletop. For a moment there was silence, then the secret agent began: "Well, well — all these ideas for civilized people are better located in the stomach. You think badly about all this, Father."

"What's the matter with you, man, you don't have any self-respect," said the priest.

"That's just it, he's uncovered his lack of sense,"

"Well, let's let it alone. I haven't the strength. You call people evil-doers, but you call them that in order to treat them like evil-doers. You've learned from someone abject the right to despise others. Therefore it is necessary to aim for complete forgetfulness of self; it is necessary to destroy in oneself the desire to exist. Is it not so?"

"Calm words."

"Oh, you're as imperturbable as a depths without slime."

"That too is for the birds."

"The total of our past deeds decides our later life and further deeds. We cannot get away from the result of previous bad deeds."

"Little Father, there is no philosophy, metaphysics, ethics. There is nothing — apart from movement and change, apart from this turnstile of death and life which is one and the same thing. For please think, Father — who is, or was, the depository and witness of love? A maple tree. And rue is the emblem of maidenly virtue. Not some ethics or other. They thought up something, probably so it would be harder to guess."

"Maybe right," said Banczycki.

"Yes. For just think, for cucumbers to come out well, they must be soaked in milk twenty-four hours before sowing!"

"Maybe you are right, Mr. Gail. For example, such a godly covering."

"What godly covering?"

"Unkempt shag, quite simply. A crop of hair, for instance — that too would have some meaning."

"Hm."

"A little wreath of lice in the bosom. Well, eh?"

"Hm."

"Ah, Mr. Gail, we are moving off at full speed . . ."

"What?"

"At full speed. It is time to seize a blunderbuss and fire."

"Do you know what, Father? You could use a tame woman. Not a bang in the face."

"Well, damn it, be off."

"What, madman? Can you throw away such an opportunity?" Gail spread his hands, pressed his chest against Banczycki's chest.

"Mr. Gail," the priest removed his guest with one fist, "what makes a spy? What is a spy's screen? A loose tooth?"

"Aha, that's the way you're leading, little Father."

"What? World history, biology, sociology, heredity, criminality, or finally, upbringing?"

"Construction of the world. You, little priest, could use a heavy beating in some jailhouse; then we'd know."

"And I tell you, my little spy" — the priest thrust one hand into his pocket and moved something there — "I'll tell you. The construction of this world is penniless peasant dandies, gestapos, the last of many children, and so on. I don't have to say anymore, damn it."

"I know it myself. I regard myself as something worthless, worthless as a dismantled stove . . . Please understand, father, that life here cannot pass in a ceaseless fight through this Jewry. A man must live out his life calmly."

"That means what? If, going through Szabasowa, for instance, were you certain that the sight of the people murdered there would not move you to the depths, and that in turn would not influence the secret activity of the lymph, or whatever it is called, to its disadvantage?"

"Ha! You, Father, have a strange way of saying something stupid and questioning a man out of his senses."

"As you see, so you judge."

"No. Only I am surprised, that's all. Please throw all this away to the devil."

"Oh, Mr. Gail!" shouted Banczycki, "you must have been born yesterday, you didn't spend an hour in high school, or a moment at a university."

"Excuse me. I have a degree in law. In any case . . . The war drags on, and it is already as tiresome as a failed marriage. It drags. They shoot. Any amount of blood squirts out of bodies."

"You are all fighting."

"Allow me to sit here a little longer. It's an inflation of lies and rubbish from paper sacks. Nothing more. Evenings, Bach rings out his themes on the radio. Upstairs, soldiers' brothels, while here and there eyes of prisoners peer out."

"Jails can't be empty!" Banczycki groaned, and he looked Gail in the eye.

"Oh!"

"What do you mean by 'oh!'?"

"Your rectory is empty. And it would be useful to work something out. So many pretty Jewesses are wandering around the forest."

"Would you like to have a whorehouse here, eh?"

"Well, no. But there is a difference. We are not yet rationing sugar out to you from a matchbox. And no shit-bucket is standing in the corner."

"Do I know?"

"There are some, I imagine, who are smiling. They know what to expect from the flies in a man's pants."

"How smart you are. A criminal teaching a dog to track. I am like a dog; I have everything in my nose."

"This is more or less how it must be understood: for you, there are no foreign lands in a spiritual and spacial significance. Is it so?

"Guess. Why do you at once evaluate, damn it."

"I understand. People have to stifle their passions these days. Their troubles are no longer private. They listen slyly to improbable tales which end in furious catastrophe. Each man wants to experience his fate in secret. Besides, people are what they secretly want to be."

"I'm not externalizing. If it came to shooting, then that's exactly the point that someone would call a furious catastrophe in the rectory at Huciski. I am just wondering where we shall hang you."

"Why are you all going to hang me?"

"For curiosity. Let me ask you: how long can a woman run carrying two children?"

"Why run?"

"To escape death. And the woman is chased by sturdy farm laborers in the uniforms of the Mazeppa band. They stop and beat her on the shoulders with their fists. The flash of a shot, and the woman falls to the harrowed earth with her children."

"You are a man, one does not treat me so."

"What do you know about a man. Nobody knows anything about a man. Everyone talks rubbish, which might protect them. Let's speak frankly: you are a spy. That's all there is to be said. Morally chaotic, with a conscience like a sieve."

Gail went on to mention something about bombs in London and walked to the door in his apparently never-greased boots, which seemed to be sizzling. Banczycki could fire. It was as though he were even considering the spy's death. The depths of winter. Joyfully, when little birds alight on sunny twigs amidst trees heaped with snow. And here the traces of a scuffling man . . .

"Listen to me," roared Banczycki. "When you survey your child's things, your heart aches. You see him, you hear his voice, you look into his dark, gleaming eyes. Cirla had a son too. I don't know if it was you, but it was certainly someone from that Criminal Police of yours who ran after her little boy. He chased him through frozen orchards. He caught him and ripped off his red sheepskin jacket. He took him near some undergrowth. The child hid his eyes with his little hands. The shot ripped his head open. The child kept running backwards, as if someone had struck him hard on the forehead. And he fell down, so very little, that nothing could be seen on the snow. I know . . . He, that grown man, went to Hanczarka with the little sheepskin jacket, and stifled his conscience with a gramophone. The light of day burned him, which is why he put on a steel helmet with a swastika, and black glasses."

"Just so, were you, little priest, to put out a fist to threaten him, he'd put a bullet into your chest without hesitating. You'd spit blood, seek for the fence with heavy hands, and frighten those close to you with your fishlike eyes."

"Good God! Who rules this world?"

"Shooting."

"So you say."

"Shooting. You yourself want to shoot me like a dog."

"Yes. It would be necessary to decide. What's the time? Tell me what the time is. It matters to me. I would like to take advice from someone. For apparently, when a person kills someone, it's as though one had already killed oneself."

"Very well. We'll see which is the stronger — a member of the Criminal Police, or the priest from Huciski."

"Oh, little Mister Spy. Surely you saw old Buchsbaum lying naked under a cloudy sky, whiskers to the ground. The wind tore at the scraps of shirt on his emaciated shoulders, toil stood in a cavity like a kneading trough. Alongside, two bags of coarse bread, onion, and a stave polished by a hard bone."

"Yes, I saw. Kurdiuk's work."

"And a girl sprawling on the lumps of frozen winter corn. She served at your place. One braid of hair across her lips puffed out by a shot, a jellied eye. Thick stockings on her legs, earth in her hands despite the frost. And to the left, the mother who bore her, naked, with a rag of clothing on one leg."

"I remember. Teitelbaum then taking advantage of the calm on the highway disappeared at a jog trot into a field. A patrol spotted him through field glasses and fired single shots at him. He squatted cross-legged, reached the forest, and disappeared into the blackness."

Banczycki went up to a window, opened it, and shouted into the darkness:

"Horse-face!!!"

At dusk, when it was already dark, a girl shot in the liver was dying on a heap of straw behind a stove. A gurgle could be heard in her throat; she clutched an empty bucket; her fingernails sizzled as if someone were taking chaff off a tin plate. Kierasinski, this new arrival to Chuny Shaya's band, a refugee from the Belziec camp, was groaning in the middle of the room.

"What are you doing there?" asked Szerucki.

"I've found the wick of a broken lamp."

"So what?"

"I will smear the uppers of my boots with this wick, then the water won't get in."

"All the same, she is dying," said Szerucki from the darkness.

"Is she?"

"Just listen to how she's breathing. Well, listen . . ."

"Give her artificial respiration, that is sometimes very effective. Only don't squeeze her spleen out."

Szerucki could be heard as he moved the straw, and the sick girl asked in a quiet whisper:

"Wo bin ich?"

"What?" asks Kierasinski.

"Wo bin ich?"

"Got any matches, Szerucki?" I asked.

"My matches got wet; everything on me got soaked down to my shorts."

"You're a dolt too, aren't you. To let your matches get wet."

"Nach Hause will ich."

"What's she saying?" asked Kieraskinski.

"Don't you say 'what?' over the sick girl," says Szerucki. "Kneel down here, closer, and rub her forehead with your dry hand."

Straw rustled, knees banged, and quietness fell, as if everything had been hit by the blunt edge of an ax. Footsteps flapped in front of the hut. Someone impatiently sought the door handle.

Kierasinski went to the threshold.

"Who's there?"

"Dudi."

"Let him in," said Szerucki, "one of us. Hitler needs him for good luck."

Kierasinski removed the barrier, and the door burst open.

"What's happened that you're alone, Dudi? Eh?"

"Flying-carpet sent me here."

"What did he say?"

"To run away."

"And where is Flying-carpet now?"

"In bed."

"Where?"

"At Sitwa's. He caught two bullets."

"By accident, or what?"

"They were shooting, he got hit."

"He is not careful enough, that marinaded prick. You'll stay with us, it won't be any worse for you."

"You, ask him who was shooting, and how many of them there were," says Kierasinski.

"Where did they hide you all in such rain?"

"What?"

"Where were you all, Dudi?"

"In the undergrowth, beyond Podlaskie."

"That is entirely OK, now I know why they hid you there. Flying-carpet had not seen Hoch for a long time, as previously his daughter brought him news nearly every day that things were very bad, for he fell sick and also some gang had designs on the dollars sewn into his red jacket. Do you know anything about Hoch, did he say anything to you, Dudi?"

"No."

"Sure, you're a child. Oh, goddamn this world."

"You must be hungry, Dudi, and we too didn't eat today so my head hurts."

Meanwhile, the sick girl got up and ran to the window, from which could be seen a fire going out in the drizzle. A head loomed in the windowpane, and the girl fell down as heavily as a sack stuffed with wet logs. Wind hurled the door of the empty pigsty, and as it returned to its place, the door squeaked on its hinges like a well by a busy road.

"Light up, Szerucki, for she's certainly dead by now, and we shall not succeed in finding her by groping. To leave her here half-alive?"

"There are two matches in the box, and there is a great danger that neither will light."

"Where do you have them?"

"Inside my shirt."

"It must be damp there, for you are agitated."

"I'm not at all agitated. Help me to carry her to the straw, so she won't turn cold on this clay. Slowly, give me your hand under her legs."

"Yes, she's dead already."

"Can it be?"

"Well, it feels like it. Don't act the fool, Szerucki. Obviously you are very sorry for her, as though she were your own."

"Neither mine nor yours. She was ours."

"It would be interesting to know who she was. We could sit here till morning, feel through her rags; maybe she has some papers sewn in them. She certainly had something on her, perhaps a scapular or other thing for identification."

"She has no scapular; she was Jewish."

"What if she was? Maybe she pretended to be a Catholic with a scapular, for a cross is worse, especially if gold. Bang a Jewess on the head, and the gold cross goes into a pocket. But what's a rag scapular — it smells of the deathly sweating of a pursued man."

"We won't stay here till morning. We must get moving now. We'll set fire to the hut. She too will burn, but it is better that way than to have dogs drag her around the forest footpaths."

"Szerucki!"

"What?"

"Does she have a ring on?"

"Aha," said Szerucki, "now I understand. Now I know what you are."

"And what do you think, Szerucki, that pigeons are cooing outside the window, and there's sun in the morning? You could give the ring to this little Dudi, and it would keep death away from him."

"Don't kid me, Kierasinski. Let her ring alone. The dead are almost holy. One can search a dead person for papers, find out who they were and what country they came from. Flying-carpet keeps a record of such cases."

"I tell you, papers won't bring back a smile to anyone's face. Feel, I tell you, to see if there is anything; then pull it off. A ring would be useful to Dudi; he came out into this black world without any money or experience. As for holiness, you can tell that to someone else."

"Have some respect, Kierasinski. I don't care for you. Probably you joined Chuny Shaya as a provocateur. It's none of your business to interfere in our work. From today you will be regarded as a provocateur. I will tell Chuny Shaya this, and Horse-face will shoot you in the head, so that your eyes will pop out."

"Calm down, Szerucki. Quit sticking your revolver in my chest. I will prove to you by my own death that I am not a provocateur. Take the dead girl's ring, or in other words, save the life of this little Jew boy. He can't manage to run around in the mud, and will get lost some black night. You yourself said Sitwa will gladly keep him at her place for a week or two, in exchange for the ring. Maybe Hitler will break his neck during that time. There will be fewer informers, the forest will turn green, and we shall get closer to hope."

"It seems you've gone crazy. You've been a week with us, and already that has caught you."

"And you want to be famous for honesty. What's your fame to anyone, if you're registered in other books."

"What books?"

"Police records. In one they have written down: Kuba Szerucki — bandit. In another: Kuba Szerucki — Soviet diversionist. In the third: Shabbasgoy, hooligan, spy of the Chuny Shaya gang. There are also those who have a grudge against you, because you know something about this Hoch and his red jacket with dollars. Fighters of the Galician division will hang you one of these days, and will drive people from burned-out Podlaskie, Zalesie, Huciski, and will order them to grease you after your death with sticks — It's his little business, son of a bitch, that your villages went up in flames — That will be your fame. You want the shortsighted praise of your own men. Help Dudi with the dead girl's ring; when a man is drowning, don't merely murmur a song to him."

"Ha, you talk like a priest's propagandist. You are raving, man; I am registered in Chuny Shaya's records, and no one will rub me out of them. Your dealings in the hallway stand and follow you. You explained to Chaim that you escaped from a Belziec prison transport, that you're a Jew from Tomaszow. But that's not true, you're — God knows what you are! Some sort of earthworm. Be off, or I'll spatter you with shot you before anyone comes. Why did you call yourself Kierasinski?"

"And why does he, over there, call himself Flying-carpet?"

"What's it to you? That's our affair. Don't you question me, Kierasinski, you won't find out anything, and don't grind your teeth as though you were asleep. He calls himself Flying-carpet because he doesn't resemble a Jew."

"Nor do I."

"I don't know that for sure. One day we'll take a look in your pants."

"He, he, he. What are you doing there? Going on, eh?"

"Don't drive a man crazy with questions."

"Is that why you won't stop rooting about in the straw?"

"No, I am covering her with straw so it will catch fire and burn up."

"Well, let it be as you think. Dudi, go listen on the threshold to see if anyone is coming."

"Why are you sending the child out? Stay here, Dudi," I said, "don't listen to anything he says. Sit down and cover yourself with that girl's blanket. She had a blanket here under her. Take it and fold it in four, cover your back and neck. I'll set a match to it all, we'll get warm, and then go."

Kierasinski went out into the hallway in silence. Several footsteps flapped under the window, a sole rustled on the stone threshold.

"Who's that?"

"Me, Chaim. Is that you, Szerucki?"

"I'm here. Come inside. Shine a light, maybe you will recognize who this dead girl is."

"Who's that standing behind you?"

"Dudi. He will come with us. He must come with us, because someone laid Flying-carpet out flat today. There is no one in the village anymore."

Chaim shone his flashlight into all the corners of the room, and then at the pile of straw from which the legs of the dead girl stuck out into the room. Dudi was cowering behind Szerucki, without his cap, his nose swollen and plastered with congealed blood.

"Take the straw off her face," said Chaim. "It's Lula Heim! Flying-carpet knows all about her. It's certainly Lula Heim. Do you know the way to Sitwa's? I'd like very much to be there by tonight. Flying-carpet must be looked after. We'll take him to Czaczkies' gang."

"Put out the light! Or no, don't. Shine it here on her left hand."

"Yes, she must have been a very rich girl. Please, Szerucki, we must go without delay. Do you all have some weapon or other?" Chaim shone the light on Kierasinski, who had spread the fingers of both his hands wide to show they were empty. "Why are you, hope of mankind, still unarmed?" asked Flying-carpet.

"He doesn't succeed."

"Who doesn't?"

"Oh, this whole Kierasinski thing doesn't work."

"Do you really think so? Try not to make it any worse for him, maybe he's broken down, or still not used to our gang. Maybe he hasn't yet corrected everything that is necessary in these circumstances. It's only too easy to say, 'I joined a gang.' "

"Do you have matches, Chaim? I want to set all this afire. I don't like huts standing solitary in fields. Dangerous ambushes for gendarmes. Well, aren't they?"

"Do as you think fit. Let's go, my friends."

It was necessary to set off just before midnight; rain was beating the February earth incessantly, and it was dark as an abyss, but over Szabasowa a puddle of fire was quivering. Somewhere far off, as though behind the Trojnoga forest, a rifle fired a volley. Szerucki set fire to the straw in which this poor girl had breathed her last, and everyone went quickly into the darkness of this world. It was impossible to measure, either by sight or hearing, what was in front of us in this darkness.

We walked in a group along the field edges, our feet jogging, sometimes clapping, as if five men were threshing. Alongside stood the forest, quiet and dull, like a coffin, with scraps of unhealthy expanse in the gaps. All the slope behind us was exposed by the fire in which the girl was burning. Over us an aircraft flew, humming, to the East. And once again only our footsteps were to be heard, little and stubborn; Dudi could be heard limping: pa-tich, pa-tich. That's bad, I think to myself, he won't go far. There's a long road ahead. Don't think, man, that the end will come at once. For us, this day's night will surely have no end. We must break its back, otherwise a dirty grave covered with turf awaits us. To encourage Dudi, I ask him, "Well, how are things? Did you hurt your feet very much? Eh? You don't even want to answer? It's nothing, Dudi. We shall get to Sapisko; there we shall rest, eat something nice and fat. It seems your father is encamped there, we shall meet him and, how happy you will be! But suppose it were necessary to run away from bullets? Eh? As soon as we grab a revolver, you will have to be armed," say I, but no one smiles, no one jokes. Worn out with misery, we are silent. Maybe someone makes a gesture with eyes or lips, nothing more.

We came out breathless on a high escarpment, following Szerucki, who knew every hollow of the ground very well. From this escarpment jumping glowworms of bullets in the black dimness could be seen to the north, in the direction of Talesni. It was not possible to see our faces, increasingly sore and burned and changed into those of badgers; we could feel our clenched fists sweating. Memories ebb and flow, thoughts go backwards, sum-

mon up the murdered, acquaintances slip past in the closeness of
the walls of the alleys of Szabasowa, centuries and generations behind them, as in a cave filled by the noise of groans and curses, in
alleys populated by the murdered, and a gang of robbers prowling
the long passages of the Jewish consistory, cries of children slaughtered in the concrete ritual bath. And when you drag yourself into
the depths, the history of your little descent gets more and more
dense — here's the face of your grandfather leaning over in the
morning, here work-worn hands touch the still slippery and cold
surface of the earth, gather up daily bread handful by handful,
and the confused noise of women at a wedding; and then a song
you had forgotten reaches you:

> A poor Jew is driving along,
> Got no straw, oats is dear . . .

Cold after cold, care after care, and the children not dressed for
the winter. The road is too long for a fall afternoon; Chaim's
grandfather is coming back to his hut with a small sack of yarn;
going in he tries to put two and two together in the darkness. His
children and wife are plunged in the dark. Mawkish recollections
fall without effort, like ripe fruit; others burden heavily. Tonka
continues to stand behind the curtain with her hair in one braid:
she smiles bitterly: 'Well, Tonka?' 'Fine summer weather,' she
replies. Song after song . . .

> He's driving, he's driving, his horse is dying,
> And he's pushing the cart after it . . .

Little candles, burning at certain intervals of time, throw short
beams of light on certain people and places — in the snowy
square a water-carrier quickly nods, to be in time for the shabbas.
And a December sky stands out pinkishly, like a globe scattered
with salt; frost grips from heels to eyelashes. Groups of shadows
are crowding to evening prayer, it is dark in the alleys, it is necessary to grope one's way, and before dawn people, groping in the
darkness, go to dawn Mass — oh, you horned devil.

We passed the Trojnoga forest and continued on, upwards,
along a path drenched to the consistency of paste; we push amidst
frozen ferns to the little Tatar Peak. Kierasinski took Dudi picka-
back. Rain is whispering around; puddles stand in the fields; a
red valley long and wide as an island is to be seen beyond the
glow. And we walked on to reach Sitwa's that night. The heavy,

gluey earth stuck to our boots, rain kept striking us sideways. We walked one after the other in silence. The route Szerucki chose was difficult, the Miodobor slopes were heavy with winter deadness. We dragged across the bridge by the mill on our knees. Through the rattling a shriek in our direction could be heard, and a shot from a sawn-off rifle. A bullet whizzed as though from a catapult. We slid down the embankment and ran a whole mile. Two more times, the sawn-off shotgun goes off behind us, and barking dogs fly up. We gather in the undergrowth, Kierasinski runs up with Dudi on his back, and he breathes heavily, as though soffocating. A wind rises and blows straight in our faces, so that we stagger and move on, taking short steps along a hill. We plunge into pinewood seedlings, water in our boots, our shorts sticking to our bodies.

"Damn nightmare," whispers Chaim.

"It will be necessary to burn the mill down. Well, won't it?"

"Do you think it was an ambush?"

"The rain drove them into the mill; they were sleeping late by the merest chance. Else, brother, we'd have been asleep in the mud."

"Do you think it was Ciszka's doing?"

"And how! What do you see, Chaim, with your eyes? You don't see anything that is happening around you."

"And you are trying to render in words Ciszka as a monster persecuting you, and your heart sinks into your boots. It is necessary to catch him and kill him. I consider this a most urgent matter."

"Did you see him, Chaim?"

"I never saw him. I would like to."

"Well, you will," said Szerucki, and after a moment, "I won't forgive that feeling of my heart sinking into my boots."

"So what if you don't?"

"I will prove to you that in a week there will be no Ciszka. Yes," Szerucki went on, "I want to prove it to you. I am hard. Even when I was a little boy I was hard. Because that is how I wanted to be. I thought how to be hard, how not to let myself be eliminated from the world. For you know, Chaim, that they always want to eliminate a man from the world, behind a ladder, in all manner of ways. I am still investigating their Kierasinski. Chuny Shaya must decide what's to be done with this little golden bird."

"Well, as you think best. It's possible to be wrong."

We walked an hour through dense scrub, passed a rippled forest lake. Toward dawn a slight white frost pinched, cocks crowed somewhere far away, dogs barked, the dawn showed red. Rabbits ran across the black earth, the quacking of ducks over them. When we passed the black skeleton of a burned-out gamekeeper's hut, a terrible shriek tore the air.

"Hunechke!" cried a woman.

"It's Cirla," said Szerucki.

We walked on, and behind us the watery and icy freshness bore the shriek of the insane Cirla. There was no Hunechke in this bald landscape, there was nothing except a gang of informers tracking down Bernstein's diamond and Hoch's red jacket with dollars sewn into it, apart from a dozen children wandering around after a dog, and Chuny Shaya's gang, which kills informers and provocateurs. In spring, bedunged cattle will come out into the wet pasture; covered with a sack, Cirla will begin to search among the cowherds for her Hunechke. O paradisal beechwood, o hundred-legged thicket!

A thin, reddish dawn widened over the obscure hillock of a cloud, under which to the right a glow was dying out, but it was no clearer near us; black coverings continued to hang over our eyes, and our eyelids watered.

"Does Chuny know Cirla has gone mad?"

"What can he do about what is happening to her? Nothing. Well, go on, Chaim, don't halt the march," I said.

And again we walked an hour through open fields, in an infinity of mist that pressed into our mouths and noses.

And we walked on into the dark fields. Snow clouds clogged the world, and in the sky was vaguely to be seen something like a gray horse with pigeons, or some letters already darkened with age, or a wall of black stone. Then again, a valley, as if you were looking at it from a high window, and in this valley people were despairingly stretching out their arms to something great.

We reached a parting of the way: the left went to Talesni, the right to Sitwa's.

"Is there a wayside shrine here?" asked Chaim.

"Yes. There it is. It is to Saint Ann."

"How do you know it's Saint Ann?"

"Well, because we buried Wasicinska here, under this shrine. Then someone left two vases made of shell cases, and in them a little barley and oats with centaury."

Walking along, Chaim began recalling: Yes, Klara could be heard climbing the ladder, twisting some plank. She had led him into a small room with a low ceiling, cut obliquely across the steepness of the roof, illuminated by a small crack in the floor.

"Is your head reeling?" asked Klara.

"No, not at all, only everything stands out in my memory. After all, you were lying sick in this attic; I visited you secretly."

"If you had known how I loved you, and I never spoke of it. Doctor Chaim! What a young girl I was then! Please stay here quietly, and I will visit you."

And through tears, her face brightened with a girlish smile. I pressed her, moved. We stood a moment, embracing.

"And you, little Klara, what will you do?"

"I will work, I will support you."

"You're a funny person, little Klara. Where will you earn money?"

"How's that?"

"Well, yes . . . where will you earn money?"

Then Klara had taken him sick with typhus on top of potatoes under a tarpaulin to Huciski. She herself walked in the dark at the horses' heads. Rain was pouring down, and the fever rattled in his ears.

"Why did you bring him here?" Horse-face was indignant.

"And where is your promise?"

"What does 'my promise' mean? It got burned down tonight. He is sick, he will die on your hands like a dog under a bare sky."

Klara fell silent in confusion; she stood beside me motionless. "Come with me," said Horse-face, and they went somewhere to the left of the road leading from Huciski to Tatar. There, behind a hill heavy with rain, a church could be seen, with a red roof, old linden trees beside it . . .

"So it was you, Szerucki, who lifted the tarpaulin?"

"I was sorry for you."

"Splendid girl. She will do everything in her power," said Chaim. "Your face looked terrible to me, coagulated with uneasiness and fear, stern and bitter as a root bleared with olive oil."

"We killed a pig that night, maybe that is why I looked so. Chuny shaved me with scissors," Szerucki replied.

"Even then you were a talker. Without looking at me, continually watching the road, you began telling me you were thirty already, that your name was Kuba, that you were a horse-leader at Czaczkies' place, then a joiner, then you had a lot of trouble with the police. You spoke many words of praise in honor of Chuny Shaya, your friend since childhood. You spoke of him as of a faithful creature: 'You a Jew?' you asked. 'Yes.' 'What street did you live on?' 'Brandon.' 'Ah, I know,' you said. 'Your father made barrels in order to educate you as a doctor. That was a calm man: he walked calmly and slowly, spoke calmly, smoked cigarettes and ate calmly. He drank a lot. Yes, he drank a lot. It is rare for a Jew to drink a lot. He dragged oak logs into his workshop, and there chopped them into pieces; he planed entire days with his hand wrapped in a piece of leather. He was sanguine and red-faced. He never said a word to anyone. But your mother — she was foul-mouthed. 'Girls don't like my Chaim,' your mother said to Mrs. Arnstein, whom she helped in the kitchen when your father was no longer alive. 'Your Chaim isn't a handsome boy, he's pockmarked; girls don't flock after such. But she to whom he becomes attached — '

"My fate had begun making her uneasy," Chaim went on. "She asked herself what would become of me when she was no longer here. She wanted some other heart to take me into its care." 'But that girl who brought you here? What sort of girl is she?' you asked.

"Once — it was that summer — I was walking through the cemetery in Szabasowa, to find out who had survived the first massacre. Horse-face was with me. There, in the undergrowth, we met this girl. She was with several children. It was around two or three in the morning; soaked, mud-spattered, exhausted, we had stopped to draw breath. Horse-face shone his flashlight and saw these children crouching around the girl. When the light hit them, they all crawled uncertainly into the darkness. And Klara, under a tree, amidst the nocturnal silence, listened for what would come next.

"Horse-face must at some time have known a girl by the name of Tonka. He never mentioned her to me, but at such moments she stood in his memory. He sought her everywhere in this darkened world. 'Tonka,' he whispered into the darkness.

"The undergrowth rustled, and a girl drew near us.

" 'Who are you, where are you going?'

" 'What's happening in Szabasowa?'

" 'Don't go there, that's all, don't show yourselves.'

" 'Why?'

" 'There are gendarmes in Cemetery Street, killing people. You'd be foolish to let yourselves be caught.'

"A great noise was coming from Szabasowa; automobiles whined, people were running away down the slippery paths of the cemetery. Sometimes I lost sight of it all in the darkness. People were running to reach some boundary as fast as possible, and to put an end to this awfulness. I could not distinguish earth from sky. Shots went off around the gravedigger's little house. We also ran out of the cemetery. People were stopping behind a wall, as if on the brink of some perishing abyss, gasping. Clinging to the fence, we set off for Stawka, and there the darkness was complete. Then in front of us some two figures in broad cloaks rose up out of the dark. We changed direction, into the cemetery again, and these unknown men ran after us; the beams of their flashlights could be seen moving. They found one scuffling shadow, and a shot rang out. Excited and scared, I ran after Horse-face, this girl beside me. We stopped far away, on plowed land. A bright glow bloomed over Szabasowa. At gray dawn we gazed at each other's faces.

" 'Will you endure coming with us?' asked Horse-face.

" 'I will,' she said.

" 'And what's your name?'

" 'Klara Wasicinska.'

"Klara spoke very little, nobody could really say if she was educated or what she thought of it all. She stood beside us covered in a sack, and she pondered deeply, as if life had suddenly died in her for a moment. And something happened within this girl. Horse-face has eyes which one doesn't forget; everything can be emphasized by words but not by a look. Klara was the only woman I loved after the death of my wife. She knew that life is everything, and that everything in it is important."

"I found a letter on her," said Szerucki.

"And what did she have to say?"

"She bade you good-bye."

"The forest thinned out beyond Trojnogia, black wet linden trees were standing along the field edge. We decided Szerucki should go alone to Sitwa's and make a reconnaissance. If we did not get Flying-carpet out before dawn, he would be lost."

When Szerucki came to Sitwa's hut, dawn was showing behind the forest in a green line. Hot smoke was rapidly flying from the chimney, sparks scattered. Windows were dark. He stopped on the threshold with his weapon ready.

"Who's there?" someone inside the door whispered.

"It is I, Szerucki."

"And what do you want?"

"Is Flying-carpet here?"

"There is nobody here."

"Is that you, Vitalisa?"

"Get away from here!" shrieked a woman inside.

"Shut your mouth. Let me in, or you'll be sorry."

"Go on, you bandit. You think I didn't recognize you. As soon as you set foot on the threshold, I recognized you as a bandit."

You've mortified me deeply, woman. You called me a bandit at a moment like this, but I am the sort of man who would braid your hair for you."

"Braid yourself, and you know where."

"Next time you'll do it yourself."

"Get away from the door."

"What are you afraid of?"

"I'm not afraid of anything, but get away in peace."

Szerucki pretended to go away, knelt down, and listened. In the hallway someone was whispering impatiently.

"Is it you, Szerucki?" called Vitalisa Sitwa in a hoarse alto voice.

"Well, yes, didn't you recognize me?"

"And what did you want?"

"Talking frankly, you're an old hag. Why don't you want to let me in?"

"And if I don't?"

"You don't want to open the door. Well, speak. What sort of bandit am I?"

"It was she who called you that."

"Ah, you old women, damn you," Szerucki went on in mounting anger, "I have the right to demand that you open the door immediately."

"Oh, how stupid all this is. I've always treated you like a human being, and I'm always glad to see you. People don't act this way with me. Go away from the door and don't make a noise, else it will end badly. Today you're acting uppity with me . . ."

"Vitalisa."

"What?"

"Will you answer two questions?"

Somewhere, in the depths of the hallway, was heard a slurping, as though someone were squeezing butter out of water. Szerucki waited a little longer, trying to control his rage.

"Will you answer two questions?"

"Well?"

"Where is Flying-carpet?"

"And what has happened to him?"

"Dudi says he is at your place."

"Not true! I haven't set eyes on him in six months."

"And will you give us something to eat? There are five of us. Will you?"

"I've lit the stove for baking bread; it will be ready at noon."

Szerucki bit his lower lip. It was getting light outside. He turned toward the stable; there by the gate stood a cart with leather straps unharnessed on the shaft, freshly collected mud on the wheels. Somehwere nearby horses were neighing. Szerucki stopped by the gate and did not move. Dark shapes drew near. He saw them separate, saw that they wanted to encircle Sitwa's hut. There was still nobody in the garden; Szerucki ran there, stopped behind a tree, loaded a fresh magazine into his Mauser, and ran further, across a black, slippery field. The figures plunged into the mist; unswinging rifles from under their arms, they cut off his path. Dear God, they have seen me, thought Szerucki. He turned sharply right, flapping his hands, ran full speed along a ditch on the road to Wiliny. Peoples' voices could be heard around the hut, dogs were barking. He decided to creep along the ditch as far as he could, jump into the forest, then see what happened next. For the time being, he was certain his own life was at stake, and that the end was almost certain for Flying-carpet. Plunging into the undergrowth, he heard horses neighing behind him, and a rapid, stifled thumping. Someone was drawing close on his tracks. It was as though pliers were pulling the back of Szerucki's neck. A gendarme on horseback flew up, and Kuba began firing at him. In the frozen dampness of the forest, shots burst out loudly with a triple echo.

"Well, it's bad," said Chaim, "damn his ass, very bad."

The banging of a Bergman could be heard from the forest. Three, maybe four times, a Mauser fired back, and there was quiet.

Kierasinski was seized by ever increasing excitement.

"What do you think of this, sir?" he asked.

" 'Sir, sir, sir,' I am no 'sir.' They must have got him. Go there carefully. If anything has happened, we shall meet at the rectory. You understand, Kierasinski — go up more or less to the place where they were firing. But don't go there recklessly, don't let yourself be caught."

This Kierasinski was a powerful and fit man, for no forced marches, hunger, lice, or cold knocked him out; his shoulders were still broad, and his calves filled his top boots. For a moment Kierasinski could be seen as he walked, crouching, beyond the undergrowth, and ran quickly to a ravine from which projected the tops of high trees drenched with rain. A flock of crows beat into the air above the trees. After a moment he came out of the ravine to a clearing, crouching as though the colic had got him.

A violet sun rose a little way above the earth, and the earth on the slopes began to steam like yellow cream. Chaim and Dudi sat in the undergrowth until dusk. Nobody came back. Near and far, all over the clearing and in the black forest, dogs barked, and shot followed shot.

They set off at late dusk. Chaim was so frozen that his lips were pinched. Dudi, covered in Lula Heim's blanket, staggered like a sick person or someone wrenched out of deep sleep. It was seven miles to Banczycki's rectory. The way led through thawing snow, and across bogs up to the waist.

"Follow me carefully. If anyone attacks us, keep behind me. And if they kill me, then run away, throw off the blanket, run without drawing breath into the forest, into the undergrowth; hide and watch the movements of those who are tracking you down. Don't cry if anything happens, you mustn't be so clumsy," said Chaim, and he lit a cigarette and walked on in silence. Far to the left, in the darkness, a woman shrieked twice and there was a shot. In the sky and earth whiteness was rolling; snow had begun to fall, gathering on the paths, furrows and field edges. And all this, he said, brought to mind some pictures or other from schoolbooks: the red lantern of a guard, skaters with violet noses, riding down a hill on staves, old boxes, and oilcloth bags; warm little huts cuddled under snow, with the light of family happiness, sparks of Christmas, dusk with bells.

They were walking in the direction of the rectory, east of Huciski, struggling with snow and wind. The valley was drenched by a recent thaw; their feet sank in the wheezing turf. Chaim stopped, listened, investigated the nearest piece of earth. A small expanse of earth trembled under foot, and in the distance it was covered with black — it all seemed a deluge, as if he and Dudi were the only people left alive, and that further on there was nothing. Struck by a shudder, he took Dudi by the hand, and said to him,

"Never mind, we'll make it somehow." And there was nothing but the roar of wind, no shriek, no shooting or light, like an eye shut forever by a scar.

Suddenly, as though in a terrible dream, he heard rapid footsteps behind.

He turned — the stranger was already close — he was a gigantic man. He was walking fast, and he passed them in the darkness. Chaim called:

"Kierasinski?"

But this man did not say a word; only the heavy tramp of his feet could be heard. He was running away breathlessly, or he wanted to warn someone. Chaim brought out his pistol and fired, and this man could be heard running on.

Late at night it brightened from the snow. The rectory was standing quiet and dead as a grave. The black opening of the empty stable, a manger dragged out into the yard, a mincing-machine without wheels turned upside down, and a lot of scattered straw underfoot. Chaim tapped three times at a windowpane, then once more.

"Is that you, Chaim?" The priest could be heard coughing and moving something heavy from in front of the door in the hallway. And when he could not cope with the bolt in the darkness, he said as though to himself;

"Right away you'll see what happened in my room. If you have matches, light up. Basically you were always partly right, I ought not to have let him into my place, never in my life. I've been left here entirely alone for the night, and I don't know . . . I'll tell you what is happening to me. I'm glad that at least you are here. It was a fine stratagem, but too much for my ruined health."

They went into the kitchen; there was a smell in the darkness of moonshine vodka and of burning, as though someone had been boiling foot-clouts since evening on an overheated stove. Dudi sat down heavily on the floor.

"Anything to eat here?" asked Chaim.

"Yes. Do you know what happened here?"

"Is anything threatening us?"

"Not for the time being. You must agree that I too will soon be wandering around with the rest of you. I will not keep any secrets from you."

"What good would that do? Give us something to eat, man, we're worn out."

"There's millet and milk in the dutch oven, untouched, just as I left it when Gail came."

"Was Gail here?"

"He was, but he's gone. The end."

"Who cleaned him up?" asked Chaim, cutting the cold porridge with a pocketknife; he gave some to Dudi and began eating it greedily.

"He knew how to defend himself. I didn't think he was so ingenious."

"The more swine a man is, the better he knows how to take care of himself," said Chaim, restraining his satisfaction.

"Chuny got it from him with a knife."

"However, Chuny got his ends."

"Chuny! He'd pursue earth that blows away on the wind! And those children of Hynda Glas, taken as hostages for Gail's safety? What's going to become of those children now?"

"Calm down. It wasn't possible to live any longer with that spy on our backs."

"He'd gladly have disappeared or sunk into the ground. All this, together, is a very gloomy thing, to spend one's life among the tearing shrieks of murdered people, to watch the freezing of naked children in the snow. Even when a bird now appears to me on a tree, I watch it like an enemy. All this is forcing me to maintain stiff anger, suspicions. It isn't possible to live like this. A nasty prospect, for sure."

"Dangerous and brave deeds swarmed around you. Well, didn't they?"

"Good God!" Banczycki groaned. "How sad it is to struggle with all this. Do you have a weapon?"

"Yes. Why do you ask?"

"I sniff some business which may come for it in the next few hours. The business with Gail lasted two days; he was to go back to Szabasowa today from his social visit. Gendarmes will occupy the road. This is also why it is necessary to light a fire in the stove and cook something warm, before anything else occurs."

Chaim took a wisp of straw out of a mattress, chopped down the screen to the stove, and set fire to it. They said nothing, but when the fire was blazing under the tin lid, making the handle ring, Banczycki said in a cheerful voice,

"Horse-face gave me his hand, for I said to him, 'Fine!' Yes, it's not an easy matter to agree to anything like that. Chuny was different; he came back, looked around as if for something he'd forgotten. He said to me, 'We live in this world as though doing penance, damn it.' They came to me again after a half hour, not to tell me, but to wash their hands!

"I did not have any forebodings that evening, when Gail came in covered with snow and said, in his light tenor,

" 'Oh, it's like this, your reverence. We eat warm soup, and Jewish children freeze to the marrow in an empty stable.'

" 'Yes, I know,' I said, without giving him my hand, 'not in my stable. I know what you mean to say by that. This subject keeps you impatient. Please sit down, sir, and tell me what has brought you here.'

"Gail sat down to the right of me, looked me ironically in the eye, took off his cap, and said,

" 'The very same matter again.'

"I was sitting in my place with my face hidden in my hands; oh, God, how hard is the journey in the Calvary of this world.

"Staring persistently at the end of my boots, I listened.

" 'Your reverence promised to act as go-between in the case of these children imprisoned in the Hilfspolizei guard post.'

"After a short pause, he added,

" 'They'd agree, after confiscating the dollars, to let him go to the devil. But meanwhile, as is plain, the case has not gone ahead in any way. It seemed to me that we'd reached an understanding with one another to this extent. But one of us is lacking in good-will.'

"My silence, and the quiet around both of us, made my head reel.

" 'Good-day!' cried Gail, awakening me from despair.

" 'Good-day,' I answered, and rage seized me, for this was nothing but pulling a poor man by the nose. Oh, heaven and earth! You endless human hope! You bandit, I thought to myself, you bandit, catching little insects in passing, it seems to me you are running along a human path; your neck is stiffening.

" 'My heart swells at all this,' I told him, aloud.

" 'As well it may. Your reverence is already so beset by solitude that bandits of the Szerucki and Chuny Shaya type seem your only friends,' he whispered. 'You're a poor man, your reverence.'

"The informer's face grew longer, taking on a look of great depression. After knocking the ash off his cigarette with his middle finger, he gave his voice a sympathetic sound:

" 'Your reverence, you have fallen into this disgusting Jewish existence, filled with bleary-eyed terror. You know but too well what I mean. You must break away from it. It's a hard matter certainly, but it must be done . . .'

"I said a few well-chosen words to him, nothing more:

" 'If you please, sir. I am not alarmed either by what I have behind me or by the prospect you have sketched for me in your policy. I set off into the world, ready for anything. Brawls of your kind, audacity hatched under a criminal's skull make me uneasy, but I won't let myself be provoked. You, sir, are a crippled human individual.'

"I stood up to take a breath. And at this moment a bullet went through the arm of my chair. In this way destiny certainly sketches out a man's road. Gail stood up too, took out his revolver, and began gnawing his lips, as though relishing something tasty. I gazed at him for a moment with strange intensity. In my thoughts I galloped through all my life, full as you know of sky, earth, sun, and a hideous Golgotha. Somewhat soothed, I began yawning fit to break my jaws. In silence, we inquired from each other with our eyes what this shot meant.

"Gail put the flashlight out.

"Here is life in its real shape — greatness and ugliness.

"He began howling like a madman, although two rifle shots in the yard were not aimed at his stiff figure. Man's cruelty! — you can have no idea of the drama that was unfolding in my vicinity.

" 'Who's that?' asked Gail.

" 'It's probably them,' I answered, no longer caring about anything. 'Someone else will replace the prosecutor, calm down, sir. This lamenting is useless.'

"I could see Gail slowly aiming at the window, through which I could see nothing but confused whiteness. Maybe he could see them from his place. A loud bang went off, and in fact some confusion occurred under the window; two figures drew out of the dusk. Shots answered. Chuny ran in by the kitchen door and shouted; Gail threw down his weapon. For a long moment they left him apparently alone. I saw a match light up several times, and went outside, for I felt sick. I lacked something. I breathed in fresh air on the veranda threshold."

A dense warmth came from the burning red stove; light was running over the furniture and ceiling.

"Don't doze, Dudi," he said. "Chaim, you could catch cold sitting on the bare floor. Get up, take off that wet blanket."

Banczycki and Chaim went out on the threshold to listen, but there was nothing in the expanse stifled with snow. It was monotonous and dull, an ordinary, predawn morning fettered with fallen whiteness. Beyond the crooked stable, beyond an overturned gate, there was a great, sad distance, for the moon had risen like a phantom.

They went back into the room. Chaim broke brushwood outlined with ice crystals, and pushed it into the stove. He tried putting water into a cannikin, but something began to sizzle very loudly.

"You, take it off, for it's not possible to hear a word that's said. That must have a bullet hole in it."

Chaim poured the water into a tin jug in which Klara used to take Szerucki's dinner to the forest.

"So it has."

"Yes, now nothing will keep us from dying of hunger, or something."

"You act very passively," said Chaim.

"What do you mean by that?"

"You are acting like a man who lies down on his back and will neither get up nor die. You should be ashamed. I don't recognize you, man. Have you broken down, or what? Get to work! You know how a bird, gliding a long time between two peaks, arouses pity, nothing more."

"No, Chaim, my health is altogether washed out."

"That's another matter. You must rest, feed up, and sleep well."

"Where and when am I supposed to do that? Never mind. You mentioned a bird. This is the way it is. I have for several days been feeling like that bird which floats above earth and distant horizons, sort of picturesque, but lined with a crime of our kind. We don't have any place even to surrender to our dreams. You do me an injustice, Chaim, saying 'You have broken down.' "

"You always had the habit of being melancholy, of recoiling, of pulling your cap down over your eyes and coughing. Even at the time when it was necessary to defend those arrested people who dug out and ate pigs dead of the German measles."

"I defended them, but when the mayor accused me of defending Communists, what could I do? I said, 'Mr. Mayor, I am defending poor people, Communists are no business of mine.' And he said to me that I was associating with you. It's a far-off matter, I never told you. But once it started it had to be ended. Then I fell sick and you cured me. You know very well how many suspicions there were in connection with this. I did not lie my whole life with my belly upwards, waiting for some Ascension. But a moment of dreams, some little stopgap of his own, is necessary to a man, no matter where he is — this man, stretched for centuries on all the earth."

"But in the meantime, it's so far from well to well that a man can drop dead from thirst. It isn't possible to remain silent, with a docile expression, for too long. Dreams, thoughts, and what you rightly call Ascension don't solve the problems of a fallen-in belly."

"That's true! You know that very well, looking after poor people. You have a gauge of your own usefulness. You must admit that you didn't stand like a wooden figurine in that wind which has been blowing so many years, God knows where to. You didn't look out the window and say what's happening there, outdoors? This is what I am getting at. For when you came to our poor village, covered in straw, when dogs flew at you, getting you terribly messy — then I thought to myself that you ought to occupy the best place under the sun. It was a question then of typhus, as today it is informers — someone must put an end to it. Maybe this is a reflection of my village childhood, some sort of heritage from which I have never freed myself. My mother, coming out of October vespers, met a dog on a path; she took fright and hit it with her rosary, and she went home quickly, quickly, for she was pregnant. But the dog, whining, ran after her to the house, and there she saw that she had hit its eye out with her rosary. This isn't a fairy tale, the contents of which can be altered according to one's imagination. From that time on, my mother's life passed in grief, in pity for everything, in fear, in pain and continuous returning to that tragic moment. The blind dog lived in our house five years more, and died one day, in a hot August. I buried it, bursting into tears. Then my father, a country church organist, died. 'Yes, little son,' said my mother, leading me through the forest by hand, 'we've had to leave our hut.'

" 'Why?' I asked.

" 'Because a new organist has come,' said my mother, and her face grew long with depression. This is the life you have known only too well, to tell you a part of mine. I wondered whether a wandering dog goes with the Jewish children?"

"Which dog?"

"Oh, this Bas, which was here even at carol time."

"That one! No, no. It seems it wasn't."

"Is it dead?"

"It went wild. It bit anyone who approached the children."

"Damnation! Was it necessary to kill it?"

"I only know that the children were killed first."

"Damnation. So what am I to tell you of my childhood. These are minor weaknesses. What are you looking for, Chaim?"

"Maybe there's some onion. I wanted to add some flavor to these potatoes."

"Did you peel the potatoes?"

"Never mind that. An onion would add flavor."

"I don't know, I don't know if there is any, or where. Maybe there aren't any."

After lighting the stove, Chaim wandered about the room looking for onion and salt; he broke open the empty tin cookie boxes in which Klara had stored various roots in autumn. At the bottom of a drawer, under torn socks, he found scattered beans and some ears of garlic. Steam came from Chaim's coattails, hanging over the stove. Dudi, crouching and with hands pressed into his stomach, was sleeping across the mattress, interrupting his sleep with brief cries and shudders, or he would belch, for lice were disturbing him.

"What were you getting at in your tale?" asked Chaim.

"Well, the connection with my childhood. You say I had a tendency to make allowances, flinching and coughing whenever anything came to anything. I, like every man, am filled with bad scars. After the death of my father, my mother and I went out into the world to seek bread and some resting place. We wandered several days somewhere between Belziec and Lublin, but everywhere we were sent away empty-handed, or with the murmur of words, 'You poor people, how can we help you?' In the end, completely worn out, we reached some little town, and there on the outskirts my mother became a washerwoman at the home of a rich butcher, a German colonist. We were greeted by a woman with a wrinkled face, who had a heavy knife hanging from her belt on a blood-stained tape.

" 'Antoni! Antoni!' she called.

"The man who appeared in the door at this cry was a thin old man. The woman first quieted the dogs, which were straining toward us, pulling at their chains.

" *'Was najes?'* the voice of the old man flew across the yapping of the dogs.

" 'A poor woman come, who wants to serve. She is asking for work.'

" *'Ach, ja!'* the old man cried. My mother went up to this man and kissed his hand. He gazed at me a long time with his gray eyes, and then he asked, 'He yours?'

" 'Yes.'

" 'Where did you get him? You're a young woman.'

"My mother told him our story."

" 'Well, yes, you're a poor woman. You will stay here and do our laundry.'

"So my mother ruined her health washing the linen of this very deep-rooted family: she washed the aprons and skirts of the numerous staff of the great pork-butchering industry. She sent me to school, and ordered me not to be anything in life except a priest. For she set herself this penance for striking out the dog's eye.

"Before I come to the further history of my childhood, I should mention that they were the Gails."

"Who?"

"The Gails. And their grandson here, you know very well what he was."

"Hence your weakness for him."

"No weakness. I hated him the same as you, maybe more. I don't like the way you state the matter, but what's to be done about it?"

"Well, what, a test, or what should we call it?"

"Nothing of the sort. They began hitting him, so I said, 'Let him alone, boys. It can't be done this way. He's your prisoner. Take him as a hostage or something. Or send an ultimatum to the Hilfspolizei sentry post, to let the children of Hynda go, then let him go. I hope with all my heart that this succeeds. If Chaim were here, he'd admit that I'm right. There is nothing that can't be settled in time. Destiny plays a great part in such matters.' "

" 'Chaim, just like the priest, would send an ultimatum,' said Chuny. But meanwhile Gail was drawing on that green rainproof coat of his, his topcoat and boots. Horse-face was searching his pockets, and in this position — Chuny on the kitchen threshold, and Horse-face in the depths of the room by Gail's side, with drawn revolvers to the windows — they were listening, for someone had run up to the building. I went out on the doorstep again, hesitated a moment, and finally shouted very loudly, 'Who's that?' The stranger walked boldly right up to me as if he had rehearsed the part. It proved to be Kierasinski, and he had an ax hanging from his belt.

" 'Come, come, attention,' says he, 'your man is coming.'

"Pondering over some intention or other for a moment, Kierasinski moved softly over to me, and asked,

" 'Who's there?'

" 'Chuny and Horse-face, they have some unfinished business in there.'

" 'And why are you here on the threshold, your reverence?'

" 'Because someone was walking about, was it you?'

" 'Yes, it was. Isn't Chaim here?'

" 'Not yet,' I said, and I then heard from the room: Bang, bang, bang, as though someone were throwing someone at a cupboard.

'Damn you, damn you . . .' Chuny shouted three times. 'They are hitting him, why are they hitting him?' I said.

" 'Does it bother your reverence?'

" 'Whether it bothers me or not is not the point. I had another idea for him. It is not possible to think so little. This is a lamentable time, damn it. Chaim isn't here; he would have settled it wisely. You alone, Kierasinski? And where are the rest —Szerucki, Chaim?'

" 'We dispersed, one here, one there, and Szerucki went to reconnoiter and got lost, for there was a battle. Czaczkies attacked gendarmes.'

" 'There was a battle? You must tell them, for maybe they don't know. It will bother them that Szerucki isn't here.'

"And then I heard Chuny groan with pain, and a shot went off. Kierasinski jumped inside. Someone had already shot someone else in the head, I thought to myself, and I went into the yard. I took fright and didn't know what to do. Who had so soiled the world? There you are, a scene from a great tragedy took place here a few hours back."

"You obviously want to groan over everything today," said Chaim. "Maybe that's all right, but don't make too much of it. We have more than once come to an understanding on this topic. You bellow to the point of being disgusting, and you will stop if gendarmes start chasing you."

"Not only people," Banczycki went on, "but cattle too mourn death, for death is the end of everything. Everything fears death, for it is evil, the greatest evil. Surely you understand me. The murdered also murder. But maybe it would be possible to save these children of Hynda, in exchange for this scoundrel? When they took him out, I begged: 'Boys . . .' But Gail was assuredly already dead, for they were holding him up under the arms. He dragged with his heels in the snow."

" 'Please, your reverence, don't make a big deal out of this, for it's no use,' said Horse-face. And when he came back a half hour later, I was in bed. Horse-face started again: 'Death! Accursed word. How is it: death. And did not childish lips whisper of life? O thou, life! And a tear of Cirla's? What is that worth?'

"They sat down, lit cigarettes, and gave Kierasinski one.

" 'Smoke?'

" 'Yes.'

" 'And what instruments do you have for smoking, you face?' Horse-face laughed, and the little flame of a cigarette quivered in the darkness. Kierasinski said nothing.

" 'Where's Szerucki?' they asked him.

" 'How should I know where he's got to?'

" 'What does 'where' mean?'

" 'He went to reconnoiter the premises of Sitwa, or whatever her name is.'

" 'Who sent him?'

" 'The doctor.'

" 'When?'

" 'This morning, at dawn.'

" 'Yeees,' Chuny groaned, and shone his flashlight. Kierasinski, by the stove, was jigging his knees.

" 'Did you go out into the clearing?' asked Horse-face.

" 'Why?'

" 'Because you have an ax under your arm. Where's it from?'

" 'I found it by a murdered farmhand.'

"Chuny could be heard clinking ammunition in his pocket; there was a long and sad moment of silence.

" 'What are you saying, you son of a bitch? After all, you were left with Szerucki by the shot Lula.'

"Kierasinski hesitated a moment.

" 'Come, speak up, I would like to know.'

" 'She died. The doctor came and told us to go after Flying-carpet, because someone had shot him. So says Dudi, but is it true? Szerucki set the hut on fire and we went away.'

" 'Why did he set fire to it?'

" 'He did well.'

" 'And Lula?'

" 'She burned, and that was the end.'

" 'What are you babbling about?'

But Kierasinski did not give in; he referred to the matter and spoke rapidly, but not clearly, so that it was difficult to catch what it was all about:

" 'I tell you, it's no use chopping water with an ax. Give me a rifle, and I will show you how to kill a Kraut. At first it will be a little — for slaying a man is difficult, and afterwards you spit on your hands. We're not used to fighting alone for ourselves. But when a man persists, everything goes smoothly.'

"He talked and talked a long time, but after a time the men saw that either this Kierasinski was drunk or not of sound mind.

" 'Assuredly, assuredly,' Horse-face threw in, 'you won't get a rifle from us. You'll get a punch on the jaw. Don't lay it on so thick.'

"They ate a little bread, drank water, and I heard Kierasinski also eat something.

" 'Well, let's go and look for Szerucki, and you come with us,' said Chuny.

" 'Ah, sonny, sonny — we'll see what you can do.' Horse-face patted Kierasinski on the shoulder, and they got ready to leave.

" 'Good night,' Horse-face approached me, pushed me with a hot, rough hand, and said, 'Well, now?'

"I rose up curiously, leaning on one elbow.

" 'What do you say, Horse-face?'

" 'Forgive me, your reverence, for we killed this man.'

"I could not see his face, but a great pain crept into my heart.

" 'Well, what of it?' I said, 'it's a good thing that it isn't our fault. The point is that you don't become a man always enraged against everything. It is necessary to acquire some feeling of life.'

"I said a few other things, incompletely, for I did not know him: what sort of man he was, or what he was concerned about in all this. 'Remember, man,' I added, 'that the heart is dearest when it sings a song of bread.'

Chaim put in:

"That upbringing taught him a certain range of sentimental and false feelings."

"Think so? He might have cheated himself for a very long time, but that isn't always healthy. Then comes a merciless reaction. It is possible to falsify feelings, but nobody is satisfied with that. Bothersome detachment, and that's the end."

"It all depends on a man's relation to other men, and for the time being this matter is completely dead. I consider that if we'd investigated to the bottom, as people feeling each other out, then it would have come out very badly. For the time being, assuredly every man feels some sort of threat in another man."

"Very saddening. You think it all the results of a false concept of civilization, eh?"

"We're afraid of each other. There's something in this. Maybe it's a question of individualism."

"Do you consider Horse-face an individual?"

"He betrayed himself by that reaction. He has isolated himself. He stressed that he is from another bloodstream."

"For goodness' sake, Chaim. You'd lead us into a civil war. Yet look — they went into the dark night, they went to look for this Szerucki. I wonder what you'd call that?"

"They went because they were working men; they still had a feeling of class community."

"Maybe . . . maybe you're right. They were not uneasy because you weren't here. They went off as though you you didn't exist. An hour passed. The night was long and sleepless. I got up, looked out the window. Snow was still falling. I wondered to myself if there were still any area on the earth where people smiled. The clock struck twelve. I ran into the room to look out, for someone had fired a shot in the fields. The thought occurred to me that they might have killed Kierasinski. That was impossible. I opened the window. I heard distant shouts of people and groans, and at that moment someone ran into the yard and knocked at the kitchen window.

" 'What is it?'

" 'Please, sir,' he asked, 'what is this village called?'

" 'This village? There is no village here any longer. There used to be until autumn, but now there isn't one,' I said, and I drew back inside, for this stranger seemed terrible to me.

" 'All right, sir, but what was it called?' The stranger stood against the background of the window, a huge peasant, hair disheveled, or maybe he was wearing a sheepskin cap.

" 'Zalaski, Zalaski,' I said.

" 'Oh, Jesus!' this man groaned out in great agitation.

" 'What is happening out there, all that shouting and firing?' I asked, plucking up courage.

" 'Please, sir, they are driving hostages along the highway from our village to Szabasowa, and I ran away, sir. People are shouting because maybe someone will hear them and rescue them on the way.'

" 'Well, and didn't they see you running away?'

" 'It got dark, and everyone came out after us, and walked along far off in the fields, lamenting. And each one of them, sons of bitches, was afraid to run away into the fields when it got dark.'

" 'From where are they bringing these people for hostages?'

" 'Near Talesnia. They killed a gendarme.'

" 'Come in and rest. It's quiet here.'

" 'Ah, sir,' said this stranger, 'how do you know what quietness means? It's very bad that it's so quiet. It means a village burned down, people killed. And they didn't set fire to your place?'

" 'Well, somehow not . . .' I said.

" 'Is there any gang around which I could join?'

" 'I don't know, man. There are several, each chases individually around the areas they know; they flash up here and there like stars, then go out suddenly, strung up on poles or knocked out in a fight with gendarmes or Hilfspolizei.'

"And he went away. After barricading the door, I lay down again on the mattress, shattered and ready for anything. Then you tapped, I dragged myself on fainting legs, and so flows this night.

"What do you think of this Kierasinski, Chaim? Do you know him well?"

Chaim was standing at the open door of the oven, drying his knees.

"He says he escaped from a trasport to Belziec, they were taking him with Dutch Jews. He comes from Tomaszow. He spent his youth working in the quarries as a so-called career."

"What's a career?"

"I don't know."

"Well, then?"

"He says that after two years he went down in his career, to play tipcat. I don't know what that means either. In any case, just not any sort of work. He says he got up as soon as it was dawn, and went out, and came back in the evening, and then he still had to thresh the grain of his neighbor by lamplight. His mother fell ill, and he had to earn money to pay the doctor! He sent his younger brother to high school. And it went on like this, he says, until he was twenty-eight years old. Then he worked at smuggling."

"Where?"

"He didn't say exactly. He says he went with a dog to get saccharine and lighter flints. He stayed in jail a year, under investigation. Mobilized, he fought as a lancer in East Prussia. Apparently he's of mixed origins, for his mother's a Jewess. In any case, we don't trust him."

"Such want of trust must be unpleasant. Did he earn it by his appearance?"

"Intolerably woolly-minded fellow, he judges everything crassly. He likes taking gold from a dead corpse."

"Simply, you're having trouble with him. Some sort of beastly environment formed him."

"Watch, Chaim, that the potatoes don't overcook. Get one out and mash it in a piece of cloth or against the wall, with your sleeve."

"But I tell you that this fondness for gold works in various ways. Gold is a second soul to some men. Not everyone knows how to stop himself from that. I recall that the Baroness Schnell was in love with gold. She always wore many jewels of heavy gold. For instance, big brooches, rings set with stones, earrings in the shape of plants, gold spectacles. Her husband liked looking at her when she was hung with all this to the point of exaggeration. Yet it must be admitted that she was simple, sincere, and direct for all that. She knew how to connect other things with charm."

"What other things?"

"Spying on behalf of the German government. From each trip abroad she brought back a new pile of gold. Very often in the afternoon she would stand at a window and look at the shopgirls or children riding down the street on wooden skates. She turned to the footman: 'Are genuine skates expensive?' 'They continue to be expensive, your ladyship,' says the footman. Her husband was killed out hunting. She searched his pockets one more time on the catafalque, for it seemed to her that the footman had pushed to his master a golden cigar case for the eternal journey. Then, with a concentrated and tragic expression, she snuffed out the candles."

"Yes, if you please, man's destiny flows simply from himself, even in his cradle. It seems to us that this nature vanishes with the course of years. It merely dries up under a layer of trivial culture, and under the influence of hot blood it immediately melts."

Chaim strained the potatoes, picked one up, and bending to the light, began to scrub it with great dexterity.

"Shall we wake Dudi?"

"Let sleep," said Chaim, "fortify him."

"But he might eat two or three hot potatoes, for who knows what will happen in a little while? You can't be certain he'll get anything to eat all day? White snow for wiping away tears — that's too little."

It was darkish on the mattress, the shape of the sleeper could only barely be discerned. Dudi ground his teeth in his sleep, his jawbones labored over something unbitable.

"Get up, Dudi. Get up, eat something hot, and you can go to sleep again, for it is quiet," said Chaim.

Dudi sat up. He tried to say something, but fell backwards, groaning.

"Hm," says Chaim, feeling Dudi's pulse, "this isn't good. Something terrible must have been scaring him in his fever, for him to grind his teeth so."

They moved the bed with the sick boy to the wall. Chaim threw twigs into the stove, and Banczycki recalled that the blanket Wasicinska had had was still in the cupboard under the stairs, and he went through the empty room. The door squeaked there.

Rolling a cigarette, Chaim heard Banczycki call him.

"Look, how furiously some place is burning. What a terrible fire."

"Yeees," says Chaim, "it's Sapiska."

The fields twinkled with redness, and flames reached into the high boundlessness. A machine gun was firing, and an uproar was coming from the expanse suffocated with snow, like a horse's gallop over a frozen lake. And this lasted until the gray dawn hour.

Chaim felt Dudi's pulse once and covered him with Wasicinska's blanket. He went back to watch the conflagration.

"This child has pneumonia," said Chaim.

"Very likely," stated Banczycki, and he suddenly drew back in alarm, for cattle were flying across the field to the rectory, and further away two men were dragging a helpless body.

"Oh, dear God!" Banczycki howled, and having covered his head with a sheepskin jacket, slightly hobbling, he ran out of the rectory. He crossed the orchard, and beyond the turn in the road, he jumped over a ditch into the church cemetery. There, in summer, were a lot of flowers, herbs, a whole forest of blossoming boughs, sitting hens roosted, children played at hide and seek. Immediately behind the fence stood indulgence sheds, a procession walked with the monstrance. And further were little ponds — there old women soaked hemp, whitened linen on the slope by the church, washed linen at the springs, and a child and a calf walked. And around the thickets and the stiles girlish laughter was to be heard. More than one man, here on this hillock, bent the slender waist of his girl. Banczycki passed the scattered firesite of Zalaski, crossed himself by the collective tomb of his parishioners, and disappeared into the fields leading to Szabasowa.

The conflagration blurred itself on the wet thaw of morning. Only in the room pierced by frost in the corners darkness still sat, drawing at the eyes.

Half-raising himself, Dudi was speaking to someone in his delirium, shaking his head and pouting his lips as though at a breast. Chaim, holding an aluminum pan with hot water, said,

"Do you hear . . . ? Drink this."

"Hm . . . hm . . ."

"Drink it, you must drink it."

"Who's that?"

"Whom do you see?" Chaim glanced at me. "Ah! That's the man who found you in the forest."

Dudi drank the hot water and asked,

"Is Mis Kunda coming?"

"Yes, he's coming."

"For sure?"

"For sure," said Chaim. "Mis Kunda likes you, he will certainly come."

I pulled the worn galoshes, webbing foot-clouts off the boy, and threw them into the stove. I covered him with three jute sacks over the quilt, obtained from the hallway under a pile of chaff. Dudi again pushed his head to the wall, whispering and champing his lips fiercely, indifferent to everything.

Quiet everywhere, nobody anywhere. I went out to the gate to see what there was beyond the cemetery, on the road to Sapiski — nothing, deserted. Some crows on a signpost. And here a minute titmouse, clutching to the window frame for a moment, peeped into Banczycki's room and flew away beyond the chimneys. I tore down several planks from the pigsty wall, chopped them with an ax on the floor, and carried them into the room. I pushed a lot of these dry alder logs into the stove. The fire crackled cheerfully. I put a bucket of water on the tin top. Then I crawled into the attic — there Klara had dried fruit on the chimney in fall, but there was nothing — mice had devoured everything. There were a few uneaten bilberries on a piece of newspaper, two empty slices of sunflower by the chimneypiece, a large gray pillowcase with down, window frames, strings hanging up with old slippers of gray spider web, and a pile of snow blown in through the broken smoke-holes. Going down into the hallway I saw a dog. It was sitting crouched on the threshold.

"Whose dog is that?" I asked.

"That one? I don't know. Banczycki's dog is dead. There should be another omnadina." Chaim poured everything out of his haversack on to his spread-out coattail. "Omnadina . . . omnadina. Damn, there isn't any. I must have crushed it."

"Didn't you give the omnadina to Chuny?"

"No, I had it after him. Well, there isn't any. He should be given a little Eleudron, because this will be flaky pneumonia."

"Is there any?"

"What?"

"What did you call it . . . ?"

"Oh, that. No, there isn't any of that either. Would you go to that girl of Leit's in Szabasowa?"

"Well, why not?" say I, "but for the night?"

"Well, yes, yes. Take my pistol and go and buy the medicine; I will write down what you have to buy. Drop by at Flying-carpet's girl's place; I'll give you a letter to her. If she asks about him — if, for instance, she asks why he didn't write — then you tell her he went out unexpectedly and suddenly for medicine, and let her give you a few dollars to pay that Volksdeutscher woman. Don't tell her anything beyond this. Everything else is irrelevant. Besides, we'll discuss it. In any case, what can have happened to Flying-carpet? Didn't Gail mention anything during his talk with Banczycki?"

"Nothing."

"For sure."

"There was talk of you, Chuny, Horse-face, the children of Hynda Glas."

"What did it start from?"

"From Hoch. Banczycki, I must admit, started right away like this:

" 'Sit down, sir. Did you let the children go?'

" 'What do you mean 'let them go'? That is a matter for the Ukrainian auxiliaries. I mediate. As your reverence mediates with these Jews. They will agree to let the children go, but it is necessary to give them Hoch alive. He walks around the forest with these dollars, and no one has any use from them. There's a lot of it, and more than one thing can be settled with the Germans for that money. And the old man has already lived long enough. He'll kick the bucket one day in the forest, and nobody will have any use from it. It's necessary to hurry, someone worse will come from district headquarters, and he'll shoot the children. And will your reverence be satisfied afterwards, will everything afterwards be as it is? Surely not. They reckon that your reverence will mediate. They might shoot him themselves, it is perfectly simple. But there is such a proposal, let your reverence repeat it to them in the armed band. Unless your reverence thinks up something else.'

" 'What can I think up! Please, think what?' says Banczycki.

" 'Maybe your reverence will reach an understanding directly with Hoch. Fix a place and time.'

" 'No, that is shameful! How much are they paying you, Mr. Gail, for this shame?' The priest laughed, swinging one foot as though he had kicked something. Gail flashed his electric torch. He placed it on the table, and all the light fell on Banczycki.

" 'Is it shameful?'

" 'Why do you wonder; after all it is easy to understand. I didn't say it for fun. I wanted to know,' said Banczycki, 'what it is you want to settle with me?'

" 'If they come here tonight, then please tell them to arrange the place, time, and person with whom they want to talk over this matter. No one will know what lies at the heart of this.'

" 'Exactly . . . nothing will come of this. You all slaughtered poor Lula Heim. What did you kill her for? I see no reason.'

" 'What does "I see no reason" mean?' Gail stood up from his chair and fluttered his hands over the priest.

" 'Well, I don't. The girl had lived through so much, she escaped from a camp, she survived all summer in the forest. You shamed her, she got pregnant, but she should have been left alive.'

" 'Your reverence doesn't have the right to involve me in this.'

" 'How not to involve you in it, when it was so?'

" 'They declared she was a spy. Reports were written daily and sent to Flying-carpet. Better not involve yourself in this case — I say that in confidence.'

" 'Ah, what a stupid, false, and fouled-up matter! A poor girl from Holland, who didn't know the language or the people. A spy. You know what, sir? Her one sin is that she trusted all of you. And everything you're accusing her of is after she's dead, and unjust. It seems to me you've gone a step lower, persuading yourself that this person killed by you was a spy.' The priest raised his white hands, as if he wanted to push Gail away."

"Did Gail have any defense?" asks Chaim.

"Yes. Someone was prowling around the house. There may have been several of them. One was whistling at the gate."

"Well?"

" 'Your reverence is telling me fairy tales,' said Gail, after lighting a cigarette and again pushing his right hand into his pocket. 'There's no need for us to quarrel about these things. One day you'll find out that fairy tales aren't worth a damn. Why can't your reverence and I come to an understanding?'

" 'What do you really want with me?' Banczycki exclaimed. 'Nothing will come of what you are thinking. The end.'

" 'That's precisely the point, that there is an end. Otherwise it will be the end of the rectory. But we're human beings, the land-kommissar may turn a blind eye, and somehow it can be gotten away with.'

" 'No,' said Banczycki, 'no, nothing will come of this.'

" 'Someone came from the Gestapo to investigate the past of your reverence. We got away with it somehow, so it was still possible to erase it from the records.'

" 'I am not afraid of death.'

" 'That's another matter, but to be investigated insistently, so everything comes up into your throat. It sometimes happens that people shoot themselves in the head.'

" 'That doesn't suit me. I will not lose my train of thought in all this. In any case, there's nothing to discuss.'

"The man who was whistling at the gate came up to the window and tapped lightly.

" 'All right, all right,' said Gail loudly. 'I must go. So I'll come tomorrow. Your reverence will tell me something on this subject.'

" 'I tell you frankly what I'll do: I'll make a voluntary confession to Chaim on the matter. I am prepared to tell him everything. And apart from this, I never want to see you here again.'

" 'Never? But I thought we would wait, time and sense will have their effect, times will change. Your reverence will come to the Special Service, and somehow it will work out. Now I would like to go calmly back home. If Chuny Shaya's men kill me on the way, your reverence will be responsible. You must also fix it with Chaim so I can get about here and there without interference.'

" 'Please leave,' said Banczycki, and he got up. 'You are a terrible human individual. It will be bad in the world if you don't stand trial for murder.'

"And someone fired a shot outside the window. He would have killed Banczycki."

"Did you find out who fired first? Didn't you notice that those men running away wanted to finish him off?" Chaim leaned a foot on the bench and stropped a razor on the boot upper. "Was the first shot from a rifle?"

"Yes."

"It's possible to make a mistake, I tell you. I didn't investigate this matter, but it doesn't seem likely to me. It's possible to make a mistake when a man aims at some shape in the darkness. There's nothing I don't know about Horse-face, I know almost everything. Except one thing . . ."

"What's that?"

". . . whom, apart from Germans, he considers his enemy. I had no opportunity to talk with him on this subject. I thought it was you who fired first. You were inside, near."

"I was in the door to the veranda."

"Ah, yes. It was impossible. Did the priest say anything more after these shots?"

"He talked, he talked a lot. When Chuny ran in, Banczycki immediately went out. Staggering in the hallway, he hastily sought an exit to the back of the rectory. It occurred to me that Mis Kunda also staggered like that, when they shot him in the brushwood near Pasieki. Only then it was light, day. But he also nodded his head somehow, as boys are in the habit of doing. Mis raised his hands, began running, bending as though playing tag, and he sought something with his eyes. 'Drop down!' I shouted, for I was sitting close by. They kept firing. This boy went through great torture."

"Yes . . . You think Banczycki also got it?"

"He surely did. Look" — I took Chaim close to the veranda door. A lot of blood. And look there — spattered blood everywhere. It can't be Gail's blood. Him they took out through the kitchen door. After our men went out, Banczycki groaned, fumbled in the darkness looking for something, and lay down. I went out. In the hallway I heard him shout,

" 'Chaim?' I stopped under a tree. A shot was fired ten minutes later in the cemetery. I lit a cigarette and waited an hour. Someone was firing on the highway to Szabasowa, people were shouting. Then some man appeared near the rectory, and talked with Banczycki. Afterwards, I saw you and Dudi creep into the yard. It would have been nothing to lick you both."

"Thanks. I did not have misgivings. I was happy to be there on the spot."

"What are we going to eat?" I asked Chaim.

"There's only these frozen potatoes. Banczycki used to keep rabbits once, in the stable, look there. We can bake them over the fire somehow, over this brazier."

"Very nice, it's a good thing you remembered," and I went to look for them, but there was no trace of rabbit any place. The new snow around the byres was smooth, and there were no traces of foxes or birds. Such a dead household is sad. Already the stable no longer smelled of cows, the manure had frozen under the piled-up snow.

Chaim let his pants down. Crouching, he picked the lice off his shorts.

"Well?"

"There isn't even a rat," I said, "yet we are not going to live like wolves. We must change location for we shall die here."

"Die, well . . . for the time being we must stay here, until Dudi gets better. Or because there's no help for it. It's even a pleasant thing to hunt lice, I tell you."

"Yes, except that it's possible to fall sick from them suddenly. Chaim, take your shorts off and bake the nits over the fire. It's precisely a question of nits."

"I would not like to undress entirely. Then I'd have to take off my boots."

"Do as you choose, but you would be doing the right thing if you burned this filth. I'll keep watch; you can do it at your ease."

"Yes, I wanted to ask you precisely that. Go out and see what is happening; in case of anything, whistle. But take a look at what time it is, too."

I crept into Banczycki's room — five thirty, I say.

"It's stopped, surely?"

Suddenly, ten yards in front of the house, I saw Chuny Shaya and some women coming. They were walking with vigorous strides, carrying bags. They were already on the threshold.

"Good-day," says Chuny, and he throws his sack into the room.

"May God give you health, what news have you?"

"I've brought you something to eat. Sit down," he says to the women. "Here are little pieces of bacon, there are also various baked things, but too little, for it's from this night's fire in Sapiski." Chuny sits down and at once takes off his boots, soaked rags. But the women stand by the threshold scared, watching us. They were dirty, poorly dressed, in patched coats. Three were elderly, with large bellies, and the fourth still young, a girl certainly, for she cast uneasy glances at everything.

"Sit down, you!" shouted Chuny. "They're the only survivors from all Sapiski. A man could die there!"

"Yes, it was bad luck. Sit down," Chaim invites them. "Nothing threatens you here."

"Until darkness falls," adds Chuny. "Well, take it out of the bag, you're surely hungry. Various little bits of bacon and bread, even little cakes. You go into some not entirely burned hut, you look — here someone is killed, there someone burning, and there . . . Oh, I found this bread under an overturned tin washtub."

"Well, sit down, you women," Chaim again invites. "We aren't from the police."

"Don't you believe him," Chuny smiles, and he winks at the youngest woman. The women sat down on the bench and began quietly crying with their puffy eyes.

We ate the smoked bacon and the bread, and drank hot water.

The women sat as though in a picture, clasping their red, worn hands in their laps, and they wept fervidly.

"What is left you from all your medicine? Two fingers to take a pulse?" says Chuny, and he puts a hand on Dudi's forehead, whose face is already entirely red. His thick, drawn-back hair lies on the back of his neck.

Chaim is silent, having cut off the margin from an old *Sunday Bell* with scissors. He is writing a letter to Flying-carpet's girl concerning medicine and also something from himself. A prescription goes on a separate bit of paper.

"These three women will go with you. For what will they do here, they became widows tonight? Do you women want to go out into the world? Really? They will go to Szabasowa with you," says Chuny. "Dominka will stay with us. She's still a girl, this Dominka . . ."

"Is she?"

"What did you think? A friend of Horse-face's, she used to do little spying jobs for him in Sapiski."

Chaim, cleaning his lips with his tongue and champing with relish, says as if he had it by heart:

"Two or three ampules of omnadina, then there should also be salipiryna. I've written it all down but remember, you. A few bandages, iodine or Rivanol, a few needles for injections, a thermometer — understand?" I nod. Chaim sighed. "Well, damn it, I should have antitetanus."

"Will you manage to be back by dawn?"

"We'll see, how can I know? I would like to. But who knows if that . . ."

"Ksavera."

"Whether she will fix everything today."

Chaim, scratching behind his ear, says mildly,

"Oh, yes. She's a very efficient girl. Too bad, it seems, that she will not see Flying-carpet again in her lifetime."

"Well!" Chuny threatens with a finger. "Just don't you mention it to her!"

"I was only joking to myself, as we say among ourselves."

"Do you know for sure that this man we talked of on the way didn't go into hiding in Sapiski? Speak up, Dominka."

"I'd have known."

"Horse-face will find him out, even if he's dead. What's worse is that Szerucki has disappeared like a stone in water."

A dog crept out of a thicket, and gathering crusts from under our feet, wagged its tail all over the women's skirts.

"You recognize them, Bas!" Chuny shouted. "But wait," he added more calmly, "this means something happened to Kalma."

But Chaim didn't pay any attention, or didn't want to start on this topic; he said to me, "You will take my rifle, try and come back quickly. Perhaps it's better that you leave earlier with these women, for it starts getting dark at four."

Chuny pats Bas on the shoulder, looks at him from all sides, and strokes him.

"If you hadn't found us here," Chaim frowned, "Chuny, listen to what I'm saying, you're crazy, this dog will get the staggers now," he ran his hand through his hair and snapped his fingers, "It is necessary to arrange . . ."

"All right, all right, I'm listening," says Chuny, cutting a slice of dirty bacon for the dog. And we decided that if I didn't find them here, then I would be at the burned site of Zalaski or in the potato cellar under the burned-out barn of the late Mrs. Arbuz.

"All right," I say, slowly and stiffly, "all right."

"Or you will see us as corpses."

I say nothing. Chaim hands me his revolver. The women also get ready, hoisting their sacks. Suddenly my hair stood on end, something touched me painfully. Short Chaim stands on tiptoe and kisses my cheek.

"What sort of joke is that, Chaim?" I say, moved. "Why are we saying good-bye as though it were the end of the world?"

Chaim punched me in the shoulder, and we moved off. Chaim accompanied me beyond the gate, recalling there was a man in Szabasowa who wanted to sell a weapon.

"Ksawera knows about this, you'll find out from her. It's supposed to be a five-shot hunting Winchester. Take a look, you're an expert. It's possible to buy it."

"Buy it, quite right. Do you think Ksawera is equal to it? And if anything happened in the house? So that there isn't this money?" The women had already walked about twenty yards. Chaim took a deep breath and pondered, half-closing his eyes. "This old man who goes around with dollars in his coat," I say, "it would be worth getting at them. He could give us a share. Sure, it's a dirty trick, but not altogether. Think about it."

"I'll talk to Chuny about it," Chaim gave me his hand.

"Yes, do that. It won't be a sin on our part."

After a moment I looked back. Chaim was standing and gazing after us. The old women were walking briskly in front of me. We were passing the gray undergrowth that stretched with ice by the cemetery. We went by burned-down Zalaski, and through glens by one human track to the north, under oaks and by fields, to the clearing. We crossed the forest, parallel to a duct, and then went by way of the ravine of a pool to Pasieki: there, on a fine day, it is sometimes possible to see from the hillock the tiny dots of roofs in the valley — that's Szabasowa.

Silence around, sometimes an airplane flew across high up, from west to east. In the glens a fine mist was lying, clear and frosty on the hillocks. The old women kept up their brisk trot, they blew their noses, snapped their fingers, and then were silent. At once my mother came into my memory; she also was walking in front of me, crying and going no one knew where.

"We're going to Talesnia," says she.

"Well, and what shall we do in Talesnia and what shall we eat, you think they don't kill people there? Surely Mama doesn't know what is happening in the world. I suggest we stay here. Partly in the forest, partly in the fields. And here I feel everything is stupid. What does 'in the forest, in the fields' mean?"

My mother said nothing, and walked on. I caught her by the hand and began shaking her.

"Where do you want to go?" I asked.

"Surely I have the right to ask you to take me to Talesnia. You act toward me as though I didn't love you, as though I'd treated you badly one hour . . ."

"What stupid talk," I shouted. "All right, I will take you to Talesnia, and there they will kill you, at the custom house. I don't want to see them kill you. Let's both be sensible, why do we have to be so nasty to each other?"

"Listen to me." My mother stopped, and she spoke calmly. "Listen, don't be so stubborn. Take me near Talesnia, then you can go. I will make a living. I will wash floors or something, maybe there's a public urinal, I will do something."

"Everything has changed there in the past few days. Talesnia is dead, it is dark there, there is nothing and no one apart from the police, who are digging in the ashes."

I did not wish to order her. My mother rushed ahead like a wild duck startled in her sleep. We walked by the field edges to the south. This day my heart warned me of something, and this day I was weakest in all my life.

"You won't playact to me here, now," she said, when we were already near Talesnia. She picked up her skirt in one hand and jumped across a ditch full of red water.

"Look to the left; how many people are lying naked."

My mother stroked her forehead.

"All murdered?"

Close before us lay a corpse, its head burrowing in slime, without trousers, shirt ripped. Only here did my mother understand everything; turning around she walked heavily back into the fields. And all around, everything was the same: early summer, the day finishing its course, larks singing. Then something splashed.

"Run, mother!" My neck swelled from the terrible breathing, both hands beat together — I ran away. 'Stop,' my mother sometimes said to me, 'don't run like a lunatic! Take a piece of warm cake for the journey!'

I heard a shot and turned. My mother was lying lifeless on the path without a kerchief. Life poisoned forever! All the way I beat my breast and walked. In the morning I came to Zalaski. A crowd of people was standing in the pasture beside a tied-up bull calf, looking from under its eyebrows; it hung its face to the earth, then tossed its head, broke the string, and ran down a crowded alley, casting up mud with its hind legs. People groped after the animal with sticks, and laughed. Boys set off after the bull calf and caught it, then tied a noose on its muzzle. Some man or other came up, threatening them with his fist.

"You boys!" he shouted, "you boys, if you take that bull to a Kraut, we shall beat you. Whose is it, this bull? Mrs. Arbuz's?" He turned back and fixed a gaze full of suspicion on me. He took me with him. Then I fell ill. I lay in the stable at Mrs. Arbuz's place, and Klara Wasicinska came. At once she addressed me on familiar terms.

"What's the matter with you?" she asked.

She stood over me, her hair braided into one pigtail, smiling bitterly.

"How should I know what's wrong with me?" I said.

In the afternoon something rustled around me — Emilka had come, wet, sweating, holding a bottle in her hand. And after a moment Chaim crept in.

"What's there?" he asked. He undid my shirt, looked at my chest. Emilka came several times a day to the stable; she gave me a drink from a bottle, and in my head a battle with the Germans on the Prussian frontier went on. The sound of bells announced the quarter hours of the battle, and always someone took me by the hand and invited me to rest; the horses fed; the leader of a unit winked at me, and said that somewhere near here was good eating. We go behind a church, to the sisters of charity. As soon as we stop on the threshold, a lancer runs up and says we are setting off. Supply wagons are to be heard, thundering without pause on the highway. We go back to the horses. People are sleeping in a meadow. German artillery play reveille. To horse! We take the pouches off their muzzles. We ride fifteen minutes, and bells ring — we had gone into the forest. Rifles start playing, the first lancer falls, my lance chances upon someone . . .

Emilka shook me by the hand, and said, "I will cover you with straw, lie quietly, for there are gendarmes in the villages," and she ran out, agitated. And no one came to me until the third day at dusk, when some man or other in a leather jacket appeared in the stable, short, lean, but compact. He said nothing, but gazed at me fixedly with glittering pupils; he went away, leaving beside me a bottle of buttermilk. Two weeks later Chuny came in the night.

"Get up, colleague, we're going." Staggering, moving my hands like a swimmer, I crept after Chuny into the dark yard. Three horses were standing there, also Szerucki and someone silent. They put me on a horse, and we set off at a light trot. I put my arms around the horse's neck; a fine rain was drizzling. We passed piles of grass, potato patches crackling underfoot. Chuny and Szerucki held me up, their hands were like iron. They had no time to talk to me — my brothers, defenders, comrades. At a walking pace, cautiously, we rode down a cliff into a ravine. At dawn we dismounted in a forest. Szerucki gave the reins to Chuny, and crept into a dark hallway. After a moment he came out and beckoned. Chuny took me into a room in which several people were sitting, and children were sleeping on straw by the wall.

"Take him out," says a man in a leather jacket.

I sat in the undergrowth until broad day; Chaim came and ordered me to strip, and Chuny and Szerucki brought a tub of warm water.

"You, get washed," they said, "for there are children among us, and it is easy to infect them."

I carried the dirty rags from myself deep into the undergrowth and washed myself thoroughly. They gave me a woolen shirt, a jacket of some rich person, and new military breeches. I ate some potatoes.

"You, Leit, talk to him," said Chuny to the man in the leather jacket.

And Leit (Flying-carpet) explained to me what it was all about. He said that all the people gathered together here were brothers, my new family; not all were Jews, but that it was one family. One for all, all for one. Nothing to anybody about anything, it was necessary to talk only with a person who had to be talked to, but not with a person who could be talked to. Give up everything, share everything. The enemy must be killed; by knife, crowbar, whatever came to hand. Never by prayer. It seemed to old Buchsbaum that he could drive away the enemy by prayer, it seemed to old Hoch he could bribe the enemy with dollars.

Leit gave me his hand.

"You're young, what can you do?"

"I am a typesetter."

"What's your name?"

"Heindl."

"Did you go to school?"

"I went for a time," I said.

"Are you a Jew?"

I said nothing.

"Well . . . It's a question of formalities."

"A little."

"What does that mean?"

"My mother was Jewish." I told him the history of my father, manager of the Parnes and Company mill.

"Would you like to do a reconnaissance?" Leit looked me in the eyes, and that was all.

"Somewhere in the neighborhood," he said, "is Czaczkies' gang. It is necessary to go out into the countryside, contact them for work. They are men from the quarries. They escaped in the spring. They wander around somewhere in a group in the forest, living half-naked. This must be investigated. Well, so you will do it. Yesterday, around Pasieki, they killed a man; they say he was one of Czaczkies' men. You must inquire from people in the neighborhood who the murdered man was. Who saw him, and what he saw. If you meet Czaczkies, you will recognize him immediately, because he is very tall, taller than our Chuny."

That same day I went through the forest near Pasieki to confirm whether in fact the dead man was from Czaczkies' gang. But no, nowhere was anybody killed there. Not until the hillock by the path to Wiliny did I find a pile of bodies. There was a murdered woman and three children by her. A spider web and dew were already lying on the children's poor clothing. That was more or less here, where now these women had stopped.

They are straightening the bundles on their backs, blowing their noses. We put our hands to our foreheads, for something is burning with black smoke in Szabasowa. Far away on the high-road several sleighs are to be seen. It is becoming a violet early evening; light frost is settling on the trees; the path before us is becoming glassy like salt, and far off is a dull wall of smoke.

"Didn't this man spend the night in your village? You certainly know him, the man who was shot once in the yard at the priest's house — Leit was his name," I say to the nearest women.

"It was so," says the nearest one.

"Did he stay the night?"

"That mad woman Dominka cuddled him in her alcove. She walked about, pretended he was going away someplace, and someone must have seen everything. I was sitting and sewing. One of the peasants came, and said something was going to happen that night. People went to Dominka, and told her to take herself away from the village. 'Listen to us, it will be bad.' But she stood on the threshold of the recess and hit the first man with a plate. She's a violent girl, and no one dared open his mouth. The German police came toward dawn, and that's how it happened."

"But he? This man, this Leit?"

"He got burned. This Shaya of yours took away what wasn't turned to ashes, down to a cap found under a tile. As for her, the healthy mare, she pushed out a window and doesn't even know what happened at our place in the hamlet afterwards. My mother ran out across the threshold, and fell down on the railing, shouting something. And here was terror, Jesus, how much terror! I flew out of the house and into the garden, and was afraid they'd catch up, and I would not have strength to tear myself away from those terrible hands."

"And what about that cap?"

"They buried it near the wayside shrine. The earth had frozen like a bone, it was hard. They broke it with an ax and scattered it."

"Did they take your men, or kill them?"

"They killed some and took others for interrogation. I did not see mine anywhere."

"They certainly took him," say I. "We'll find out from the railroad man at the barrier, he must have known whom they took last night from the highroad to Szabasowa. Well, eh?"

But the women slid downwards in silence. Over the forest the moon looked reddish as an ember. Dusk quickly veiled the eyes. A cold north wind pinched the nose, whistling could already be heard from the Szabasowa railroad station, somewhere the sounds of dogs barking in the distance were flattened by night. We were passing dark little houses on the outskirts of Foresta. Nobody is to be seen. Someplace someone like a black ball rolls quickly from yard to yard.

In front of the barrier I pushed one hand into my pocket; the revolver was cold as ice. Someone is standing in a dark raincoat.

"Good evening," say I.

"Evening," rumbles a low bass.

"What was burning here?" We stop, the stranger quickly lights a cigarette, and examines my face in the glow of the match.

They burned down Jewish huts, he says, and he puts the ember behind him, taking a step toward the women. "In your place I'd sell the moonshine here, in town the gendarmes will take it from you. And you, man, go on living no one knows how. Let's go into the hut, I'll pay."

"What will you pay with?" I asked.

"That depends," he says, and coughed.

"We have to go to the Criminal Police," I say, "for they took these women's husbands away last night."

"Too bad, what's more urgent?"

"Did you see anything in the night?" I ask.

"What do you mean 'see'?"

"Did they bring anyone from the highroad to the town?"

"Why not, how many times is that seen? What of it?"

The railroad man walked away beyond the track, and at once a goods train came up from the east. Cows' heads with big horns could be seen against the sky, calves were mooing, pigs grunting. We stood for a time — the train was long. The top boots of gendarmes could be seen beyond the boxcars, in the flashes of an electric torch.

I left the women and fled rapidly along a bank between piles of planks. The train flew past. Around the building could be heard:

"Moonshine, moonshine! *Donnerwetter! Kom . . . kom . . . kom . . .*"

I was running along some ditch, cartridges rattling in my pocket. Beyond the barbed wire was the empty white space of the sports ground, and now from the side I saw electric lights moving along the bank. There, further on, someone whistled twice through his fingers. In Railroad Street I met a girl, maybe fourteen, going in the direction of the town, carrying something in pails.

"Allow me, miss," I said, "I'll help you."

The girl did not reply, one could suppose she was frightened. She began to cry.

"Please, sir, I bought for myself . . ."

"Never mind," I whispered, and ran on.

The street was deserted. Shutters closed, only from the Grand Hotel a ray of light burst upon the street; over the roof, smoke flowed straight into the sky. Behind the hotel the alleyways of the ghetto, broken door frames sticking up like an overturned windmill. A crowd of people had moved around here not so long ago, in summer evenings. In the winter, children went skating; they gathered snow from the railings of the marketplace and ate it, to find out if it was tasty. Laborers and women sat around on benches, joked and bit sunflower seeds.

Flies buzzed, turkeys walked up and down. And in windows wreathed with ivy the green light of the moon gleamed until late; lovers kissed in summer houses. The flat paving stones were warm, and children on all fours or clutching with their little hands at the fences took their first tottering steps on them. Merry dog chases, and after them gentlemen out for a stroll. In gates, beggars wrapped up mouthfuls of bread, pancake, cakes in newspaper.

A band was playing in the hotel, colored lights twinkled, went off and on. Feet scraped in dancing. The moon stood above Szabasowa, mists drifted over the ghetto, the alleys were a maze beyond the barbed wire.

Alongside, below, New Street. In the shade, behind trees, a gate ajar. A path trodden to the porch in back of the house. I stood a moment on the threshold, rang, and moved into the depths of the long hallway.

Ksawera cast a dazed look around.

"No help anywhere, I'm completely alone," I was thinking as you came in. You stood on the threshold a moment, carefully inspecting all my room. Someone walked around the house, passed close to the window, pushed the gate. I was waiting with beating heart. Did you ring, sir?"

"I rang twice."

"I'd fallen asleep from exhaustion. Please sit down."

She was silent, confused.

"I don't recall you very well, sir. Yes, a little. Somewhere by a campfire of potato leaves, in fall. You said something funny to my girlfriend. That which was two years ago is already confused in my head."

"Just so. My name is Heindl."

"Yes . . . To calm me down, please say what brought you to my place."

Ksawera had thick, fluffy black hair. My eyes wandered over her graceful figure, avoiding her gaze. Alarm flooded me, like a wave a drowning man. I pulled out the letter. A terrible hubbub of events. It seemed to me that Ksawera had been trampled on and ill treated here, even in this quiet room of hers. When she was reading, I glanced quickly, secretly, at her half-closed eyes. My heart heard her despair before it reached my ears.

"But where is Leit?" she whispered, and looked at my hands.

The thought came to take my cap and go away whistling. It would have been possible to do that. It would have eased the girl. Wherever you are, whatever you do, such a moment comes when you see through a mist of tears. You play the lunatic, throwing up your hands.

"He's a shrewd guy," say I, "he'll manage. He got caught up some place temporarily."

But it is only for a child that such gestures have more significance than real things.

Ksawera looked at me with a strange expression on her face, as if she had already guessed everything, had caught the whole secret. And here it was proved that with words it is possible to lie, but there's no way to do it with gestures. Later, nothing more comes out. I smiled.

"Yeees. We'll do everything in our power to find him."

"Funny. Why do you speak to me thus?"

Growing uneasy, she once more raised the letter to her eyes.

"Why funny?" I asked, for something to say.

"You'll admit in a moment that it's funny."

She was trying to draw me out, she knew very well what she was getting at, but impatience overcame her. She rose and pumped the Primus stove. And I began asking her how she was getting on, and all about life in Szabasowa.

"Poor man . . . Each of you lives, but he had to die," Ksawera kept reverting to this.

"Nothing is known yet," I said. "Nobody has seen his corpse."

When I uttered the word 'corpse,' it was as though a wind hurled Ksawera. She ran up to me.

"Surely he's dead. Surely," she screamed, and turned with a stifled sobbing to the corner with the Primus.

I stretched my weary legs in front of me and sat thus, motionless, pondering and moved.

"You're a funny man." Ksawera turned her face in my direction.

"Why?" I asked.

She was silent, spreading jam on bread.

Ksawera's apartment was long and narrow, like a yard in an inn, but clean. Two windows were tightly covered with blankets. There was a table, two chairs, a cupboard with mirror, an old-fashioned chest engraved with iron flowers, a large black chest of drawers with two pairs of small doors, and a little sofa with a shelf over it. Above the sofa was a wooden cross, a party favor in cellophane, and a wreath of catkins, in the corner a pile of books a yard high. A picture was hanging over the books — merely a view from a window into a gray sky, with trees fleeing along with clouds. Over the cupboard was a dark-red violoncello.

I ate bread, drank a pot of ersatz coffee.

"Do you smoke?"

"Yes."

"Has Chaim anything to smoke?"

"Sometimes. Cheap stuff mostly. Or some days nothing."

Ksawera nodded in agreement, and now she did not move her eyes from my face for a moment.

"Where are you all at now?"

"In Zalaski."

"All the same . . . When do you want to go back?"

"Right away, if possible."

"I will go fetch this medicine for Chaim, and I'll lock you in."

She stood behind the closet door, threw me a pack of cigarettes and matches. She put on a dark linen coat, drawn in tightly at the waist, and a woolen cap.

"Please put the lamp out and sit quietly until I come back."

She went out. The lock rattled twice in the hallway. I extinguished the lamp, pulled off my boots; groping to the sofa, I lay down on it. Long ago I'd lain on something just as pleasant. It was warm and dry, somewhere close to my ear an alarm clock was ticking healthily. Now a quarrel was clearly to be heard in the next apartment.

"You'll see," a man shouted, "you'll see if I'm scared. He won't jump, I'll kill him. He doesn't know me. He has nothing to show here!"

"He'll do as he likes! You always suppose he's afraid of you. Now it will be your turn . . ."

Sleep began to come over me. I smoked one cigarette after another. Then, beyond the wall, there was a great uproar, shouts of satisfaction, the laughter of women, a dog barking, stamping feet, and an impossible noise, as if someone had won something great. Some party was at an end.

I rose, so that the lice from me would not get on to Ksawera's bed linen. I walked from the window to the door, thinking about this and that, as happens when a man is in such a situation.

"What do you know about Ksawera?" Chaim asked Szerucki one night.

"Why?"

"Flying-carpet gets letters from her, food packages."

"She has no trade. Her father has been in France for ten years. He used to send her a little money. In France it is possible to make more money than here. She played the violin in a funeral band, but she isn't a Jewess."

"Oh, that's her! I remember," says Chaim.

"She lived in Zawodz with three working women from the bristle factory."

"Yes, yes, yes. That's fine," says Chaim, "I know who she is."

"You, man, don't ask stupid questions."

"What does that mean?"

"You know all about her, and you ask questions for the sake of it."

"You're angry because you don't know anything more about her. You lived so many years in Szabasowa, but you don't know the local people there."

"Talk away, tap the window with your beak."

From such an insidious conversation it was possible to find out that Ksawera was not a girl; she had a husband, lived with him a year, then left the drunkard, a smooth hypocrite of irreproachable behavior among people, a sharper and secret agent with sloping hips. It was possible not to believe one's own eyes — he was so pleasant on the surface. He beat her, brutally dragged her to him, trampled and kicked her; with a terrible feeling of nausea she yielded in despair. She suffered for a year; one night straight from bed, snatching clothing, she ran away from the alcoholic. Then she lived with Leit. He played the cello, she the violin. She gained great trust in this man, told him of her life, her childhood, the death of her mother, with whose death everything in the world ended except music. Her father, an Austrian, did not take an interest in his daughter; sometimes he sent her a few pennies. He always loved money more than he loved people. And no sooner had she drawn breath in this new life with Leit than the war came. But Ksawera's husband, Ciszka, knocked on the door the night after the Germans entered Szabasowa, "with the purpose of preventing any unforseen happening which might come upon her" because she was living with a Jew. Bultz and someone else were at the windows. A July downpour was roaring without pause. Ksawera awoke, a rustling by the wall came to her, a plank on the threshold squeaked. She woke Klara, who was spending the night there, having hidden the Arnsteins' valuables under the floorboards. Klara opened the window:

"Who do you want?"

"Does Mrs. Ciszka live here?" said Bultz.

"Yes. Through the hallway."

And Bultz and Ciszka began scrambling over the planks in the porch. Only the stranger, cunning dog, crept in by the window. Leit took heart, and hit the secret agent over the head with an iron rasp.

"We'll break the door down!" they shouted at the entrance.

Klara and Leit fled into the gardens under the embankments. At night German patrols walked around the town, and shot at the windows. Leit lay in the potato beds until dawn. And from that time he did not see Ksawera again. He got letters, food, money from her. Nine tenths of Ksawera's life was hard work and stony self-will in a wool-carding factory. She did not free herself from the annoyances of Ciszka, his importunities, blackmail, and provocations. Never in her life, as she sometimes told Klara, never had she been as happy as now, when there were so many opportunities to protect people. Since Leit had been wandering in the forests, she had not touched her violin. Music was good for nothing when a person was weeping inside, when they threw children against a wall in full view. It was possible to watch a gendarme's night from hiding. Every day, toward dawn, violent banging at the door awoke someone for death. Only animals were left, and they died on the threshold. Ksawera took several children out of the town one stormy evening, and gave them into the care of Chuny Shaya, who was waiting in Lipki with Szerucki. Only Kalma survived. She walked around in rags with a sack on her head, and lice bit into her bones.

Lighting a cigarette, I glanced at the alarm clock; seven thirty. I pulled the belt of my pants and began doing squat jumps, because the shivers were beginning to get me. In the next room, someone was again talking to someone else. I crept barefoot across the cold floor, floundered through recollections, shortening details. Ciszka came to mind. It would be worth asking Ksawera what that scoundrel was doing. But was it proper to speak with her, to go into these detailed basenesses? For as it was, it looked like punishment was approaching. No matter what would happen afterwards, Chuny and Szerucki would slaughter him. Who told this bandit to suggest hunting down children to the police? Not one had risen from the clay hillock. And then, with several of them, he waited in the undergrowth until evening, so they could catch more in an ambush. They could be seen; they went off around midnight in various directions without saying good-bye. "All this must be remembered," said Leit, "even though I don't know in what little streams it flowed. Don't let yourself be trodden on, don't let yourself be killed, don't yield to lice and hunger."

Leit was almost short in stature, thin, with an ugly, pock-marked face, but he knew how to fight as well as the sinewy Chuny or Szerucki.

He inspected everyone with a cold, sharp eye; he struck a blow cunningly; in talking he did not gesticulate at all, and was stubborn as a rock.

One time, we were lying with Flying-carpet on a field edge near the highway where a battalion of Jewish laborers with yellow patches on their backs were working; we were lying in wait for the chief ganger, who had made a fortune by supplying scapulars with mercury against lice to the workers. He made an exchange — the mercury in ointment for a ring, a watch, golden rubles. Lying thus, we were thinking out how to make this criminal harmless, for none of us yet possessed a weapon, except a large pocketknife with a tin handle and the inscription "Magnetic Horse" in Russian.

We had not had time to think of anything when Leit jumped out and stopped a yard from the ganger.

"Throw it," he shouted at the top of his voice in German, and moved a step with a rock lifted over his head. The blow fell only once. Blood flowed out of the ganger's ears. Leit did not have time to search the recumbent man, he only grabbed his revolver. Sentries began firing. Fifteen men from the battalion escaped, crouching in the undergrowth. Szerucki looked at him in amazement when he learned about this. It was the first time anyone had

acted in this way. Leit's face changed out of recognition afterwards, only sometimes the same thin smile wandered on his lips.
Also he told us more often: "There is no law on earth that can for-
bid a man to defend himself against death. With goodwill and
effort, we will liquidate more than one." That same evening, everyone in our band drank moonshine at Mrs. Arbuz's place; only
Leit and Horse-face did not touch liquor. Amidst the noise and
the enjoyment, out came things we ourselves did not realize the
value of. Also Piegza and Bambucher, perverts and provocateurs,
left our group forever and ever.

Ksawera returned at eight.

"Please light the lamp," she said quietly. "I don't even know
what your first name is. That Chaim certainly has his head on his
shoulders, he changed the handwriting on the prescription. There
was someone in the pharmacy that made me feel bad. Was I
long?"

"Not particularly, maybe an hour."

"What did you do? Did you doze?"

"Oh, well, one thinks about this and that. I listened a little to
what they were saying in the next room."

"And what did you overhear?"

"There was a quarrel."

"I'll introduce you to that man. He trains dogs, an old eccentric."

An expression of watchful impatience appeared in the bold look
of Ksawera's black eyes.

"I mentioned him in a letter to Chaim."

"Yes, he told me . . ."

"You'll be able to talk to him. You will leave here only at
dawn, for this is a gendarmes' night. Some Soviet prisoners have
escaped from a camp, the streets are barricaded. You don't have
any papers, that's for sure."

"You must be joking, miss. The patient is waiting."

"I thought of that." Ksawera looked me straight in the eyes and
shook her head. "You won't get out of Szabasowa earlier than
dawn. You are in no danger, we will sit through four, six hours in
the dark."

Ksawera handed me a piece of fresh, well-cooked smoked meat;
we ate and talked. Short bursts of firing were to be heard, someone ran past our windows and turned into the ruins.

"I hate even the very thought that anything of the kind might
happen. We'll drink tea in the dark. Please put the medicines into
your jacket pocket at once, everything necessary is there."

"Right," I said, and took the little package from Ksawera's hands. It must be admitted that the firing in the street began to make me uneasy. I would have preferred to be outdoors, and here it was possible to grow old waiting for stupid incidents, so I put my boots on and sat down close to the window. Pushing one hand under the blanket, I investigated the bolt, so that in the event of anything I would not have to loiter too long. I peeped through a crack — was it dark night or frost that veiled the windowpanes so?

"How does Chaim feel?" asked Ksawera.

"How can a man feel? Somehow or other . . ."

I lit a cigarette, Ksawera sat down, the sofa creaking under her full body.

"You won't get any sleep because of me, miss."

Ksawera did not reply at once.

"Never mind, don't even think of it."

"Tomorrow you have to get up and go to work. You won't have the strength."

"Please drop the subject. It's all nonsense. What's happening to Kalma?"

"I know little about her now. Most likely she's at Czaczkies' place, somewhere with his men. She'll slither away from death."

"And Cirla?"

"She went out of her mind, she's wandering in the forest."

"I met Leit at Cirla's wedding. Old Buchsbaum commissioned us, we played until supper. Cirla was standing at a mirror, combing her long red hair. The bridesmaids placed on her forehead a metal band, coming down on her temples, and behind her ears were two sort of flaps of gilded tin, and on this foundation they piled all her hair up, and braided it. Her forehead was bare, and her head became tall. Then she adorned herself in the family jewels, earrings, rings; she looked very beautiful. Everything took place in the Jewish fashion, only Chuny was dressed in secular style. He walked erect under the canopy, and with his height he looked very comical. Then he squatted down in a corner and listened to the music. He likes music. After midnight we played the *Erlkönig.*

"Leit liked Schubert. Chuny went up to Leit and asked, 'What was that?' 'That? Schubert.' I myself learned from Leit that Schubert was the ugly and poor son of a simple, ordinary teacher. He had curly hair like a Gypsy, dark sallow skin, and fiery eyes. He was eleven when he came to the conservatory with an application to be admitted. They mocked him, a little Gypsy in a torn shirt.

When he was sixteen he went home to his father and brothers, who were also good musicians. They performed at home. He was still very young, only nineteen, and he wrote *Erlkönig* to Goethe's ballad.

"My chatter surely bores you, sir?"

"No," I said, "I like hearing such things."

"His life was frugal, and no one shared his troubles. No one. Continuous labor on new works, and constant attempts to find some modest post, which he never obtained. In the summer, some weeks of a walking trip in the Austrian Alps with a singer friend — this was Schubert's life and fate. The happiest days for him were those when he walked at random through the mountains and thickets with his friend, and they sang for their own pleasure. They sang songs, maybe the most beautiful, which for sure nobody had ever sung before. Schubert loved everything. He died young, when he was thirty-one. And two public concerts barely sufficed to pay for his funeral. Please tell me something about Leit now. When did you see him last?"

"I saw him long ago; we were separated, and even a little mad at one another."

"Why mad at each other?"

"Because he was of a different opinion regarding one matter. In fact, I wanted to ask — how much money did you spend on this medicine?"

"Of Chaim's five dollars, I still have two in my pocket. If you need anything, something will be done. I have a certain source. This is beside the point, don't any of you bother about it. Please tell me why you got mad at one another, it makes me sad."

"Nothing big, they differed a little with Chaim. It was often said that there was no money, even for the poor children who wander with us."

"How is poor Leit guilty of that?"

"How would you behave, miss, in such an incident: a man is wandering around the forest, a very old man with dollars sewn into his red jacket. According to what agents believe, there are something like forty thousand."

"I would take them from him, share out as much as is necessary for life, let's say for a whole year, and that's it. You might, for example, have looked after him, found some shelter, because it is necessary to consider that the man is old. But what position did Leit take?"

"A different one, and here for the first time Horse-face and Leit differed. Leit said, 'Don't do it, consider what disastrous results it may have on the entire cause.'

" 'What cause?' said Horse-face. 'For example, what cause?'

" 'Just think, consider for a few days, then give me a reply. You'll certainly agree with me.'

" 'Tell me why it isn't possible to take a few of these dollars from the old man. Why, now?'

" 'Try and do it,' warned Leit.

" 'I'm not pushing. For in any case it will end with agents kicking the old man to death. The children haven't a spoonful of hot food, or a rag to their backs. What sort of matter is this piety?'

" 'Consider it,' said Leit. 'I won't say anymore.'

"Yes, this is not as simple as it appeared at first to be. I can't forgive this," said Ksawera.

"And Leit began looking at us with a look different from ever before.

" 'Maybe I am unnecessary to you, maybe I am interfering,' and he went away. He turned back once — 'consider, all of you,' he said — and he walked away, no one knows where. Dudi, who was with him to the last, knows very little, almost nothing. This incident can be variously interpreted: for good and for evil. Meanwhile, the position is that if no corpse is to be seen, then it's a waste of time talking about it all. It's the same with Leit, please think over a little what I've said.

"How am I to understand that?"

"Simple enough. I do not swear he is dead."

Ksawera fell silent; obviously she did not want to say anything on this topic. She shifted on the sofa, and whispered,

"Yes, yes, yes . . . How terrible all this together is."

After a long silence she rose, and said,

"I'll fetch my neighbor. Talk together! He has a rifle for sale. However, you must pretend that you're a poacher, that you need a gun for foxes or something, for he declares that it is forbidden to kill people. 'People are necessary,' he says."

"Who is he?"

"A retired hunter from some count's estate. His name is Trypka. Now he deals in dogs, saccharine, carbide, caustic soda. Apart from this he trains young dogs, no one knows what for, but he trains them. He is trying to accustom them to attacking people. For this purpose, he dresses up his fourteen-year-old grandson in thick tarpaulin rags, covers the boy's face with a wire beekeeper's net, hangs on his back something like a rifle, for example a hoe. Evidently he wants to arouse hatred in the dogs for armed men. I hear this sometimes through the door — cruelty. This grandson beats the dog, and the old man baits the dog, and this goes on for hours, to some end or other. He says he likes such feelings, that they relieve him. He says that after an hour of training he feels less beset by enemies. Apparently he has some enemies or other, in whose eyes it isn't enough to sprinkle snuff."

"Is it worth talking to him on the subject of weapons?"

"Yes. He is no danger to us. He has his own way of reckoning in this. He would like to make some money, that's all, it seems. Maybe you promise him something of the game; in any case he is counting on it, as I've already mentioned it to him. He's entirely indifferent to other matters."

"What does 'other matters' mean?"

"What is going on around. He wanders about the area of the ghetto and traps cats; the fur is fur, and he makes soap from the rest. He has the look of a hangman toward everything else. He says he put so much effort into his life, and that it was all for nothing. 'You're a valiant person, miss,' he says to me, sometimes. 'Why?' I ask him. 'Because you don't let yourself be trodden on; you have tasted life to the depths, but you don't let yourself be trodden on by other people's boots.' "

Yawning, I stretched my legs under the table and only now did I feel how terribly exhausted I was after the day's march, after yesterday's sleepless night. I took a cigarette out of my pocket, looking for matches, but really I didn't really want to smoke. I held the box and listened.

"God alone knows what is lurking in that man. I lack the courage to watch him, nor am I sure whether in my present state of nerves I wouldn't commit some error. In any case, a meeting with him will explain everything to you."

"I don't understand."

"You will also find out what the police will give you for letting Gail get away."

Sweat broke out on my forehead. Questions crowded. Thousands of matters mixed into one heap. It was necessary to say something, but before I could think of anything, Ksawera went on:

"It seems to me that they have Leit, they took him for a hostage."

"Where did you get that idea?"

"You have nothing to fear in dealing with me. There was talk of Leit and Gail in the pharmacy."

"Did you speak to anyone on this topic?"

"No."

"Well, then?"

"If you prevent me from looking for Leit, you will bear the entire responsibility."

"What happened?"

"In the pharmacy I found a certain man. When I came in, he was saying to the assistant: 'Do you remember, miss, anything about the teacher from the Hebrew school?' 'Well, yes, why shouldn't I? A little squirt, he played the cello.' 'It was he the police caught tonight.' 'Please wait,' said the assistant, 'the medicine must be got ready.' She whispered something to Mrs. Biferster, and the latter with wide-open mouth, supporting her upper teeth with her tongue, asked me,

" 'What do you want?' She kept turning to the laboratory as though someone was threatening her from there with a revolver. She went for the prescription. A coarse male voice said,

" 'I am not a fool in love. I observe customers closely.'

" 'Take a look at his old prescriptions, you'll see I'm right.'

" 'Do you have a bottle for the Rivanol, miss?'

" 'No, I don't.'

" 'Who wrote this prescription?'

" 'Doctor Ferencki,' I said.

"A short, stout man waddled from behind the desk, holding a sheaf of papers.

" 'You know Dr. Ferencki, miss? Are you his patient?'

" 'Yes.'

" 'How is he getting along?'

" 'As usual.'

"Fatty leaned on his elbow and repeated to himself in a whisper: 'as usual.'

" 'Please wait,' and he went out. And that stranger, waiting for medicine, said, 'What's going to happen now that they killed that guy from the secret police?' Trypka was summoned for interrogation.

" 'Which Trypka?'

" 'The dog man.'

"A man's voice from the laboratory: 'You play the violin, miss?'

" 'Yes.'

" 'What's happening to Arnold, M. A.?'

" 'I don't know.'

" 'I thought you might know something. I asked because I have a good deal of curiosity in my nature.'

"He handed me a package with the medicines, I put out my

hand, but when I tried to take it on two fingers he shook it. Suspicion awoke in me that this was some signal, or that he was deliberately trying to summon up in me some terrible uncertainty, out of fear and curiosity."

"Who's the fat man?" I asked Ksawera.

"I don't know. I never saw him in Szabasowa before."

"I paid," said Ksawera. He gave me change and asked the seated man, 'What do you think, will they shoot this Leit?'

" 'And what did they catch him for, do you think?'

" 'I didn't take all this into consideration.'

"Mrs. Biferster came out of the laboratory, and put a hand on the man's arm:

" 'I hope you won't leave me by myself. It isn't worth going out. A lot of Soviet prisoners have escaped, you might have some unpleasantness in the street.'

" 'Now I can sit here with you awhile, then I'll take myself nicely off home and sleep.'

" 'Oh, I hoped that you would not leave me by myself today.' "

Ksawera said, "I said good-night and walked out."

I stood up, depressed, and started walking about. Time and again, shooting was to be heard in the town. I pulled aside the curtain on the window and stared into the darkness. Ksawera scolded me, saying it wasn't for that that I came there, to get depressed and sit like a dead pumpkin. She urged me to wake up, to interest myself in this Trypka. Maybe really there was something in favor with Leit. We should not delay, for as things were, everything already seemed to hang on one thing, everything looked loused up.

I noticed a certain excitement in Ksawera's voice; she spoke in a sharp whisper,

"I never thought that Trypka might hold more than one life in his hand. Despite everything, however, it is necessary to talk to him. You'll go back to your own people with certain material. For me too things will stop being so confused."

"Fine," I said. "Bring him in, miss, we'll talk. I've nothing against it. I'd like to ask a question beforehand."

"Well?"

"Are you not by chance, all unwittingly, serving some scoundrel?"

"Can you think so badly of me, despite all your experiences?"

"I have no experiences in the region of Szabasowa."

"Good heavens . . . nothing of the sort," said Ksawera; breathing in with a whistle, she approached me and convulsively seized me by the hand.

"Have you all regarded me as such a woman?"

Some explanation had to be found. I was ashamed of the brutality shown to Ksawera.

"Sometimes chance leads to that. They must already have beset you. They coax for their own purposes, and that may happen in the twinkling of an eye. A person notices he was stupid, lets himself be drawn into criminality. He would like to hide someplace in a dark corner, but his life is already threatened."

Almost instantly Ksawera cried,

"It's not true. No, no!"

Her voice had a sort of dignity and passion of its own.

"I believe you," I said, and we both fell silent.

Someone knocked on the wall. Ksawera nervously knocked back twice. After a moment the floorboards in the hallway creaked, heavy footsteps were to be heard. Something flashed through my mind. I felt as though I were suddenly melting into air. It was all the same, someone must give up his last breath here today.

"Come in," said Ksawera.

"You won't believe it, miss," said a treble voice from the darkness, "but I tell you that this escape of Soviet prisoners is not any ordinary escape. I can swear to that by the most holy words."

"I'm not alone," says Ksawara.

"Oh . . ."

"This gentleman has come on account of — you know — "

And she began telling highly colored things about me as a bandit. In this brief narrative I grew to the role of an eccentric, singing as I murdered animals.

Trypka came up and seized my hand in his coarse but very warm hand. Sighing, he uttered a philosophical statement on the subject of unhappy human fate, and of old people in particular. He spoke through his nose, in a benevolent tone.

"Please sit down," Ksawera invited.

I lit a cigarette, glanced at the alarm clock: it was ten thirty. I saw Trypka's face in a flash from the match. Now I recalled it all; suddenly the thought seized me that there would never be any end to the whole crime. So on, continually without measure, as if walking by a terrible mountain; everything suddenly changed — something flashed and brought everything to me: he was Bultz's cooperator. So, as with one's conscience — suddenly, amidst pondering, or in the night, when I awoke scared from bad

dreams — this burdensome recollection attacked me with as
much accuracy as though it were a moment ago. This does not let
itself be erased even by a cheerful thought; it remains forever like
a sin against one's mother, or something even worse. I was to kill
him, back in the fall I was to have killed him. The heart is always
the most precise of judges; it delivers a sentence in a moment, on
the basis of some small gesture, often a look or one thought. Trypka's step, his knock at the door — all this lay heavier than logs on
my chest. The clumsy thought came to mind: kill him . . .

And I, like a horse in darkness, pricked up my ears so as not to
trip and fall over.

"Somehow, one lives somehow," I said.

"Ough," as from a very slimy depths.

Ksawera sat down beside me.

"Are there, let's say, a lot of foxes this winter?"

"Quite a lot," say I.

"More or less, judging by sight?"

"That depends. Where there are more, there are more; where
there are less, there's less."

I felt the content of his aggression; the night had not shut in the
circle of our thoughts and experiences. One absorbed the other,
the other gave way to a third, ever more lively, like birds from
burned-out nests.

"Now's the season for them. It would be good to come."

"As long as it was with something."

"Yes, that's so, surely. Poverty squeaks when the pocket is
empty."

"Something could be found," say I.

"More or less so?"

"Let's talk."

"Well?"

"What is it?"

"A rifle," said Trypka, and he started coughing.

He had coughed the same previously. A fine rain had been
drizzling, it was dark. Chuny went first, and the dogs threw themselves at him. He jumped over the fence. His face pressed against
the windowpane.

"Nothing doing," say I, "there are no customers for rifles now."

"What do you know about it? It's possible to mangle with a
rifle bullet, for it's a twenty-two. It will rip a cartridge case, but it
will kill at a hundred yards."

"It would not penetrate a watermelon."

"Waste of time talking."

"Surely."

"That means no?"

"What do I want such useless trash for?"

"Well, then?"

"Something with which it would be possible to kill at a distance. Some carbine with ammunition, if there were one, that's something else."

I turned my face away; it seemed to me that Trypka was seeking my eyes. My fear was stupid and absurd, but I could not control myself. It was too dark for him to penetrate to all my secrets.

"From a distance. That doesn't depend only on the barrel. The same barrel, let's say, works different in frost, different in heat," said Trypka, tapping the tabletop.

"One kind of ammunition for a bat, another for a duck."

"Why a bat?"

"Sometimes it is necessary to kill a bat, because there is something hidden in it."

Silent, I felt like someone looking for something not yet lost, but it was already slipping from my grasp.

"It so happens that what kills a bird won't kill a bitch. There must be different ammunition for one and the other."

"I know that."

"Now the eye too. If one hasn't the eye, let's say, it's a waste of time inflicting pain. Let's say one shoots at a duck. It goes on flying, with its legs hanging down, and will fall far away into the willows. This means the shot caught her in the belly, and a search. Then again she joggles, strains, and flies awry, flees on foot like a fox. Such a wounded animal disappears from sight, burrows into the mud. Grass and sky."

"That's the point. From this rifle you can get the very same bits and pieces. And a man comes back from the forest with his head low, very tired. There is even a song about it: the titmouse says she fears a hawk, but she fears a person with a rifle still more."

"It's so, it's so. A shotgun's a shotgun, an eye's an eye. It, this eye, does everything. Like one time my father and I went after an otter. The dog saw a black hole and didn't want to go any further. I saw with my young eye that the otter was sniffing the air for the exit. I showed my father — he lifted it to his eye, but he had not cut the hairs in his nose, and one black hair tickled him, and there was no end to his sneezing."

"What has that to do with it?"

"It has. A man, when old, smells himself. When he remembers his youth, then he knows it. What can be done when he has a

burning in the eyes? For a bandit, youth is necessary, for sometimes an animal defends itself. Let's say it's necessary to trap a
bird. It is shot and must be caught. A duck offers no resistance, a
crane is an eyesore and can hit out an eye for good and all. And
it's necessary to try a kite, if one doesn't lay it out at once with a
well-aimed shot. One must squeeze its beak with one hand, for it
won't give itself up any other way, it bites. Limping, it hastens to
its place, it turns back its head, and bites, and bristles, and hits,
and defends itself."

"Because that's the kind of bird it is," I said. "It trusts no one."

"No animal trusts anyone. Only a toadying dog, sometimes a
horse. But the rest are alone. A wounded animal runs away, and
likes to await its end in solitude. If you come up to seize it by the
beak, it will defend itself with might and main."

"Not like us."

"Everyone knows, a man wounded at once falls down and
shouts. A shot fox will scream, a wolf shouts, a hare shouts very
loud. But other shot animals keep silent. Once my master almost
missed an eagle; we were afraid to go up to it, we set a dog on it,
and he seized the bird by its broken wing. It defended itself with
its claws. A lot of curious people gathered to watch. The eagle set
its heels in the undergrowth and looked at the people, and that
was the end of it. For a few days children came and brought it
water in a shell, but this has nothing to do with it."

Ksawera's room grew cold. Trypka was talking, and his voice
clattered and echoed several times from the wall. I felt alone, entirely alone. It seemed that at any moment the door handle would
grate, several more of them come in, and then what? I would not
be able to cope in the darkness; they would creep in and grab my
legs.

"Why don't you open your mouth?" asks Trypka.

"Somehow," replied Ksawera in thought and sorrow.

Beyond the windows, somewhere further down the street, shouts
could be heard, someone's footsteps ran past the house, and after
a moment someone else pursued, with a limping step.

"What time is it?"

"What's time to you, you don't do anything all day, you can
sleep it out," says Ksawera. She clutched me by one finger and
was trembling all over. Evidently she understood everything, but
did not want to admit the idea that the cause was hopeless. And
here it was the question of a man — surely being beaten at this
moment in the Criminal Police guardroom.

"You're joking, miss. It is children who have the habit of talking to one another before they go to bed. Except that we here today behave differently. Children say everything at once, one child doesn't interrupt the other. One says: this fairy tale has no ending. One says: the stove is standing there. Nothing will come out of it. The rifle doesn't suit you, sir?"

"Not at all."

"And a Winchester?"

"Yes."

"Five-shot?"

"Is there a supply of ammunition?"

"Yes. A good thing for a bear, a wolf, or for bigger game. A shot in the head from it will penetrate the brain, knock down an animal on the spot. If you happen to fire it at a roe deer and hit the ventricle, you may be surprised, for the deer flies ahead sharply, as if blinded, trips over a tree stump, and falls. There's no need to double. It tempts a man. With it you can hit a point straight or crooked."

"Caliber?"

"Forty-four, with ejector. It ejects a spent cartridge by itself, and draws the next with the trigger cocked. Only the foresight and a finger at work."

"Is there a safety catch?"

"Two, even. It can be safeguarded, for let's say you fired and broke an animal's leg, you go up with the catch on and hit it on the head with the butt. You'll be grateful to me for it."

"Thank you very much, sure . . ."

"But you won't get it for a 'thank you.' "

"Well, I guess not. What am I to give for it?"

"Would twenty be too much?"

"What does that mean?"

"Miss Ksawera knows, it was already spoken of with her."

"That's something different."

"The price must be that. Nowadays everything is reckoned in dollars."

"For the time being I don't have so much."

"Sure, I understand. Life doesn't always work out as it should. Sometimes a few pennies — that's all. Like once here I went into the ghetto for planks for fuel, came to a cellar, with some rags along the wall. I shone a light and saw a woman inside. She came out into the light with me, and I helped her up the rotten stairs. We set off along the road by which so many people had already escaped.

" 'Halt,' says he in a dry voice.

" 'Who is it?'

" 'Ciszka. Why do you say "Halt" when you know Polish? A few dollars, if she had any, or a brooch. She shows her fingers crushed.

" 'You with rats? What? Were you fighting?'

" 'No, I was not fighting.'

" 'Get out of there.' It's known, a few dollars or not. Even so, it equals death, for I never saw that woman anymore. Until today they called me to the gendarmerie. One says,

" 'Are you scared of us?'

" 'Why?'

" 'Because you have such a scared look,' he insisted. 'Are you scared?'

" 'Sure,' I said, and he laughs.

" 'Listen, old man, you know Bernstein's secret hiding place?'

" 'Where?'

" 'In the foundations of the temple. It's a matter of demolition. Trojhender is to demolish it tomorrow. The rock will go for bunkers, because things have gone badly at the front.' Then they brought in some man or other.

" 'You know him? Is this Bernstein?'

"Then this old gendarme whistled; once loudly, then more quietly, and their officer's servant, Kaliko, came in.

" 'Is that him?'

" '*Jawohl!*' Both frowned. 'You can go.' "

"Was it really Bernstein?" asked Ksawera.

"Difficult to tell. Beaten, livid, unshaven — try to recognize him. Bernstein was tall, and that man was short, in a tight jacket. There was no opportunity to look him in the eye. That officer's servant kicked him. It is sad to be a man and not understand life. A few dollars, a diamond, and accursed poverty for a time."

"When shall we do the business?" I ask Trypka.

"Right now. I need the money. My life is hard."

"That's understandable, only today I don't have the money."

"Then it was a waste of time to talk such twaddle for so long."

"I'll bring it tomorrow. Miss Ksawera will guarantee that."

"So people say. A man turns his back, and that's the last one sees of him. You look out the window, look to the gate. Even if I wanted, I'd have to dig it up. Go out of town. People are happy to sell. Money is useful. Now they are bringing cows by train from Russia. They can be bought from the stationmaster for dollars. There would be something to get cream from, a man isn't alone. I don't know what your business is, but nowadays it's something for something."

"How shall we settle it?"

"I have said my piece. For the time being the rifle is in the ground, the dollars someplace . . .".

"In the forest."

"Oh!"

"Can I ask a question?"

"One?"

"Yes."

"Very well."

"If the gendarmes ask what happened this night in Miss Ksawera's house . . . ?"

"What will they ask, when nothing happened?"

"Do you have money, miss?"

"Yes."

"Please pay him . . ." I jogged Ksawera's elbow. She understood. She went into the depths. The door of the closet squeaked.

"No, no. I won't take the money until I bring the rifle."

"That's fine," I say. "Miss Ksawera will have the dollars. The rifle must be dug up tomorrow; in the evening someone will come for it."

"Sure, that's understood."

I brushed off the wretched uneasiness, my exhaustion left. I lit a cigarette; it was three on the alarm clock. A new day was approaching. I'd survived, and would see my own people again.

"That's fine," I repeated, and decided not to speak any more. " 'Nothing purifies a man of dirt as silence does,' my mother always used to say." A man must think and act. I drew the curtain back. It was dark; there were stars in the sky, but in two hours it would be day.

Trypka rose and both of us were silent. Ksawera rustled papers.

"I am leaving now," whispered Trypka.

"Thank you, sir," said Ksawera, with concern in her voice.

"What for? No reason to. I myself wanted to come and say . . . this and that. There's a rifle, it's possible to sell it. Now one should ask: to whom is it being sold, for what? The terrible hour will come when everything is straightened out, then someone will laugh in my face, spit, and throw me out. The hour of judgment is upon me, as though this rifle were to kill people."

"What has suddenly come into your head?" says Ksawera.

"Everything comes suddenly. A man whistles, seeks, looks, sniffs, walks around, instead of taking a close look, under his own feet. You're young, what's it to you? I am old, I am already departing from this world, so it is necessary to consider how to depart. I will go back to my apartment, I will sit and think, for whose death will I dig up this rifle? And I will not stir out of the house until it stands clearly before my eyes."

"Don't tire your heart with this."

"Well, it is a terrible hour, when one thinks thus of everything."

"Killing people never amused anybody. It is no pleasure; it is despair that may force a man to it," says Ksawera.

"That's what one says, but one does it one's own way. There are those who live by it. They kill, and they live by that."

"One doesn't kill by a rifle alone. It is possible to do it by word, and still more terribly."

In a flash Ksawera's room filled with troubles, stupefied by the weariness of thoughts, the head strained with hatred; two steps from the door, take the old man out and kill him; drag him over the threshold, under the fence, and go back to one's own people before the dark of night lightened. Huddled to the window, I did not let my eyes leave the flashes of a searchlight in the sky; three rays joined into a mass, they shifted westwards.

My ears caught the closest rustle behind me.

"Yes, it was Leit. There's no doubt it was him. I was standing two yards from him. He had not even changed much," said Trypka. "Just the same as when I saw him out for a walk with the children, before harvest time. One little girl brought him a daisy, he sniffed it, and sighed deeply. Then they looked at a rainbow which stood over Trojnoga. Warm rain fell, and the children jumped over ditches, and with so much impetus you'd think straw were lying there on the highway. I was pasturing my daughter-in-law's cow. One remembers it all, because it was a few weeks before Hitler's bombs."

"Well, and what about it, that one remembers?"

"Sure. When one remembers everything, then one feels bad."

"Did Leit say anything?"

"Nothing, nothing, nothing. Rapidly. They asked, 'Bernstein?' Before I could rack my brains, the second man comes in: 'Bernstein? Fine, take him out.' The door opened, someone seized Leit by the hair, and threw him to the ground. They brought in a peasant smeared with clay. This man took a revolver, stuck it in his face, which was bleeding. And he gave it to him some ten times. He beat him without a pause, on and on. 'Sapiska! Sapiska!' he shouts. Oh, God, be merciful to the people. He threatened me and gazed at me like death at the final hour. The peasant was strong; he stood where he was and grabbed his head. They took him away. The end of everything. Sapiska! They took me: 'You will show us the temple.' So I did. The stone can be seen, under which are steps into a cellar. Nothing to get it up with. To the carpenter who has everything. The son is turning a bevel, the father working a chisel. They took two levers and kicked the son on the way. At once they got down to work. Downwards with candles. The officer's servant comes and says Soviet prisoners have escaped, twenty men, three killed. They closed the heavy lid of the cellar. In the evening, the foreman shouted to Ciszka, 'Shirker! The prisoners have escaped, you're scared already! You think the police and other such things are already superfluous.' They ordered me to go home. I set off, and now everything is staring me in the face."

"An unpleasant business."

"It's good that you understand me a little, miss. In the evening my younger brother came and hit me; he kicked me all over like a bitch. As if some insanity had seized him. What is it, man. 'Shut up, shut up, shut up,' he says through his teeth, 'and run, for I will shoot you.' It is shameful when your brother hits you. Someone had said too much. Then I recall that I have to sell the rifle, because my brother knew everything. There may be trouble."

"Maybe you're mistaken?"

"Would to God I were. But . . ."

"Will you come for the rifle yourself?"

"Yes."

"That means — see you in the evening."

He went out, coughed in the hallway, and blew his nose loudly.

"You trust the first comer who strokes your sleeve, miss."

"I'd like to see you in my position. You might have a little respect for my sufferings."

But I was knocked off my feet by weariness; I felt like a deaf horse. I took my boots off, unwrapped the foot-clouts.

"Miss, you'll see a lot of the world before you know people well."

"What of it? I will make you tea before your journey. Yes, it's true all the same . . . when joy is taken from a person, the earth becomes a cemetery."

"Please have hope at least."

"That much is left."

Ksawera lit the primus. Now, in the glow, her figure could be seen, narrow in the waist, with full breasts; one braid of hair quivered down her back.

"You'll be a little surprised by what I'm going to say, miss."

"You have persuaded yourself of something."

"I don't like that old man. Any further — you'll go into their abyss. Has Trypka lived here long?"

"He moved in after the death of Dreifus. In October."

"He made friends."

"After a few days he came and declared that if I needed help, chopping wood or anything, he'd be glad to oblige. He keeps an eye on the apartment whenever I go any place on business. I at once appreciated that there was nothing hidden about him, I wouldn't have to reproach him. But here, meanwhile, the last hope has gone."

"Does he know Leit is a dear person to you?"

"I didn't confide in him. There was not a word on the subject."

Ksawera leaned over the sofa, brought out a small bundle from under the roll on the pediment, and handed it to me:

"These are the letters of Chaim's wife. Please take them to him."

And suddenly, as though feeling a pain.

"Oh, no . . ."

"Sure," I say. "You are tired."

Ksawera shivered, her mouth opened as though she wanted to smile, and she fell down, breathing heavily; she groaned in a voice of fearful pain. I struck her in the face, as one strikes a person who has fainted, as Chaim often struck Cirla.

"Dear God, what happened?" Ksawera whispered.

I reached for the water bucket and sprinkled her brow.

"Miss Ksawera," I said, "we all love you. Please calm yourself. I'm leaving now. Please rest, open the window a little, you need fresh air. You mustn't break down!"

"Yes, but I feel that energy is pouring out of me in an ever thinner stream. I am tired . . . exhausted, barely alive."

"Please calm yourself, it will be better. Someone will come this evening, either Horse-face or me."

I took her cold hand and pressed it; I set out. I stopped a moment on the threshold, nothing but silence. From the distance was to be heard the stifled rumbling of a locomotive. The sky was still full of stars, the air frosty and calm. The alleys were in darkness; only the rooftops glistened with hoarfrost. Not for a long time had I seen the sky over Szabasowa, but I remember what those nights were like — the blue went into infinity.

The window opens, and Ksawera's face appears:

"Till we meet again," she whispers to me.

I at once turned into the ghetto area. Already there was nothing there, a few blackened chimney stacks still rise, but there are no yards, fences, walls. Nothing moves, everything is dead or turned to stone, scattered with snow. Here and there are blackened cellars.

Paths cross, but not one of them leads home, to a garden, a girl, a school, or a window from which a loving greeting would wave. Further on, several little empty houses are still standing, with the overturned stables of droshky horses.

No, not that way. I had got lost. The cold shook me. I walked slowly, listened, looked around. I was looking for our house; maybe it wasn't true that they tore our house down. A white house with red windows. I was thinking calmly, without bitterness. Never, anywhere will there ever be a prettier little house, a more beautifully blossoming garden, nor such flowers in the window, nor that rustling sunny field immediately beyond the garden. I heard a song that had already died; everything went after the song. I saw the hallway, ax, yard, and the dead body of Josie Propst, who had nodded his head a moment before his suicide as though he'd suddenly seen the whole truth through the open door to his grandson's empty cradle. 'Where are you going?' Knopf asked me, looking at the ground. There is no road anyplace. All her life my mother never dared go far; she only knew her own neighborhood. Sometimes she went out to the tollgate and looked at the fields: there, in the wind, the corn waved, the fields stretched to the hills; they gleamed with gold, died out into green. Suddenly there was a shriek in the streets of Szabasowa, the strange and hitherto unheard voice of a murdered child. Here, where the school was, stands only a widely arched hallway; the entire yard can be seen empty, dark, with a heap of barbed wire, a high wall with bullet holes in it. All the doors are wide open, the windows blind and black. People, children — all had sunk into the earth; nobody mourns for many.

The road beyond the ghetto widens, flies downwards, and turns to the tracks by which ammunition rolls to the east day and night.

Behind me, in the darkness, is drowned Szabasowa. The smell of
the distance wafted in my face, to the right and left the sawmill
buildings, three high chimneys, corridors of planks — no people.
Open fields beyond the factory. I quickened my pace, ran across
frozen lumps of earth hardly hidden by the snow. I wiped the
sweat off my face; when I looked back, my town was no longer to
be seen. I told myself at once that the road was a long one, and it
was necessary to be ready for anything. It was still night; the stars
still trembled in the sky, and there were so many of them that I
staggered, looking at the sparkling heights.

And everywhere my mother was greeting me with memories.
The pain penetrated into my heart.

"Where have you been? It's already dawn outside."

"It was a fine evening. We had a talk," I said.

"Fine evening," my mother repeats; she spoke slowly. I did not
hear all the words. I leaned over — face touched face.

"Nowhere salvation, nowhere rest, not a quart of water, not
even a calm prayer," my mother whispers. "People are eating
bread and lard, apples. If only I wanted to, it would be the end of
my hunger. If it were not for the little birds — it would be worth
spitting at heaven itself." My mother hated God, she could not
forgive Him for once having besought His aid all night, and in
vain. Afterwards she wept, for she believed that such an injustice
will not be erased in this or the next world; it will remain to the
end of the world . . .

I set out by a short cut in the direction of Pasieki, then took a
field path to the Deberki hill. A blue dawn was coming. When I
was on the shoulder of the hill, I heard shots behind me.

In the valley, small shapes were to be seen running out of the
wooded cemetery into the fields. Everything was white; the sky
was white, and the fields almost blue. Only the crosses stood out
naked and black among the gray birches. A woman with several
children was running across the fields; she was already far beyond
the fence when she swayed, dragging her feet and the children
through the snow. A kerchief dragged after her. It seemed to me I
heard a person shout, crying in fear, that I could see before me the
great eyes of a child round with deathly terror.

I shouted once and then again: "Hooop! Hoop!" The echo carried to the forest. My mouth was open, and I heard my own voice
again.

After the gendarmes had jumped across the fence, they stopped and looked in my direction; one raised his elbow, evidently watching me through field glasses. I shook an empty fist at them. There were five of them. The woman and children were still running; three ran after them; they raised their rifles. Then I drew out Chaim's revolver and rushed in the direction of the fleeing people. The forest was not far off. My hand trembled; the butt was damp with sweat. There was a whistling around my ears, they were firing. I was already near. If only to God I hadn't done it. The children caught sight of me, they shrieked, and the whole crowd turned to the left. Piles of manure were standing in rows as far as the forest. I squatted and fired in the direction of the cemetery. Crouching, hiding behind the heaps, I ran into the undergrowth of the forest clearing. My eyes sought a hiding place. I looked around; the gendarmes were standing in the field, one waving a hand. Those two from near the cemetery moved forward, taking long paces.

And I'm on my way. Everything here in the forest like always: snow, rabbit tracks. The easiest time to catch animals is winter, across damp, new-fallen snow, on which tracks remain like seals. Szerucki says it is possible to tell from an animal's tracks not only its species, but even its sex, size, weight, and age: it is also possible to tell whether a bitch is pregnant. It is not allowed, for anything in the world, to fire at females in rut or at ducks in spring, when they haven't yet brought up their little ones, or at harmless and sick creatures, at a hare in the moonlight, or at animals driven by beaters, exhausted by long-lasting snow.

I stopped to hear whether they were following in my tracks. It was quiet; somewhere far off cocks crowed. Despair began to seize me; I felt shut in my own weary body. Snow came up to my knees, I warmed myself, I undid my jacket. The thought came to me that they would follow me, mount their horses, and catch up. Where to hide? My tracks are to be seen, here and there rabbit tracks, and here behind me livid and deep holes. Everything becomes excessive, the forest extends like an endless echo, is deaf. Such experiences have no meaning for a man, for they neither pain nor teach him. There is no advantage from such terror. As with memories, they remind a man of sad experiences, and that is all. What it was, where it was — the new picture is inaccurate, like a dream, not alive. But here it is necessary to walk on without a single word of encouragement. I was only scared that something might knock me unexpectedly off my feet, for I would lose my senses and maybe be humiliated. I tell myself that a man has his own measure, according to his character and strength. The heart knocks, the understanding hears.

The forest suddenly gave way, the high trees ended, and I recognized the slopes of Trojnoga. Five miles to Zalaski. The sky became gray, the fresh snow over the fields whirled like an infamous nightmare. Alongside was a brushwood field edge. I walked down this edge, continually looking at the forest disappearing into the snowstorm. The panic of my heart eased.

Such uncontrolled terror seized me once when I was a child. I was alone at home, it was black in our great room, late dusk. I cuddled up into a corner near the kneading trough and looked at the stars winking outside the window. Then our neighbor, a friend of my father's, remembered me. He covered himself with a blanket, put a decayed stump in his mouth and gummed it over his brows. He knocked in the hallway, the door handle in the kitchen rattled. He took five steps in the dark, stopped over me, crossing his arms. He spat a blue ember over me. I fell to the ground along with the kneading trough, and he went home, whistling on the way. I did not sleep all night. I wanted to tell my father, but dared not, as he came home angry in the evening. "I shall be out of work from tomorrow," he says to my mother. It was sad to look at my father's face. He fell asleep toward morning, his brow wrinkled in his sleep, his lips tight. Tousled hair, sprinkled with flour, hands under chin, fingers livid and swollen as in a biting frost. "Don't wake him," said my mother, "as it is he won't be able to cope with all this." Heavy worry devoured him. He walked around a few more weeks with sunken cheeks, then died. The man who had frightened me came in, took off his cap, grimaced, and went to carry sacks. And in the evening he brought us a loaf of bread. To this day I resent that man. I did not want to exchange words with him, not even when still more terrible events began happening in Szabasowa. When the gendarmes and Mazeppa gang, with the calmness of great soldiers, led the children from the Jewish orphanage toward the Great Gate, the pavement almost thundered. Only the leader had contorted lips — he looked at the greenfinches fluttering on the wires by the steep road outside the town. Old women weeding the corn looked at this procession, and so did children, crossing their hands over their bellies. It was barely possible to fasten this picture to the rest: green summer, a roadside cross with Christ hanging on it, nailed on, with a wreath on its cracked forehead, larks in the blue, calm trees, a gendarme spitting black saliva, and a cloud of dust behind the people marching on the sand behind the Great Gate. Sweat came out on the foreheads of the children, it ran down their faces, down their chins, and they walked on without a word.

Far beyond the town, the road widens into an expansive ravine, and goes to a dirty local pasture; it is parceled out among thin fir trees, under which piles of trash have been heaped. Further on, the world suddenly was lowered to the sandworks, and there several women were crouched, covered by kerchiefs. They shrieked, but there was no wind to carry their shriek far. Maybe some cliff or tree woke up and heard. But there was nobody with rosary in hand, no one shouted out the names of saints.

The road is long, I cannot feel my feet. I am hungry and thirsty. I squeeze a lump of snow and throw it into my mouth. I recall all this. Will there be no end to it? As in a circle, at times someone said something to comfort, advised me to hold out until the merciful sun came. Only Chuny grew more stooped every day, his eyes popping out with exhaustion, but he only believed in his rifle. Without Szerucki he saw a great abyss before him, in the hardest moments he sought the hand of Horse-face.

And once more, already near the rectory, terror seized me at the thought they were coming on my tracks as after an animal. I began looking around. Nothing. Deserted. Thick, wet snow scattered over my tracks.

There was no change in the rectory yard: the trough under the snow, a gantry, the black opening to the stable. Only there was already no window, the empty frame was hanging obliquely. And no smoke was to be seen over the chimney. A straw mattress was lying in the hallway across the threshold. This is no fairy tale. Sometimes people think up various terrible tales, which are nowhere in the world. Banczycki was hanging in the hallway on a harness hook; on his arm was a silver and white tallith. Through the thickness of his formerly shaven chin angry stripes could be seen on his cheek. A cross expression, as if he were rushing blindly someplace. I leaned against the door frame. The straw mattress was bespattered with blood. The light went out in my eyes, there was no difference between night and day. I saw not a beam of light. Now it was really necessary to get my knife out and cut him down. I shudder at the thought. Something sad is falling, like a sheet of shame, like some disgrace; I should have seen it. I closed the door, but it opened again, slowly. It fell off its hinges, thundering like a coffin. I ran to find Chaim.

In the cemetery were footprints. A storm had dumped snow near the site of the Zalaski fire; here and there chimneys stuck up

black. I am walking and whistling the tune: "From a high mountain a youth comes down into the valley." Nothing but whiteness
around. Nobody speaks. I found the door handle. Three miles
journey to Mrs. Arbuz's cellar near Pasieki. I barely dragged myself there. Horse-face was standing behind a tree.

"Is that you, Heindl?"

"What happened there?"

"Where?"

"At the rectory."

"So you don't know anything?"

"How can I know, when I wasn't there," say I, and I look for a
place to sit.

"See what a decent guy I am?"

"Why?"

"I was waiting for you."

"Well, that's obvious. But where's Chaim?"

"He and Chuny went away in the night with that sick person.
We shall find them somewhere, never fear."

"Who told you to wait for me?"

"This girl from Sapiska. Don't sit down even for a moment,
you'll freeze. Let us go and look for Chaim, for something nasty is
going on around us."

"What?"

"Why should I scare you, man? Let's go to the cliff by
Trojnoga, you will give back what you brought to Chaim, we'll
talk. Then we'll set off after Szerucki. This must be cleared up."

"And who was the man who got burned in Sapiska?"

"Bernstein."

"Oh come off it. Bernstein. You don't know."

"Well, so what, I don't know."

"What?"

"I don't know," said Horse-face, and he glanced into my eyes.
He hoisted his rifle on, muzzle downwards.

"Maybe it was Flying-carpet?"

Horse-face stops, taps his forehead with one finger.

"Was it certainly Bernstein?"

"Why have you got the staggers like this?"

"Don't you have anything to eat, Horse-face?"

"They left so much to eat in the rectory. Were you still there
when Chuny brought it? Too bad, damn it . . ."

"Don't you have anything?"

"You want bread?"

"Anything," say I.

"Swallow some snow, if anything will do."

"Don't joke, Horse-face. I see your pockets are stuffed."

"You want bread?"

"Yes."

"Then pray to your God."

"I already did," say I.

Horse-face took a bundle out of his jacket pocket. I undid it. In the dark rag was quite a large piece of black bread.

"And the man who got burned, I tell you, was Bernstein. He was a bit of a blockhead, you'd have to go far before finding another like him."

"Why? He had his own sense."

"Sure, for himself alone."

As we were passing the burned-out gamekeeper's hut in which Tykies at one time made coffins, Horse-face crept into the ruin and surveyed every corner.

"What's there?" I asked.

"I thought maybe Szerucki burrowed in here someplace and was dying. In this rubbish it's possible to sit through more than one night in case of anything."

"I'd like to sit here, rest a little."

"No, man. Keep on, let's go. Chuny is wounded, the little boy sick again. What do you think?"

"Chuny wounded?"

"Don't you know anything of what happened? Where were you?"

"Didn't she tell you?"

"She forgot you went to Szabasowa with the women. They're searching for Gail. They're using dogs."

"And where were you at this time?"

"I and Kierasinski set off at night to the hut of Vitalisa. They were firing a machine gun until it rang."

"Who was?"

"Czaczkies and his men. Because there was a company of German police at Vitalisa's place. They might have grabbed Szerucki, what do you think?"

"They might . . . how should I know?"

"You're somehow depressed or else you don't believe me."

"What do you mean 'don't believe' you? I'm tired as a horse after spring labor, and I have somehow to get it all into my head."

"Sorry for you being so tired," says Horse-face; he thrust a hand into his pocket and brought out a flat but long crust of bread. "You, fit this bread into your belly."

"Thanks, you're a nice guy." I clap him in a friendly way on the arm.

"What of it that I'm a nice guy?"

"Manner of speaking. Surely you understand what I mean."

"Did you look for Chaim at the rectory?" asks Horse-face.

"I was in the hallway on the threshold and that was sufficient to find out about everything."

"You, go with your chattering where they can't get by without it. Speak simply. I would like to know what happened there afterwards, whether there really were gendarmes, like Dominka said."

"There were. Banczycki is hanging on a peg in the hallway."

"You're joking!?"

"No, I'm not. It's you, obviously, who doesn't know anything."

Horse-face stopped. He was black, unshaven. Three wrinkles quivered over his thin nose.

"What then?" he asks me.

"I don't know what came next. Isn't this enough for you?"

"Wait, you," Horse-face goes on. "I'm concerned about whether this girl was telling the truth. She told me that before midnight they had to run away, because someone came up, firing. The first dogs ran into the yard. Chaim and Shaya seized the straw mattress, but Dudi fell off on the threshold. There, some rubbish got in their way. They left the mattress. One of them took the sick boy on his back, but she doesn't know which. Chuny began limping. 'Why?' I ask. 'Because they were firing,' she says. They were thickest in the garden. It seemed there was no way out. They went back and hid in the stable, but a dog started to bark. The other ones at once ran into the rectory. Meanwhile Chuny overturned several planks on the stable floor. They jumped out into the cemetery and squatted there. 'They squatted down and what happened then?' I ask. So she says that Chaim ordered her to go away. I don't believe he told her that."

"Where was it you met her?"

"On the road, beyond Sapiska. She says the rectory was surrounded. 'Where are you going, Dominka?' I ask her. 'It's all the same to me, maybe some work will occur. What shall I do around you all; I get loused up and that's all.' 'Stay with us. We shall soon have a few dollars, and you'll gain too. As it is, where are you going? There are no Polish gentry left, and surely you won't work for a German.' 'Surely . . .' She stayed. She likes me. It's another matter that this girl needs shoes. In foot-clouts life is unpleasant, and there's no work."

"And where is she now?"

"I left her with Kierasinski in a hamlet near Pasieki. Let them wait for me until tomorrow. In case of need, the gathering point is near Trojnoga.

"You'll find out later if Dominka was telling the truth."

"From what moment will that 'later' be?" demanded Horse-face.

"When we meet some one of them."

"And if we don't meet anyone? You think that when we get to Trojnoga they'll certainly be there?"

I knew very well that Horse-face was sounding me out. He subjected everyone to just such a wearisome test. He also knew how to annoy most painfully.

"I believe they'll be there. You've a sharp nose," I tell him. "When I get there, I'm not going to move another step, I'm so tired."

Horse-face looked me deep in the eyes, shook his head. I also told him:

"We don't know where they are, and they don't know where we are, and so it will go in a circle now."

"What else did you see in the rectory?" Horse-face insisted.

"I was only on the threshold, in the hallway."

"That's too bad."

"What do you want to find out, Horse-face? You yourself were certainly there and saw everything."

"No. I looked through field glasses. The snow blurred it a little, but some people were to be seen walking in the yard, crowding around something. And then, about an hour later, I looked and there was nothing, nobody. Nobody came out on the road."

"They were surely looking for Gail."

"Maybe," says he indifferently, and suddenly loudly,

"Ahhhh . . . only that old hag came out from the yard. The one who hid Lula Heim."

"Aha . . ."

"She ought not to come in my direction."

"Why not?"

"The old hag didn't expect I would be her death."

"Why are you so agitated?"

"Is it obvious?" asks Horse-face.

"Sure. Horrible thing. She was a spy, that old hag . . ."

"I already regret doing as I did," said Horse-face, and waved a hand in front of his eyes as though lazy, biting flies were attacking him.

"Please . . . only don't say anything to Chaim."

"If it matters to you . . ."

"He wants a 'vote to be passed' on everything."

"Done, couldn't be better," I said. "Let it remain between us."

Horse-face leaned over, squeezed a handful of snow.

"Thirst," he said, and he walked on, rubbing his hands like a man who has completely lost patience.

"Today I saw them hunting children again." I said this deliberately, to introduce a new topic and draw him away from that other trouble. "Five gendarmes . . . they were chasing children. This can't go on."

"Surely not. And we're wandering around, one after the other."

"Don't you start. For the time being there was no weapon."

"It's known why there aren't arms," said Horse-face, with mild reproach. "It's known, there was one man, he had a diamond."

"You talk like the others."

"And the man with dollars too is walking around the forest."

"The old man earned them, now he has the right to defend himself with them."

"He's the first man who never shared anything. I already told Chaim that someone else will benefit from that money. And Flying-carpet fobbed me off, as if he'd closed a door in my face."

"Not an easy matter," I said. "Everyone defends what's his own. And you, Horse-face, defend your own, that will suffice. Is your mother still alive?"

"Yes, and what of it? Don't change the subject. Now I've joined you, I want to know what to do next. We wander around aimlessly, it can't be so any longer. It's a shame I didn't catch that old man and take the money for an urgent need. When we begin sniffing what stinks, and what doesn't, then I tell you, it's for the birds. That's how Banczycki came to his end. Oh! See, you have an example of botching."

"Well, Banczycki wasn't a botcher, you'll admit."

"He even asked mercy for Gail in that mild voice of his."

"That was his business. Consider it calmly. It's self-evident, and there's not much to be said about it. Nothing was left to the killers of Banczycki, or to the killers of Chuny's children; they'll not find anyplace where they can take refuge; there won't be a home for them anyplace. But we must still have a home. That's the point in all this business. You gave Chuny a hand in his distress, so take also and think with him over all this, what should be done, and what will never be repaid as long as you live. I'll tell you, a man must undertake his obligations sternly, else he will collapse."

"This means you don't realize it's blood for blood. To forgive

your enemy for all this, or what? Banczycki tried to wash mud
away with gold, Buchsbaum with a prayer."

"You're touching on matters that aren't your affair. Sit down in
the forest some time, and think of the road you've started out on,
where you want to get to. There's the road of murderers and the
road of truth."

"Well, wait, Heindl," says Horse-face, "and what if murderers
meet you on your road? Then what?"

"I'll defend myself. With whatever comes to hand, a stone, a
stick . . ."

"But let's say you have nothing, no stone, no stick. They've attacked you. 'Give me a moment,' you beg someone. He doesn't
want to. So who is he? An accomplice of the murderer."

"Not necessarily."

"Who then?"

"Some indifferent man or other. He'd advise you to start investigation, perhaps come forward as a witness, or to shut your eyes
for the time being, so as not to be involved. It's not possible to call
such a man honest, for an honest man helps everyone in need,
whoever happens along; he chases the guilty with you. Such is
duty."

Horse-face was silent, his mouth open, and he was looking at
Trojnoga hill.

The short winter day rapidly plunged into dusk, a snowstorm
moved in. As we walked, snuggling our necks into our damp col-
lars, we stumbled over lumps under the snow. Horse-face was
hunched up, as though his rifle weighed half a ton. He was silent,
and it was apparent that he was sad; maybe some sickness was de-
vouring him, or something was upset within him, with which he
didn't yet wish to come to terms. In any case he must also have
been loused up, for he raised his elbows and rubbed his loins. On
the march lice bite when the body is heated. They frolic from top
to toe. A man moves his arms, hits his shoulder blades, and gets
mad at no one.

I'd gladly have lain down in the snow and slept a few hours
through, so as finally to get rested, stop wandering around from
morning to night. No measure, no end. When I go back in
thought, it seems to me that I never was a child, never had
enough to eat or sleep.

It was difficult to guess from Horse-face's few words what was
depressing him. Some irresistible force was drawing him; he was
walking and I following him, no longer feeling my bones. And hatred permeated me toward everything, so there was no way to rip

it out of my chest. I looked around; behind us lay the track and danger for which there was no name. We walked on in silence — with us there came a voice that judged us without words.

It was already dark when we entered the cavern in the cliff. Chaim was there, also Chuny and some woman with a child swollen with poverty. A fire was burning behind some stone blocks; further was a pile of spruce branches, and on it the sick Dudi lay. In the glow could be seen handmill stones, thresholds, and crosses. Lying around underfoot were cudgels, washboards, poles of bark, steel wedges that rang underfoot on the solid rock. Chaim lowered his voice and covered his eyes with one hand when he heard that Banczycki was dead.

"He went out early and flew off someplace, no one knows where. It wasn't even possible to guess," he said slowly.

Chuny brought in a utensil full of snow, placed it on the fire.

"She said you were limping."

"I was limping, because I rushed out in one boot."

"What sort of woman was she?"

"Mrs. Bernstein, you might say."

Not until late evening did a conversation start on the subject of past events. It was necessary to fetch snow and let it melt into water in a little utensil so Chaim had something in which to prepare an injection. Only a drop of water from a lot of snow. And when it became necessary to wash his thigh before the injection, Dudi began struggling with us, would not be moved. He protested violently, so that everyone wondered what it meant. Then it was necessary yet again to melt snow to give the patient, who, after the injection, was lying collapsed and quiet, staring at something with glassy eyes.

When this ended, we all went out for wood. Snow was falling all the time, and the wind was roaring in the forest. We looked for a moment at a distant conflagration and carried wood to warm up the frosty cave. Mrs. Bernstein had sixteen potatoes in a bag, which she shared with us. We took off our boots, and standing close to the fire, dried the foot-clouts on our feet. Horse-face gave his bread to Mrs. Bernstein. Her child was soaked and cold. We advised Mrs. Bernstein to boil a piece of bread in water and feed the little one.

I still had two cigarettes from Ksawera.

"Light up," I said to Chaim. "I almost forgot. I got a whole pack from her."

"Did she tell you anything interesting?"

Chaim leaned over the fire; rocking the cigarette in his hand, he read the inscription. I gazed into his face, which suddenly this day became like the face of his late mother. Bony cheeks, a nose descending to his upper lip, a brow full of weariness, cut with wrinkles.

"She asked me to greet you. She praised you for your ingenuity."

"What ingenuity?"

"You changed your writing on the prescription. They know your writing in the pharmacy. They rooted in old . . ."

"Old what?"

"Prescriptions. Or maybe it was just a whim, or an undefined suspicion. She still has a little of your money. It's possible to buy the rifle you mentioned. The matter was settled, but with great reservations. Ksawera is storing your souvenirs."

"They are letters from the most recent times. Do you know if there's a photo of my mother there?"

"I didn't have it in my hand. It's a small package. She began saying something on the subject, but news came that Soviet prisoners had escaped. Twenty of them, three killed."

"What do you think of Ksawera?"

"Very well. Such a picture of trust and faith against an unbearable background. I teased her a little, then reproached myself for it all the way back. The cost of the rifle was to be twenty dollars. I agreed. I was to be there this evening. But there's nothing doing, because again things have happened . . . the escape of all of you, Banczycki's death."

"Yes. No one foresaw such a turn of events to the last moment. You surely saw him?" Chaim turned to Mrs. Bernstein.

"Yes."

"Where, in what place?"

"Behind the beehives."

"Was he alone?"

"No, he wasn't alone, he was walking with some hag, some old hag."

I turned my face away; Horse-face caught my glance and afterwards began furiously blowing into the lock of his rifle, as though goodness knows what had got into it.

Now I recall that never in my life did I meet an uglier woman. Banczycki hated her, feared her, always wondered uneasily what she really wanted from him.

During the course of a long hour Chaim besieged me with questions, but I replied rather inaccurately; I deliberately omitted the

Leit affair for the time being. I wanted to reveal to him this flaw on the next day. Then we considered the Lula Heim incident.

"It never entered my head that the old hag might be a spy."

"It's as I said," said Chaim. "It was easy to foresee."

Chaim declared that Lula's hiding place was sniffed out by the old woman.

"But to kill her for this little matter isn't right. All this may be just your guesses." Chaim tried to defend himself.

"Untrue, you. I don't agree with this."

"The question is simply one of investigating her movements. She mustn't be let out of sight."

Chuny shifted uneasily, coughed, and glanced at Horse-face.

"Too bad Szerucki isn't here, he'd tell you what experience this old woman has. And too, when I asked him whether he'd kill her, he said not on his life, for she's a witch. He begged me not even to suggest such thoughts to him. He advised me above all to cut off the hands of her patrons — the Hilfspolizei."

I went out of the cave with the intention of pulling down a litter of fir branches for myself — as if there weren't enough already. I had to sleep a little.

Horse-face came out after me.

"What are you going to do now?" he asked.

"Pull down a little of this to lie on and sleep," I said.

"Will you be talking about this old woman anymore?"

"Not on your life. If Chuny wants to go back to the subject, I'll shut his mouth for him. Let him think what he chooses."

"Fine. And don't blurt out that he got burned, not in Mrs. Bernstein's presence."

"Does it matter very much to you that no one should know of this incident with the old hag?"

"Yes, for it's a question of how one looks at it. Chaim doesn't like this, or does he?"

"It'll be explained. And why are you so uneasy? Cheer up, man."

"Well . . ." said Horse-face, "not too much. But in any case, let it be a good deed for you in the end. Who knows whether I won't take off from your group for good."

"Why?"

"I don't like it all put together."

Horse-face was silent, waiting for a reply, but I had no desire to add any thoughts.

"As you think best," I stammered.

"If things go any further like this, before you can see, they'll slaughter us all. As things are bad with all of you now, they can't be worse."

"What have you in mind?"

"Everything put together."

"Then oughtn't you to speed up your flight from us?"

"You'll regret what you said. I'm leaving at dawn, and you're coming with me."

He said it with so much conviction that it was as if I'd no choice.

"Where shall we go?" I asked him.

"To Czaczkies' group."

"You know where they are?"

"Yes. I've even come to an agreement with them in the matter of rescuing Leit."

"Sure . . . It's worth considering. This is something different. I thought you had some other plan. Will you say the same to Chuny?"

"He already knows about this."

"And what, does he agree?"

"Yes. He doesn't like walking around all the time either."

"I don't understand a word of this now," I said, struggling with a heap of branches. "I don't understand who you want to run away from."

"From Chaim."

"You're surely trying to sound me out. What for, tell me clearly?"

But he did not answer, he walked slowly in the direction of the cave illuminated by the campfire. I'd cut down too many branches. There was no way of carrying them all, and I had to leave a part behind.

I lay down and covered my eyes with my sleeve so as not to see the terrible life of Mrs. Bernstein's child. I dug myself deeply into comfortless thoughts. Chaim was shuffling around my feet. I heard him say to Chuny,

"And now come to an agreement, the three of you. Banczycki must be buried. When you come back, don't forget to bring the ax, it will be very useful. Don't warm him too much at the fire, madam . . . it's not healthy."

Chuny and Horse-face went out of the cave at a brisk pace. My hair stood on end. What had they thought up now?

They continually have eyes that gaze somberly, that hide something in the depths. Maybe it's an unsatisfied longing for home. Something there gleams in their heads and at once expires. "Let me into the house . . . I didn't do anything wrong to anybody. Let me in," Tonka once begged, but he pushed her so that she staggered against the wall. I recalled that maybe Szerucki had again had some vision of Tonka. But they'd already trampled her into the dust. A large group of children gathered around Klara and are looking at her with contempt, for she was loused up. Everything is going home, without looking around, not asking anybody about anything — let's go home. And not just any place. You come to your own street, your own yard, your own hallway, across the threshold into the room. "We're home," said my mother . . .

Something clinked near my head. Horse-face leaned over me and said in a whisper,

"Get up Heindl, it will soon be dawn."

I set off with them on the journey, for so I'd decided in my bitterness. We left Chaim behind, also the cave smelling of fir and fire, which juggled with our shadows on the gleaming walls.

"When are you all coming back?" Chaim asked.

"That remains to be seen. In any case we'll send you food by Dominka," said Chuny.

Chaim rose and looked at me, and when I gave him back his revolver, he laughed loudly. My friendship for him was too deeply rooted to let it be veiled by anything. There was no reason to hide in myself everything that he deserved, no one would unlearn me that, or refuse.

"Yes," he said, "give me the revolver back."

He looked me straight in the eyes and shook his head.

Ah, to come back happily and just explain everything to him.

"Well, and now," said Horse-face, "look after yourself." He gave him his huge hand and sighed deeply; it was easy to guess he was moved.

Only Chuny didn't say a word; slinging a rifle around his neck, he raised a hand to his brow. We went out into the forest, and turned left into the depths, in order to cover up our tracks. We walked in silence, keeping close to one another. Horse-face was holding his rifle, looking at the ground, swaying steadily as though beating time to some song composed by himself. High lofty trees, shadows under them, and not a voice anywhere. We didn't look around, or ask one another anything. The journey was interminable, constantly white with shadows. It wound uphill, sank into a valley. We got warm, but famine bothered us.

While walking, I thought of Chaim; it seemed to me I'd done him an injustice, and this injustice, like a sin against a person I loved, would not be absolved now or ever. It cannot be erased, it will remain forever. I comfort myself with a good thought, but comfort is a lie. When a man looks into the night, he confesses to himself, and until the final hour he cannot forgive anything that was a sin against the people he loved. My step changed, my loused-up clothing weighed like a rock.

"Why are you dragging behind? Keep up!" said Horse-face.

By force I led my thoughts to something pleasant, to a pile of disconnected recollections, as long as they were bright, and didn't fall in depression on the snow.

"Is she still young?" asks Horse-face.

"Who? What's come into your mind?"

"Leit's girl."

"Sure," I say, reluctantly.

"He let himself be caught, there's an idiot for you."

"If he was wounded, what do you think?"

"Don't you believe what Dudi says. What does he know? I am so ashamed I could swear. The worst is that he'll think we deserted him because he didn't agree to slaughter the old man for his dollars."

"Oh, get away," said Chuny in a bad-tempered voice.

"Well, let's comfort ourselves, though it makes my heart ache."

"Is it true he's stuck in the Hilfspolizei guardhouse?" I asked.

"Sure it's true. He was in Szabasowa, but now they've brought him here; they expect to exchange him for Gail."

"Who said that?" Chuny turned.

"It's what someone told Dominka."

"It's fairy tales. We shan't see his face again," says Chuny.

"Well, that remains to be seen. Tomorrow everything will be explained. One thing could have helped us. Oh, if only Czaczkies had given us a grenade. And we'd have squatted down there, God knows what would have happened."

"Whatever it was, don't you squeak a word to Chaim," says Chuny to me rapidly. "Well, for when he begins to dwell on what's possible and what isn't, then we'll never shake off his protection. Then again, it's hard to stop in an open field and shout at the devil what is happening around."

"No one wants to shout," say I, "but it's possible to consider what will pay off, and what won't. Chaim is often right. Sometimes something is done, but then it's regretted."

"Don't you say anything, he's right," said Chuny brusquely. "Sit quiet you, and don't gabble."

Horse-face turned back, looked at me, and stopped to draw

breath, for when we came out of the forest the wind burned our faces. I held one hand in front of my mouth, but that didn't help. Words were torn away, my windpipe swelled, my fingers turned to bone.

"What?" Chuny shouted. "What?"

"That way!" crouching, Horse-face pointed to the right. That portion of the sky was yellowish — it was the East. Small gray clouds, close together, were flying in our direction. It was becoming day. Thus we plunged into a shortcut in the direction of the rectory. The wind blew through and through us.

We stopped behind undergrowth. Horse-face brought field glasses out of an inner pocket, placed them to his face, sniffing very slightly. I opened my eyes wide, trembling with the cold. I saw how it was there. Over the roofs the trees leaned, a path of dust wound behind the stable.

"You, take a look," said Horse-face to Chuny, "some woman has come out of the yard over there. Now she's behind . . . Take them, look, my hands are frozen. Well?"

"Yes," Chuny left his lips apart, chose his words, "she lifted something."

"What was there?"

"Want to see?"

"What did she lift?"

Chuny's eyes must have observed something, for he said:

"Goddamn it!"

"Why don't you want to say anymore?"

"It would be a good thing to catch her up."

"Why?"

"She carried rags from Banczycki."

Horse-face smacked his lips.

"It's surely that old hag," Chuny added.

"What are you saying?"

"Take these, look. She's already on the other side, beyond the shrine."

"She ought to have her life shortened, once and for all."

Chuny handed him the field glasses, but Horse-face stowed them away again in his jacket, and at the time when Chuny was saying, "Sure, there's no need even to think it over," he looked into my eyes, and I saw something very strange in his eyes, something pleasant in any case.

We stopped in the yard, Horse-face took his rifle under his arm, the gate slammed softly behind us. We looked a moment at the building, as though a specter were walking behind the smashed-out windows. The door was lying in front of the threshold, with frozen straw on it like lace. Yellowhammers were pecking by the wall.

"It can't be helped, we've got to take a look," said Chuny.

The silence in the hallway was such that when birds fluttered out, we crouched. Straw rustled underfoot, tipped out of a mattress by someone. We looked at Banczycki's worn boots. In the kitchen was an empty pickle barrel, overturned. It had never been this way before, but our eyes did not blink for a moment — a pile of garbage ransacked to the bottom. Only one terrible lousy shirt of Dudi's was lying on the kitchen table. We walked about the rooms, to and fro, looking fearfully through the windows. Among the gathered twigs around the stove lay a sliced loaf of bread, rotten through and through. Something smiled sweetly to us inside, it wasn't possible to prevent saliva from coming into our mouths, when Chuny divided the bread into four pieces.

Sitting down by the wall in Banczycki's bedroom, we gnawed the cold lumps of dry bread, the saliva trickling as though poison were leaking into a tooth. A draft whistled in the chimney, the door on the veranda rattled with an insistent knocking.

Horse-face went to the stable to look for the ax, and came back. "Nothing there. Not even a pickax to be seen."

We sought high and low, but there was no ax or spade anywhere, nothing with which it might have been possible to break the frozen ground.

"So how to bury him?" said Horse-face, and he went into the hallway, Chuny after him.

I stood in the gate to watch the road, lest anyone came.

They carried him in back of the stable. They came back a half hour later, snow-covered, their sleeves soaked. We went into the kitchen again, and lit the stove. It was necessary to warm up a little and heat bread over the flame, after wiping it first with snow. Chuny was coughing, he leaned his hands on his knees, and his body shuddered, as though someone were striking him hard on the shoulders.

"You must wrap up your feet," said Horse-face, "else this weather will knock you down."

And, pointing at me, he said,

"Heindl, in the attic there's an old mattress, rip that mattress up, rip it up. We'll make a supply of foot-clouts."

I brought the striped rags from the attic; they had reddish stains from nails.

"This will be a delight for our feet now," said Horse-face, scraping away the scabs between his toes, his smile remaining on his face.

"Well, what now?" asked Chuny, when we had all got our boots on.

"Let's bid farewell to the rectory, once and for all. What do you think?"

"How shall we bid farewell to the rectory, Chuny?"

"What's there to consider? We'll go our way, where we must."

And we went away, once more replacing the door on its hinges. But Horse-face, in the gate, fired into the sky until our ears rang; the forest near Pasieki replied twice: bang, bang.

"Let's take Kierasinski with us, and Dominka will go back to Chaim," said Horse-face, and he pointed: "There, in the rear, beyond that forest, we'll meet this evening with Czaczkies."

"Do you know him well?"

"Why not, before the war I had various troubles with him. Once I was hungry and thirsty, and it so happened I had to stretch out my hand in need. You know how it is. Sometimes a man lies like a rock in the street and is no use to anybody. But someone puts out a hand, and that's remembered."

Around two or three in the afternoon we came to a hamlet beyond Pasieki. We crept from the fields into a cramped room, maybe two yards wide. An old peasant, with his nose stopped up, was burning grain on a tabletop. Smoke veiled the little window by which Kierasinski was sewing on the ripped buckle of his boot. Dominka was sleeping on the stove, and some girl was leaning over the table, combing lice onto a piece of paper.

"God bless," said Horse-face; he put one hand on the old man's shoulder.

"Dear Jesus, he, he, how many more of you will get into the hut," said the old man, with a whistling between his teeth.

We stood on the threshold as at a wedding feast. Our eyes met those of the girl; in mortal terror, she quickly estimated us, seized the table as though she were about to slip over. Kierasinski spat the shoemaker's thread out of his mouth and clapped Horse-face on the back of the neck. The joke didn't please; Kierasinski got pushed, hit the wall with his shoulders, and sat down again in his former place without a word. Horse-face didn't move his eyes from the girl. Her face was small and pale, with two tranquil eyes looking out of it. She cast back her thick, flaxen hair. I saw something shiver and glisten around her lips, her dark brows went up. I looked at her feet, which were wrapped in rags. She glanced at me; her hands trembled, and she lowered her head a little. We went by her, sat down on the bench. She didn't stir. A pretty, tall girl.

"Add some water, so there will be enough coffee for us all," said Horse-face to the old man.

Dominka rose, letting her feet off the stove.

"Well now, how was it for you waiting for me?"

"But you all were a long time someplace."

"Sure," he said, "nothing goes easy today," he stroked her cheek that was red as though from fire.

Chuny spoke to the stranger girl in Yiddish. Every now and then one of us went out to the threshold to listen and watch. A little lower than us three more huts of the hamlet were standing. All three were closed, windows fastened, without a footstep on the snowy thresholds. By a decline on the riverbank stood a thatched laundry, with a footbridge further on. Immediately behind the huts was a broad field road, set with little trees, turned into the forest, which covered the view to Pasieki.

A dog, hanging its head, sniffed the foundations of the empty stable, and a crow rose and came down in time to the dog's barking.

I felt a powerful thirst. My tongue felt like dry leather. Meanwhile, far to the left, where some solitary hut was standing, a rider appeared, moving gradually in our direction. There the ground declined, for the rider disappeared from sight for a moment.

"You, come here," I beckoned to Horse-face.

"Look," I say to him, "look there, straight over the chimney of this first hut."

He drew back to the little hallway, fixed his field glasses, and called Chuny.

"One man?"

"So far."

"He's going to the forest. He'll make a turn there. Look, Chuny, isn't he to be seen?"

"Yes, he went into the forest. That's all that can be said for now . . . we'll see."

"What girl is that?" asked Horse-face.

"A friend of Lula Heim's. She was at Czaczkies' place."

"Pretty, too bad she hasn't any shoes."

"Come on, we'll talk."

We crept back into the room. The fire was roaring in the stove. We took our jackets off. The old man quenched the burned barley with a little flask. Horse-face didn't take his eyes off this girl.

"She doesn't speak Polish?"

"Only a few words. She speaks German or Yiddish."

"Well, you, Chuny, talk to her, ask whether Arnold is in Czaczkies' group. Because Heindl says that Ksawera was asking about him."

And Chuny began jabbering with her.

"Well, grandfather, what do your children write from Germany? Are they bombing? Move over, Kierasinski. You've been sitting long enough, and Heindl here, his guts are bleeding from the march. They took away all this old man's children to work in Germany," says Horse-face. "Whenever I'm here, the old man pampers me with food. For him eating is an urgent business."

Dominka went into the hallway for wood. The coffee was boiling; she tossed four saccharine tablets into the pot, and poured out a little mug of this beast's blood for each of us. And thus, sitting silently, we sipped it with relish, sipped the desired warmth. After thinking a moment the old man cut six slices of bread, each exactly like a sole.

"God be thanked," laughed Horse-face.

"Chuny, how long has she been at Czaczkies'?"

"You know what she says?"

"Well?"

"She says they caught Leit. This is true. Czaczkies has definite information. She says they had good food for a few days, because Czaczkies took a bull from the Liegenschaft in Pasieki."

"That's praiseworthy, sure — But what's she doing in this hut?"

Chuny wanted to say something, but he waved a hand; it was possible to discern from his expression that it was permissible, but not in front of everybody and not today. Chuny was always like this; he had taste.

This girl confided her troubles: it seemed to her, poor creature, that when she told someone everything, then it would at once lighten her terrible narrative.

"Is she pregnant?" asked Horse-face, softly.

"Yes, but don't look at her, for she'll know at once that I told you."

"It was surely just the same when Lula was wretched, may revenge burn him up! Do you think Chaim will be able to do anything?"

"She just came out to look for Chaim. They told her he's at the rectory. Czaczkies surely doesn't know what happened."

"This girl, surely . . ."

The girl's lips began trembling, and tears appeared in her eyes;

she sat down behind Chuny, covering her face in her hands. Her small breasts could be seen through holes in her ragged sweater.

"You, Kierasinski, go out and see if that gendarme came out of the forest. In general, see what's happening. You sit like a bull with protruding eyes. Dominka, see where she's got to, maybe she was taken ill."

Kierasinski went out, and walked behind the hut. And Chuny began telling us what terrible things this girl lived through with the bandits of the Hilfspolizei. Suddenly Kierasinski's footsteps thudded in the hallway, and almost simultaneously, an automatic banged once and again.

"It's near the forest," Kierosinski yelled. "A raiding party has gone into the forest."

Horse-face ran out, dragging the butt after him over the muddy threshold. Four men were going in single file to the wood; two horsemen stood opposite the duct. Numerous and ever-increasing shots thundered about the forest.

"Who's making the raid?" Chuny asked Horse-face.

"Hilfspolizei; and those two are gendarmes."

"Well, let me go, I want to see it."

There in the rear, under the high cliff, people were struggling and falling in the snow. It was a most interesting spectacle of a raid on people in winter time, for almost all the forest lay before us in the valley, and it was possible to count the chasers, who, digging in the snow, surrounded those by the cliff.

Chuny glanced at us very strangely, and said,

"Well, now it's us to work." He seized his cap, felt his pocket. Kierasinski came into the hut, looking through the old man's box; under the cigarette ends was bread and a stout piece of bacon.

"Don't get angry, little uncle. I am taking this for a hungry man."

"But why?" the old man defended himself; "are you all Communists or some other plague?"

"Better not ask. In the hallway, I saw, is grain in a sack, grind it for yourself in a handmill. You'll get by somehow, the main thing is that there's grain. You'd give your guts a rest."

"You, Kierasinski, and Dominka," says Chuny, "you'll go to Chaim with this bread."

"But this girl?"

"Let her stay here, we'll look after her."

Chuny whispered something to the foreign girl.

"Do as we order you!" Horse-face shouted at Kierasinski.

"Where to?"

"To Trojnoga, understand? And take care, it's warm there."
Kierasinski carried out the order. Dominka dragged after him
without even looking back.

"I'm not doing you any injustice, Dominka. Tomorrow you'll
have shoes, even if I don't know how," Horse-face shouted after
her.

Chuny went out first and led us in the direction of the road to
Pasieki.

"Go carefully, you're reckless. It's necessary to look around
well, because they can shoot you and that would be no use," said
Horse-face, and he began to get agitated; his rifle dragged its barrel in the snow twice.

Meanwile, the hunting of people went on in the forest, bullets
splashed, whistling boldly. By leaping from tree to tree, or crawl-
ing, we approached to within three hundred yards of the gendarmes standing around the forest tollhouse. Magpies rustled in
the vicinity. Horse-face glanced at them furiously.

Chuny jumped rapidly; his lean, tall figure fastened itself to a
snowy tree stump. From the moment I took Horse-face's revolver
into my hand (it was an old Schtajer), I was ever more uneasy. I
hesitated whether to delay and check if it was loaded; each touch
of the rusty muzzle scorched with coldness like living fire, the frost
scorched my sweaty hand.

Chuny, standing behind a tree, jumped up and down. He gave
a signal to us with one hand. Agitation shook Horse-face; he
moved his head, rubbed his right hand. We were lying ten paces
behind Chuny. Shots were firing closer, more often, more clearly.
The sky beyond the forest was darkening deeply. Bending his
neck, Chuny lifted his rifle, placed the butt to his shoulder with
elbow raised; a shot rang out. It sounded as though someone were
flying at a sharp trot to a hard bottom. Trot-trot, trot-trot, trot-
trot a horse galloped. Horse-face moved me away. We jumped
forward. The trees began to move from place to place for us.

The distorted shadow of a gendarme flew upwards and fell behind the cliff to Pasieki. For a moment it was very quiet. Chuny,
clutching his rifle to his chest, was running in a crouched position.
Another gendarme turned off the road and moved upon us
sharply on a black horse. Someone ran obliquely across the duct.
Horse-face fired, the horse tossed its head, and at once Chuny
fired from a half-seated position, and the gendarme jumped off,
holding the bridle to his chest like a whip. Bent over, making several more steps to the side, he fell headlong into the snow, and the
horse with its head high flew into the forest.

Someone fired a volley from beyond the cliff from an automatic rifle, over our heads. Having hidden behind trees, we listened and watched to what would happen next. A Mazeppa-ite from the Hilfspolizei came out on the edge of the forest. Chuny fired at him but missed. And we no longer moved from where we were; we were ready for anything. Horse-face drew five cartridges of ammunition from his pocket and put them in front of him, on his cap. We were silent a long time, and we lay motionless a long time, until the day started to draw out into the grayness of evening. Somewhere far away, village girls started singing something very sad. And at such moments one thinks of the dead, everything passes as though in one second before the eyes.

Chuny whistled. We moved down the slope to the dead body. We wandered in the dusk seeking a dark stain in the snow. It was dead around, and as venerable as under a stone arch. Then again we listened urgently, since three shots from a rifle were to be the answer and the assurance that Czaczkies had accepted the proposal of seeking Leit and Szerucki with us.

DATE DUE

FEB 1 6 1972			
GAYLORD			PRINTED IN U.S.A.